How in the world did thi

BUNDY

...The Childhood of
a Serial Killer

HOW IN THE WORLD DID THIS GUY HAPPEN?
BUNDY
...THE CHILDHOOD OF A SERIAL KILLER

Published by Wisdom House Books, Inc.
Chapel Hill, North Carolina 27517 USA
www.wisdomhousebooks.com

Wisdom House Books is committed to excellence in the publishing industry.
Book design copyright © 2024 by Wisdom House Books, Inc. All rights reserved.
Cover and Interior Design by Ted Ruybal
Published in the United States of America

Paperback ISBN: 979-8-9891398-0-4
LCCN: 2023918754

1. FAM001030 | FAMILY & RELATIONSHIPS / Abuse / Domestic Partner Abuse
2. SOC004000 | SOCIAL SCIENCE / Criminology
3. FAM052000 | FAMILY & RELATIONSHIPS / Dysfunctional Families
4. BIO024000 | BIOGRAPHY & AUTOBIOGRAPHY / Criminals & Outlaws Books
5. SEL008000 | SELF-HELP / Codependency Books

First Edition

25 24 23 22 21 20 / 10 9 8 7 6 5 4 3 2 1

psychopathorigins.com

How in the world did this guy happen?

BUNDY

...The Childhood of
a Serial Killer

"I am the meanest
son of a bitch you will ever meet."

Carol J. Oas MN ARNP

Dedication

**For everyone
that did not
deserve any of this.**

Table of Contents

Preface

For decades, the psychological underpinnings of Theodore Robert Bundy have been considered and described by mental health professionals, law enforcement, and lay specialists. His formal evaluations while in prison have also proved to offer informative insights on his psychological structure.

Here is what most people know about Ted Bundy's story:

Starting in his second decade, he floridly increased his siege on young females. He indicated that his prey totaled over one hundred, but that may have been bluster to impress I don't know who. He admitted to about thirty deaths in his very last hours of life, and that was only in hopes of a stay of execution. Bundy erroneously surmised that we would want to mine his mind to discover what made an amazing being like him tick.

He also thought we would want to learn from his sage wisdom regarding the others in his line of work who were still active that he could generously help us find. He *was* helpful with the investigation of the Green River Killer. Not only that, but he drew a checklist for investigators about the habits and processes used by serial murderers. The checklist, hand written by himself, was six pages long (Nelson pp. 159-164).

Bundy had an unimaginable lust for killing and a Houdini talent for escaping. He accomplished two famous jail breakouts and attempted two lesser known escapes from Utah State Prison and Florida State Prison. Once free after an escape, he went right back to slaughtering women and girls. Because of his evasion tricks, he had an uncanny ability to avoid detection and capture for months on end.

He would travel large distances by airplane, train, bus, and automobile from one end of the country to another, successfully evading detection while readying for his next attacks. Ergo, the Florida Supreme Court and Florida Governor Bob Martinez refused to grant yet another stay of execution for Bundy.

Denying any more stays definitely saved innocent lives. Ironically, at the same time, his death snuffed information that might have been useful to save even more lives. Because of what Ted was, however, they did not want to take that chance.

At the time of Ted's final arrest, I felt a ping of coincidence since I was born in Pensacola, Florida. I'm not a superstitious person, but several coincidences in my life have reinforced my intrigue with Bundy specifically. We were in Pensacola for about a year when my brother and I fell off of the turnip truck and ended up with our grandparents in the countryside near Seattle, Washington. We were raised by our grandparents, who we called Gramma and Grampa, but I was puzzled why we didn't call them mom and dad like other kids did their parents. It wasn't until years later that I asked, and contrary to Ted, was gently told.

Since I had a small inheritance following the death of our parents, I desired to use the money to attend the University of Washington. Had my life been on track, I would have entered the UW Psychology program and been in classes with Bundy. Fortunately, an unplanned pregnancy sent me down the road of popping out babies instead of being a UW Coed. As the years progressed and the case against Bundy evolved, with every news release I put down the broom and soaked in every detail.

Ted targeted young brunettes with a center part—as was the style in that day—and I did the same with my long brown hair. I got a tap of relief and a heart squeeze when I learned that one of his first victims, Linda Ann Healy, had been in three of the same psychology classes with him. I would have been as trusting and naive as every one of those lovely women and feel grateful that my children may have saved my life.

Years later, I was finally able to study at the University of Washington, where I focused on psychiatry with psychopathic origins in mind. Over the years, I have read everything I could find about Bundy. Rather than sinking into the crimes and investigations, I wanted to know how the heck he became who he was.

Up until now, I have waited for someone to look at his developmental material in depth and share with us how these people, primarily Ted, came to be. As of yet, I have not seen a clinical evaluation of his not-so-obvious psychological *detachment* caused by interrupted bonding and developmental trauma from his early years. For decades, whenever new articles, documentaries, or books came out regarding him, I looked expectantly for his early years to be covered psychologically since the first several years are where psychopathic development starts. Perhaps by the time I publish this book, someone will have done that. If not, or even if so, here are my thoughts regarding his developmental years.

Ted's unimaginable emotional disengagement from living beings started early and remained fixed for his entire life. He was dangerously detached from other humans, resentful, and terrifyingly murderous, yet no one could see it.

How in the world did this young man reach a point that he would hunt, steal, and massacre young women and girls? And what was it about him that helped him get away with it for so long? The individuals in his path and their subsequent families deserve an explanation. Many say there was no reason, that it didn't make any sense at all. I disagree. It is clear to me that from the very beginning he had limited, if any, human attachment opportunities and markedly distorted impressions of women.

Society has been fed a positive impression of his upbringing in movies and documentaries. Believers in his innocence emphasize that Ted was raised in a good Christian home, was a Boy Scout, had a paper route, was a college graduate and a law student, aspired to political leadership, and was trusted and supported by political acquaintances and professional associates.

Much of this is true. Because of his seemingly untainted past, the world was in disbelief when learning of his luring women by pretending to be injured and removing the inside car door opener so they couldn't escape once there, bashing their heads in, running and grabbing them, sneaking in their houses, and so forth. The whats, whos and hows of his crimes have already been published at length, or at least as much as has been discovered. We need to understand and be able to explain rationally *how* he came to be who he tragically was.

I will do this for you.

These serial murderers do not wake up on a random morning and decide, "I think I'll start attacking people now." This thinking is a long time coming and detectable if we understand the psychological process behind their decisions, which we didn't when Bundy was alive. We have more information now for *detecting and preventing* psychopathy, which is the solution for ensuring a safer future.

We can glean quite a lot from Ted's developmental years that can illuminate how this human distortion came about. Perhaps this volume will shed light on the pathway that brings about characterologically disturbed individuals and yield understanding of what elements to watch for—if not prevent—in our youth.

You will notice my inherent bias toward Bundy's story throughout this book. The vignettes are the elements that come to my mind based on what I know about how these killers come about. You will have your own ideas, but these are mine. I do become somewhat irreverent at times, but this *is* Ted we are talking about.

I have no intention whatsoever of blaming *any* individuals that are related to, cared for, loved, or befriended Bundy. We were all fooled. He was able to fool anyone he wanted to deceive. I leave the unnamed individuals in the book unnamed in order to honor their right to privacy. The individuals to which I refer are folks that have already been in the news, books, or have made public statements. Regarding any inaccuracies here that may be determined by the reader, I welcome your corrective feedback.

More than anything else, I want to respect the beautiful, intelligent, promising women and girls that were robbed of us and their loving families by ensuring this volume grants them eternal, dignified peace.

Introduction

"I don't think anybody doubts whether I've done some bad things.
The question is what, of course, and how and, maybe even most
importantly, why?"

~Ted

There have been many well documented and highly informed publications describing the crimes, the investigations, the court proceedings, the death row interviews, the information given by personal acquaintances, intimates, and more. This book is not intended to be a scholarly dissection of the information to date. My intention is to clarify once and for all the "why" of his crimes, as well as how according to social sciences his personality was launched.

Ted himself struggled with the underbelly of his personality disorder, but he was too close to it—too injured by it—to enable or even *allow* himself to put an end to his behavior. He certainly did not want to give up his sadistic pastime if he could avoid it.

When it came to our subject, Theodore Robert Bundy, when and how did he get his corrupt start, and why didn't we see the signs? Were they detectable? If they were readily detectable and understood, we would have been alert to his red flags from the get go.

Usually, however, we are blind to warnings either because we can't imagine such a thing could be possible or because we fear that we could have contributed to or prevented it in some way. We must give his friends, family and coworkers grace on this front. We have all missed and misinterpreted signs unknowingly.

More importantly, the perpetrator will do all in their power to reassure us that they are okay by eliciting our *admiration* rather than our concern. But there *is* reason for concern that we overlook or at least optimistically deny.

So this is *our* side of the story too—how we are built and why we can miss aberrant behavior.

Every infant and child needs the opportunity to feel safe, loved, and certain he or she *belongs with* and is *held responsible to* others. This unfortunately did not happen throughout the unfolding of Ted's developmental years. While reading along, it might be useful for you to spot the warning signals in Ted's life as they appear. Many of these warning signals are based on what we understand now as attachment failure risk elements, which I submit is what goes awry in criminals such as Ted. At the same time, notice when those around him had blinders on and why.

In my opinion, the childhood of Theodore Robert Bundy represents the disorganized experiences which bring about angry detachment. This is a condition where bonding with the child is interfered with due to the child being repeatedly emotionally neglected in some way. Enough of this and the child reacts with a rage against others that leads to disordered conduct.

Bundy experts may disagree, but I want to explore his detachment since it has never been, as I have stated, considered seriously from stem to stern in the literature regarding Ted's singular development and his tragic social outcome. This book is my attempt to start a conversation regarding exactly that.

"What is it about the human mind that makes this kind of behavior . . . and if there's anything that can be done to reduce the possibility of a person who'd been predispositioned to this kind of behavior, uh, of actually engaging in it."

~Ted

Considering what information we do have about Ted's introduction to life, here are some risk factors for us to consider when it comes to children forming detached rage, which can develop into delinquency and culminate into Antisocial Personality Disorder or, in Ted's case, Narcissistic Psychopathy.

The most common risks are:

- Live or have lived in a children's home or other institution

- Frequently changed foster homes or caregivers

- Have parents with severe mental health problems, criminal behavior, or substance abuse that impairs their parenting

- Have prolonged separation from parents or other caregivers due to repeated out-of-home placement, hospitalization, or death of a primary caregiver

Yes, all of these risks and their various permutations applied to Ted repeatedly, and each one will be explored in the coming chapters.

You may already be thinking about other serial murderers that many of these elements apply to, and I will refer to others as we go for the sake of examples, but this volume is most specifically related to TRB.

Chapter One

Environmental Loading 101

Outside the prison complex, the sun was just beginning to rise. Satellite news dishes were mushroomed among the drunken revelers gathered in the cow pasture adjacent to the buildings. Death penalty protesters gathered among the crowd as well, but they were not effective at keeping history from being made that day. There was a Bundy BBQ planned for later that afternoon at a local saloon, and there were numerous other creative gatherings elsewhere on the planet. About two thousand glee stricken folks were shouting, chanting, and cheering on this long awaited Tuesday. As fireworks filled the sky, people sold electric chair pins, t-shirts, and other memorabilia to mark the momentous occasion.

It was so chaotically wild that morning that at the next electrocution, no one was allowed within a thousand feet of the building unless they were only carrying a phone, a pager, their medicine, a candle, or a Bible. But on this day the spontaneous circus had gathered as though for a rock concert outside the state prison in Starke, Florida. It was January 24th, 1989.

Crowds were cheering so loud outside that guards and prisoners alike could hear it just fine from the inside of the prison. Although the cacophony from spectators was thrumming inside the walls, the death chamber setting itself was quiet, like in a church when waiting for service to begin. The individuals filling this room would be Ted's last audience as they watched through glass just feet away from his officially reserved seat. Justice was finally going to be served. The chosen assembly of witnesses consisted of detectives, journalists, documenting reporters, and a minister—forty-two in all.

Ever the actor, when guards brought Bundy in from the cheering sounds, one witness said he was smiling like a performer on opening night, wanting as much attention as he could possibly have. It's true that the world was watching and he knew it. Ted always loved the spotlight and this was one more performance.

Once in the chamber, even though there were gatherers behind the window to charm, he staggered a bit when seeing the chair. Capital punishment has never been a deterrent to crime, but Bundy was a brutally deadly escape artist always plotting his next getaway. Florida law saw to it that Old Sparky, being just as infamous as Bundy, would soon stop him in his tracks and wipe that smile off his face.

We all know how that day ended. The world watched as the white hearse pulled away slowly. Why a white hearse was chosen, I don't know. It didn't seem appropriate, white symbolizing purity and all. Perhaps it was the only one available if no innocents had died that week. I guess the occupant had at least been *born* a soul. Some would say he never had one at all and if so it was an evil one. The only thing I know for sure is that we don't understand such mysteries, so we each pick the understanding that suits us best.

After the execution, John Wilson, a journalist and news anchor for Fox 13 Tampa, actually summed up my entire reason for writing this book. Thank you, John. He said, "We need to know more about our society and who we are, and what makes us what we have become. We don't know nearly enough about that."

Well, here goes my attempt at this very conversation.

How did it all start? Where in the world did this guy come from? We will commence Ted's side of the story with the very first sign that anything was awry with him or the people around him. It is an eerie example of behavior and an alarming glimpse into his beginning years that shaped the killer.

The following is a grim tale based on true events and it goes like this:

A little boy lived in a house with a main floor, an upstairs, and an attic. The three-story family house had been his home for a little over three of his very first years. He didn't remember his first three months of life of course, but those first months brought about an absence in a part of his mind which led him to not care as much about things. At least not about other living beings.

By the age of three-and-a-half, he had learned most of the house fairly well and thought he knew the family around him just as much. There were five other household members in this domestic scene, and he was loosely attached to each of them.

One afternoon, Teddy found himself in the old kitchen where daily meals were made by the women of the house, as it was in those days. The room housed the stove, sink, icebox, tall cabinet shelves of food, dishes, towels, and various drawers of cooking and eating utensils. As any preschooler has been warned, knives are dangerous and only to be handled by grownups, yet he gathered several knives of various sizes from one of the kitchen utensil drawers—six in all. It is unclear how the three-and-a-half-year-old thought of this or how his little body could have safely managed collecting such a precarious load, but my sources say he did. Once the weapons were in his arms, the preschooler had to sneak up the creaky wooden stairs all the way to the second floor of the house without falling or dropping any of the knives.

Once he reached the top of the stairs, the little boy carefully opened a door and went into a quiet bedroom. This was the room of who he understood to be one of his sisters. The girl wasn't sure where little Teddy had actually come from or to whom he belonged, but she knew where she came from; her name was Julia, and she was twelve years old.

When the little guy got into her room where she was taking a nap, he found her under her bed covers, breathing quietly, sound asleep. He carefully lifted one side of her blanket and placed a knife pointing at her. Then he added another one and then another until they were all next to her, pointing at her body. He somehow covered the girl back up without waking her.

Later, Julia started to stir and Teddy stood absolutely still near her bed, waiting expectantly for her to notice the knives. Over the years, it would become quite clear that he knew how to go undetected, quietly taking young women and girls by surprise. When Julia woke from the safety of slumber, she was horrified when she first felt and then saw the weapons pointing at her body. Scared and barely moving, she gazed wide-eyed around to find no one else in her bedroom, at least not at the height at which she was looking. But then she saw the little boy peering up at her from the foot of the bed. He was smiling.

Julia was now wide awake, confused, and distraught. She gathered up the knives and returned them to the kitchen's utensil drawer. What to do? Who to tell? Julia was only twelve years old. She was to be the first of many twelve-year-olds *and younger* over the years to be taken unawares by Ted. His last child victim died when he used his newly bought, or stolen, knife to slit her throat. This incident in Julia's room was only the beginning.

Who to tell . . . Julia wasn't sure who in her family was in charge of this boy. She decided to notify the whole family: her two older sisters and both of her parents. Having informed everyone about the disturbing act, she was met with another bewilderment. To her amazement, no one said anything about it, and no one did anything about it.

The boy continued his disturbing pranks, yet no one had conversations with little Teddy about his behavior. Ominously, from the very start and for the rest of his lifetime, his startling conduct was overlooked and dismissed by the ones closest to him.

At that time in Teddy's house, there were three adults available to address his behavior. Eleanor Cowell, the woman who he understood to be his mother, may not have been mentally fit to handle the situation. She was incapacitated at times due to mental illness and occasionally had to be treated by electroconvulsive therapy (ECT) at the local psychiatric hospital. Would she have been up to addressing this? Julia did not want to upset her mother if she could help it.

Samuel Cowell, the man Teddy understood to be his father, needed to be handled with kid gloves. He had an explosive temper, was frighteningly violent with outbursts that could be heard down the block, and sometimes physically abused Julia's mother. Julia wanted to avoid poking the bear on this touchy subject.

The little boy's oldest sister, Eleanor Louise, was about 20 years his senior. At the time, Julia did not know that Eleanor Louise was the true mother of young Ted. All she knew was that Eleanor Louise acted as the mother to all, including Ted, in the house of many stories. But was her sister wise enough to teach the boy right from wrong? Julia wasn't so sure.

What would you do in this situation? As a parent? As a twelve-year-old? As one of the other daughters? As a three-and-a-half-year-old little boy? This was to be only the beginning of the people in charge of his care ignoring his troubling behavior. But Julia's question remained: who *was* in charge of his care?

Physiologically and psychologically, our earliest life experiences forever impact each of us. Chase Hughes, an expert on Human Behavior and

Behavior Profiling teaches (*Law enforcement and Military*) (*YouTube*) that we must keep this in mind: "We are *all* a product of our childhood experiences, good and bad."

Yes, it's that simple. As the brain is growing and downloading, the limbic system is programming how we relate with and respond to the events in our lives. You may have bought this book hoping for blood and guts, but you are also getting some neurons, hormones, and examples of how human predatory behavior comes about and how to recognize it.

To understand these examples, we must acknowledge the importance of infant bonding success in the first place, and the outcome of failed affectionate validation. This information has been around for some time. Researchers of child and adolescent psychology gave us the first understanding of the inborn instinctive necessity decades ago.

Up until about the 1970's, the philosophies of "don't spoil the child" and "babies are blank slates" were the infant and child care understanding, although these ideas contradicted themselves. How can an infant be spoiled if they are a blank slate?

In spite of that paradox, loving parents have always delighted in their children. They cannot help themselves, fortunately. What we understand now is that, rather than blank slates, infants are alert, hungry *sponges* soaking up everything they observe and experience into their rapidly growing brains. It goes without saying that the growing organisms require a safe, authenticating world to absorb so they know where and how they fit in life.

What children absorb determines what they translate into their forming personalities and ultimately determines the behavior patterns that develop and *stick*. The information has been self-installing all along into that little scout, and once it's there, it cannot be shifted easily. For the Christian reader, this might ring a bell from the proverb "Train up a child in the way he should go and when he is old he will not depart from it." Pr. 22:6. I think Confucius said something along those lines as well, probably because it's true, and unfortunately Ted was programmed to go in the wrong direction. Unintentionally but effectively, unemotional callous disregard instead of affectionate accord formed from the time he was abandoned as an infant in an orphanage, and it only went downhill from there.

"I need some special God damn attention. I demand it."

~Ted

When it comes to *instinctually required* human interfacing, this knowledge has taken time to trickle down into our neighborhoods and hospitals. Now it is common practice and a standard of care for the parent(s) or permanent caregiver(s) to have consistent affectionate interaction with their infant, which includes holding, soothing, and talking to the child for the purpose of introducing human connection.

The purpose of bonding is protection. If we are attached emotionally to a child, we are going to do all in our power to ensure physical and affectional needs are met so as to give the child the best starting place. Firstly, a child needs to bond to survive physically and secondly, they need it to thrive interpersonally so they can sustain themselves *among others* throughout their life. Affectional bonding is so crucial that the newborn grasps for it in a very primal way like plant roots reach for life giving water.

With disconnected individuals, the inability to understand affection starts early. Sometimes parent-infant bonding is delayed due, for example, to traumatic birth or adoption, but the parents *want* to bond with their child and persist until the emotional fusion is in place. That didn't happen for Ted, and if we take a closer look into his early home life, we can see why.

Some say that we look like our dogs, and some walk in our houses and say, "this home looks like you!" It's true that we express ourselves by our choices and how we take care of our choices. Our dogs, cars, and houses express us, and sometimes quite well. Any guests in my house today might witness a puppy piddle on the floor tile because I didn't get her out in time. We all have issues.

The Cowell's lived in a family neighborhood established in the growing city of Philadelphia, Pennsylvania. The houses were built in the 1920's as the East Coast city continued to expand its borders. Most of the neighboring homes along Ridge Avenue and Domino Lane were respectable, built of brick covered with mortar, whitewashed and then kept white and washed over the years. Some boasted brick based pillars supporting columns which in turn braced the roofs. Many roofs sported dormer windows facing adjacent dormers across the street.

Unlike the other homes on the street, the corner lot house where this particular family lived had seen better days. The chalky face of the house was scarred with scaling stucco in too many places, and the upper story was nearly brown with soiled, thinning veneer. The white wash was applied up to the very base of the upper story window sills but no further. Perhaps that was as far as the ladder could reach, or the sparse touch up may have been due to limited funds and limited paint. Rather than boasting stately columns like the neighboring houses, this house's front porch roof was supported by slim, weathered posts. Two rather intact dormer windows emerged from the black roof, as well as a solid brick chimney for Santa.

Outside of the building was the nursery and greenhouse owned by the father. Customers driving there would have come to a stop in front of a potentially handsome building—if it wasn't so ugly, that is. Although the business also offered landscaping, the yard itself was unkempt, with random straggly shrubs and dying trees. The space was surrounded by three-foot-tall hog wire held upright by sawed off tree trunks for posts.

It looked like the property owner was certainly one to make use of a dead tree. A homemade sign was nailed in place by a post on one side and a still somewhat usable tree on the other side. The hand painted letters on the sign read in script *See Flower Beds In Nursery* with a bold arrow pointing toward the back of the house. The placard remained tacked up throughout the year, even when the flowers were not in season.

A naked caned rose bush that at one time may have been lush and blooming still tried to grace the wall of the house behind the nailed tree, and it looked like it grew up as far as the second story when in its glory. The front sidewalk was almost intact until near the end of the property, where it fractured into scattered broken tiles.

On the side of the house that would have been most visible to nursery visitors towered a bare exterior wall. It had been whitened all the way to the top some time ago, but was deteriorating as well, bearing large patches of wear that had been more recently whitewashed in the same half-hearted manner as the front of the house.

Connected at the back of the family home was an optimistic two story horizontally planked extension that was painted all the way to the top. Perhaps the photo was taken when they were getting ready to sell. If selling, the upkeep on the house and grounds may have been too much for the tenants to tend properly in older age. On closer inspection, though, it looks like the exterior of the older part of the house had not been properly cared for in years, if not decades. Although perhaps impressive in its earliest years, it was less so now. If the house were to be restored currently, it might be considered suitable for an upscale historic district, but the house as it appeared in the photo resembled something more out of a Stephen King novel.

This setting was Teddy's introduction to family life. As the preschooler wandered about the lodgings, daily imprinting of life occurred upon his impressionable mind. When the two younger sisters were at school, the oldest sister, Eleanor Louise, took care of the household when the mother of the house was not able to do so. Teddy, as curious little boys have always done, wandered through the living and working spaces, always on the lookout for new adventures.

While exploring on any given day, he could have found a detective magazine lying here or there. Any of us who have seen one of these magazines are aware that on the covers and pages are images of beautifully terrified women chased by dangerously handsome men carrying knives, guns, or ropes. In other images, the beauties are shown captured and bound to a chair or bed. These visual representations capture the attention of any viewer regardless of age.

Perhaps there were some Mother Goose fairy tale books around the place as well, but even those beloved stories have a dark twist when we think about it. *Little Red Riding Hood and the Big Bad Wolf*, for example, features the wolf himself looking frail and weak in grandmother's bed before attacking the terrified girl. We loved those stories and the thrill of fear that came with them when they were read to us by a safe and reassuring adult.

Little Teddy, however, did not have consistent trusted and loving adults to read to him. Instead, he soaked in pictures of a man with a frightening temper. The father of the house's dodgy milieu was occasionally accompanied by the sound of him flinging a visiting cat against the wall in the greenhouse where he worked. Those images and sounds would have had an impact on any little boy. What do you think might have been going through three year old Teddy's mind during those times? I suggest the following: *If it is okay to do that to cats, it must be okay for those men in the detective magazines to be doing those things to women.*

Another alarming-for-a-preschooler activity on the property was when Teddy would watch the father harvest a few chickens for dinner by strangling them and pulling their heads off. This was ominous activity considering what Ted himself would do with beings in the not too distant future. Regarding the chicken slayings, Ted said in retrospect those were *not* warm memories of his grandfather. The hens would be plucked and cooked by older sister Eleanor Louise, or the mother Eleanor if she was feeling well enough despite mental illness or injury recoup from a domestic.

I remember when I was about three years old and my Grampa decided to kill our big red rooster. He got out the ax and told my brother and me to stand back because the rooster might run around a bit. He put the rooster's neck on the chopping block and *wham*, off came the rooster's head with blood squirting—and it did run around! I will never forget it.

Grampa doing this was memorable but not frightening for me because he loved us and we were always safe with him. By contrast, it was not always safe at the Philadelphia house. Years later, Eleanor Louise reluctantly admitted in agreement with other family members that her father was violent. She, as you will see throughout her lifetime, valiantly ignored or minimized very serious behaviors, even Ted's criminal ones. For her to say that her dad beat up her mother sometimes alerts me as to what *her* growing up years had been like. Based on the hints we have, it appears young Eleanor Louise's developmental experiences were disturbing.

Sometimes the father would get drunk and start yelling at the mother and girls. No one could anticipate whether the father would beat on his wife or strong arm his daughters. *Apparently that's what a man has to do in order to manage necessarily subservient women*, might have been downloading into young Teddy's mind at the sight of those incidents. As you will see, that is the conclusion he ultimately espoused as an adult. At times, the house echoed yells, cries, and sounds from punches and slaps.

And these were the people little Teddy had no choice but to rely upon to keep him safe.

With confusing surroundings, Teddy's best bet was to learn how to be liked by the father in order not to be mistreated by the unpredictable man too. The preschooler did not want to be perceived by the father as needing to be subdued like the women, but at the same time he wanted to charm the females around him so they would like him. A child should not have to be in that spot. Teddy had to master the manipulations of charm and good impressions in order to survive. As years went by, however, those cons would prove to be used very skillfully for horrific means.

Endearing himself to the abuser while charming the abused would have been a daunting task to accomplish. It certainly didn't validate him as an individual since he had to morph for everyone else. Adaptation to an ongoing relational dichotomy is enough to lead someone to crack another's head open, which we know he eventually did, but not anyone's head that lived at the corner of Ridge Avenue and Domino Lane.

So, now we have set the scene of the Philadelphia house: young Eleanor Louise's childhood home, Ted's early childhood home, and the creation address of what I think of as a well meaning horror story.

"My particular view of the world is that, uh, we're probably 95% of the way we were raised and where we were raised."

~Ted

Chapter Two

Eleanor Louise's Childhood

The serious ramifications of a child's early environment is sobering, isn't it? So, in embarking on how our nightmare of a killer occurred in the first place, we will start with Louise, her childhood name being Eleanor. It was her developmental environment that planted her firmly set personality, which in turn guided her care of Ted.

Eleanor had grown up in this same precarious household previously discussed, with a mentally ill mother and a violent father. I'll give you further perspective regarding her formative years based on what was culturally common from the 1920's to the 1940's in the United States.

Since a community's cultural concerns and biases determine the personal worth of, well, everyone in town, we should note the many stigmas in terms of social non-approval that were unfortunately placed upon the members of this family.

Eleanor's formative petri dish consisted of her childhood home, school, neighborhood, and community. We likely had these same personal environs, you and me. Culture is everything when it comes to influence. Many of my sources have provided information regarding the atmosphere in her household as she grew up, which seemed to have gone against the respectable cultural standards of that era. It is impossible to describe the many vignettes of Eleanor's tattered past, but you will see in my examples that she certainly led a difficult life. Young Eleanor was bright and headstrong, but she had challenges placed on her resistant yet *voiceless* shoulders right from the start.

I think public shame and the attempted concealment of her mother's mental illness and her father's brutality were the marination substances of Eleanor's character during her Philadelphia years.

The mother was described by both Eleanor Louise and Ted as obedient, never voicing her own opinions. I suppose if I were afraid of getting clocked if I spoke up, I would also keep quiet. Her mother also suffered from agoraphobia, which is an anxiety disorder causing one to rarely leave the home. Her staying at home increased as she grew older, but with the ongoing stigmata surrounding the household, I wouldn't blame her if she stayed in because she didn't *want* to socialize.

Eleanor's mother, who was also named Eleanor, suffered from manic depression, which is now termed bipolar disorder. Bipolar disorder consists of mood swings that originate on their own cycle within us. When depressed, Eleanor's mother was described as meek and reclusive. On the flip side of the coin, when manic, she was loud and talkative. It is not anything over which we have control, and when *untreated*, one must simply ride the storm when manic and hibernate in safety when depressed.

When left untreated, this can be a highly dangerous illness. During a bout of mania, one can become hyper, grandiose, and delusional to the point where, for example, folks have jumped off a roof convinced they could fly. When depressed, the individual might hole up in their bed with blinds closed for long periods of time. At the farthest and deepest end, the depressed person can give up on wanting to live entirely and commit suicide.

There were medicines available in those decades for bipolar disorder, but not any that were near as effective as our pharmaceuticals today. So, when her depressive or manic symptoms became too debilitating, the mother was hospitalized for electric shock treatment, or what is referred to today as electroconvulsive therapy (ECT). This treatment was effective to accomplish symptom recovery when all other modalities had failed.

Some mental health trivia for you here:

ECT had come a long way from its early origins in ancient empires. Electric Eels, I kid you not, were actually used during Roman antiquity to treat everything from headaches to gout, from mental illness to obstetrical procedures. What obstetrical procedures exactly I have not been able to ferret out, but I don't like the sound of it.

Going back even further, ancient Egyptians used electric fish from the Nile River for healing purposes. Those critters with electric organs can generate a shock of about 400 high voltage pulses per second, whereas a police taser delivers 19 high voltage pulses per second. Many ancient Egyptian tombs depict the healing power of an electric eel's shock, the oldest of which is the burial place of the great architect Ti located at Sakkara, dating from the 4th dynasty (ca.2750 BC). The walls of the tomb show Nile fishermen and a simulation of an electric fish. One set of images portrays a sad postured man touching an eel and then being postured as happy. Egyptians were certainly an intelligently curious people.

The hospitalizations of Eleanor's mother were directed toward relief of mental health symptoms, and a much more modern version of ECT was the treatment that worked for her when symptoms were at their worst. One cannot overlook, at least I cannot, the irony of electric current applied to the scalp of Eleanor Louise's mother to restore the mother's quality of life, in juxtaposition to electric current applied to her son's head in order to protect quality of life *for others*. For me, that is sadly sobering. No daughter or mother deserves that.

While more advanced than the electric therapy of antiquity, in the early century 20th century ECT was still more, well, shocking than today.

Specialists now understand that modified current per patient along with general anesthesia and muscle relaxants is effective to accomplish symptom recovery. But in Mrs. Cowell's days, although ECT was effective, it was considered brutal because the uninformed saw it as an indication that someone was *defective*, if not crazy, or worse, immoral. A really long time ago, and even now in some cultures, sufferers of bipolar disorder as well as schizophrenia and epilepsy were considered to be demon possessed.

In the gospel of Luke 9:40-44, Jesus is credited for having healed a boy that suffered from epileptic seizures. The boy's father said the child would fall, thrash, and foam, and when the "demon" finally left the boy was left badly bruised. I'll bet. It's curious to me that rather than Jesus having said, "This is an illness, not a demon," the Great Physician responded, "You people are all difficult and unbelieving, how long must I put up with you?" I think Jesus knew it was an illness and not a demon, but he couldn't say the boy needed anticonvulsant medication since that class of pharmaceuticals would not be available for nearly two millennia. Simply healing the boy was the wisest course of action under the circumstances.

Flash forward to neurological illness in the mid-twentieth century, and the stigma behind mental illness hadn't changed all that much. Because of the blight of being psychiatrically hospitalized, few people talked about mental health, especially if the patient was one's own kin. Much shame overshadowed the families of the mentally ill, and the persons with neurological infirmities were often kept somewhat—if not entirely—cloistered from the public. In contrast, people suffering from mental illness today are shown affection by the public and can receive treatment that is noninvasive, readily available, and effective. No longer condemned to episodes of mood, energy, and neurological dysregulation, these individuals now live healthy lives with their families and serve in many prominent professions.

In those earlier decades, many mentally ill family members were committed to asylums when they became unmanageable or shunned by family members. I do not know how many times the mother was psychiatrically hospitalized, but even if it was one or two times in her adult life, it would in those days have been *judged* by many others that knew of it. She did not deserve that, nor did her family.

Psychiatric hospitalization in Philadelphia or anywhere else in the world in the 1920's, 30's, and 40's was quite a gamble. At Byberry Psychiatric Hospital in Northeast Philadelphia, over 6000 patients were warehoused at a time. That was about 75 percent over its normal capacity, and they only had 180 attendants. When patients were fortunate enough to finally be released from the hospital, they were given a suit of clothing, $25 (about $500 in today's economy), and an appointment with the out-patient psychiatrist.

With nowhere to go, these individuals ended up on the street again before long, and with no medicine, the cycle repeated and they became delusional again. These souls were subject to the revolving door syndrome that similarly occurs within the prison population. Hopefully that particular asylum is not where the mother was treated, and hopefully she did not stay for long if she was treated there.

Each time their mother returned to the Philadelphia house from psychiatric hospitalization, life was not necessarily rosy. The psychiatric patient at home was unfortunately often in a scapegoat role. "Because of her, we can't face the neighborhood." "Because of her, more responsibilities fall on the rest of us. You girls need to keep this place up." "When I get back these things had better be done." "She's starting to get depressed again."

When deinstitutionalization occurred during the Reagan administration, you may recall that community care became available for the chronically mentally ill. I happen to have an intellectually disabled daughter (think

Downs Syndrome) that has been in community care for all her adult life. She is on Social Security Disability, providing her living expenses including health care. My daughter lives in a house with one other female resident and is involved in all kinds of activities around town. They have "helpers" that are with them 24/7. I smile to myself when thinking about her as being the only one in my family with guaranteed income and full time staff.

It was not so for Eleanor Louise's mother. Other than institutionalization her option was to be home with her family, which was both good news and bad news. Her psychiatric symptoms in our current era of mental health assessment, first of all, would be considered exacerbated by an intermittently abusive environment beyond one's control and ability to cope. But no one talked about the mother's difficulties in those days. Well, if so, it was only spoken about privately. The family of the patient often would have developed the coping mechanism of, if not a firm denial that anything was wrong, a grin-and-bear-it attitude. It would have been especially imperative to appear confident and upbeat when leaving the house.

We have all given the Pollyanna presentation ourselves when our life has been going to hell in a hand cart and we run into an acquaintance at the store. We cheerfully share a brief chat and go our own way. *Because* if we were to indicate any of what was currently transpiring in our personal world, we would be there all day conveying the difficulty, accepting condolences, and absorbing advice or recommendations. We all, when listening to troubles of others, console and advise because doing so is social courtesy. *So*, when we are going through life turbulence of some sort and are out in public, we avoid this "pitfall" by participating in brief social interaction, going our comfortable way, and then taking our problems to our therapist. It's healthy. It's just how it's done.

This was considered *especially* necessary (well, not seeing a therapist—I don't think her family did that themselves) for Eleanor's family when leaving the Philadelphia house. The family did not want to let on that anything was off-center at home, so the mother may have decided it was best to not leave the house at all and just stay in bed. Or perhaps that decision was made for her by her husband or concerned others. When folks are agoraphobic it is because they feel *trapped* somewhere in their life. She certainly was trapped in her mood cycling and difficult household.

The cure for her would have been, first of all, to live in *our* current time of medical science, which of course was not an option for her, or get rid of the source of the household turmoil (aka her husband). But if she did that, then the family would not have anyone to run the business. The source of the household miseries is often not willing to leave, and then what do you do? Grin and bear it. Or take care of the troublemaker yourself which will likely end *you* up in the slammer.

Louise's mother may not have had the heart, boldness, or balls to deal with her husband, and she for certain did not have social services for displaced mothers and children that we have today. Nor would she, for example, have been afforded the eventual outcome of the infamous Lorena Bobbitt if she had similarly taken matters into her own hands. Bullish men of the world had an onset of fitful sleep in 1993 when Lorena Bobbitt cut off her husband John Wayne Bobbit's penis with a knife [while he slept] because he would allegedly rape her. Lorena, by pleading insanity during her court hearing, lucked out and was acquitted. Too many women do not get off that easy and serve long terms for ridding themselves of their problem. Lorena is now a spokesperson for domestic violence and has a family with someone else.

Mrs. Cowell decided to stay in her lane of what was considered appropriate in her day, and her daughter followed suit in the years to come. Decades later, when Eleanor Louise's story became convoluted, much like Bobbitt's, because of Ted's actions, she was more pragmatic, dignified, straightforward, and preferred to be unspoken.

The Girl They All Depended On

With a mentally ill mother, it is likely Eleanor, as the oldest daughter, was unavoidably in charge of the household and oversight of her two younger sisters, possibly as soon as she could reach the kitchen sink. One must learn to emotionally detach in order to fulfill this assignment without undue heartache. At the time she gave birth to Ted, young Eleanor apparently also worked as an office clerk. Her father unfairly held her up as an example to her younger sisters. I think Eleanor Louise simply did what she needed to do.

Their father, because of running the greenhouse nursery and landscaping business, was occupied at work for large amounts of time. He also fussed over a collection of exotic trees that he protected from harm—remember the visiting cats story. For symbolism fans, you may be thinking about how felines are typically thought of as female symbols. The father certainly didn't treat the women in his life with much more dignity than the neighborhood strays. On top of that, the controlling actions that the father demonstrated were reinforced by his detective magazines in the greenhouse, which left a constant reminder that men are in charge of the women and can punish them however they please.

Unpleasantries like this do not happen every day, but some things are disturbing enough to remain in the atmosphere between the violent times. *Be careful, watch your step, remember what happened last time when so and so did that.*

I had a client that described finding herself in this very trap. She met a wonderful man and fell in love with him. Her family and friends adored him too, and after a sweet courtship they married. You are probably going to guess what happened next. Well, it happened on the first night of their tropical honeymoon.

He punched her in the nose, broke it, and said to her, "Just so you know, I will be in charge." Her two black eyes were gone by the time they got home from their honeymoon, or at least enough that makeup could cover, and her loved ones were none the wiser.

She stayed with him for ten years and had some children. Everyone in their life continued to love this man because they only encountered the helpful, fun, and kind side of him. He even behaved as Mr. Wonderful with her and the children sometimes. He never hit my client again, but it was because he didn't have to. Whenever it got to the place that she was reticent or dragging her feet about something he expected of her, he would softly rub the bridge of his nose. She knew what that signal meant. Gaining submission doesn't take continual brutality as long as *reminders* of the abuse are in place.

Perhaps Eleanor's father came in, rolled up his sleeves and did the dishes and sloshed the toilet from time to time; however, in that generation such chores were considered women's work and the father had a business to run in order to provide for the mouths he did have to feed. Eleanor, despite any of her father's kind acts, knew her place in his eyes and knew the consequences if she disappointed him. To whatever degree he was not able to help, she knew those duties were left to her whenever the mother was unable.

This is how the child becoming the parent usually happens. In many families, for one reason or another household tasks and caretaking responsibilities of the adults fall to the oldest child. This role reversal is referred to as the **parentification** of the child. The parentification of a youngster, rather than making them feel competent and grown up, interferes with their maturation in many ways. *Playing* house for a youngster is far different to *being responsible for* the household.

Eleanor's father expected the house to be up and running early, and in those days, women of the household were expected to have breakfast prepared. Bacon, eggs, potatoes, and toast were a common fare for the father, and oatmeal or pancakes for the youngsters. This family was at that time, before Ted came along, a household of five. Four, if the mother was away at hospital or unwell, which created other difficulties. Then there was lunch and supper. Also laundry, dishes, mopping floors, scrubbing countertops, homework, school, and grocery shopping—*Oh dear, I wonder who I'll run into at the store. Remember to smile.*

I feel I should further explain the probable feelings of young Eleanor. Bear with me here; this is important. This is the mother and sustainer of a serial killer we are talking about.

Young Eleanor, or if it were YOU, may feel:

- Anxiety regarding the care of others: It's all up to me. Am I doing this right? Did I miss something? Am I bad for wishing I didn't have to do this?

- Feelings of guilt and shame: I am failing here and there—what's wrong with me? I really wish I didn't have to do this.

- Unrelenting worry: What if this goes wrong? What will I say to my parents? What happens if a parent gets angry because something hasn't been done?

- Inability to trust others: I always get stuck doing something no one else will do or can take care of, and if I don't do a good enough job . . .

- Poor boundaries: I want to say no, but can I ever say no? No.

- More likely to become involved in violent or unhealthy relationships: My life as it is unfortunately seems to be my only option. I am accustomed to violence and emotional trauma, so that must be what I deserve. Even if I want to leave, where can I go? I've put up with it this long, so a little longer must be possible. Maybe it will get better.

- The pressure to be perfect: The pastor always talks about the Proverbs 31 woman on Mother's Day. I should strive to run the house as smoothly as her, but how can I live up to a woman like that?

Many youngsters have been put in parentified positions over the eons, but for Louise, this assignment was possibly a requirement of a dominating male rather than a much appreciated necessity. That is a big difference.

Understandably, parentified teens are often in a hurry to flee the nest in order to escape overwhelming responsibilities. Eleanor Louise was an intelligent young woman and Ted said she could have easily gone to and been successful at college if not for her pregnancy (with him).

Another sign of a youngster in a parent role is excelling at everything. She was a youth leader at her local church. She had been a successful award winner in high school and served in various class positions. Eleanor had relentless energy, which was good because she needed it. Ted also had the same vigor, getting by with little sleep but not, like Eleanor, putting his waking hours to good work.

Eleanor was likely well thought of in the community and certainly worked hard to accomplish that. Her family's limited finances or any other reason, like being needed at home, may have interfered with her going to college (Ted said it was because she did not have a scholarship). At any rate, college did not happen for this bright, capable, and promising woman. In a kinder world I think she could have been mayor of Philadelphia. As we saw on national television decades later, she certainly spoke and presented herself well under pressure.

The next best consideration for Louise was to get married in order to leave the house. Culturally in the US in the 1940's, the cardinal rule in many homes and definitely at Eleanor Louise's house was *Never Look Bad or Make the Family Look Bad*. Again, this wasn't the philosophy of only this family; it was pretty much expected in American culture at the time, right there with the Constitution and the Ten Commandments on the wall.

The family reputation admonition was invisible but understood. It was commonly voiced as *what will people think of us?* Family pride was adhered to in some families more than others, but the perfect family image projection was pervasive. For now, the escape route from the house of secrets for young Eleanor was a husband. But, before she could find one, young Eleanor had to keep a secret of her own—she was pregnant with what she didn't know would be a future killer.

Chapter Three

Looking for a Hero

. . . the rabbit died and the neighbors are watching.

The Rabbit Test was a method for pregnancy determination up until the 1960's. It was developed in, of all places, Eleanor Louise's home state at the University of Pennsylvania. Haven't heard of the Rabbit Test before? A purported mother's urine and blood would be injected into a rabbit, and if the rabbit's ovaries swelled, it meant the expecting mother was going to start swelling too. The general public thought that the rabbits would only die if the woman were pregnant. That was not so. Actually, all of the rabbits died because they had to be cut open to see if their ovaries swelled. The myriad deaths of rabbits were finally brought to a halt thanks to the African Clawed Frog, which yielded pregnancy results without anyone having to cut the amphibian open. Today, of course, we have the pregnancy test thermometer-like device that is effective and animal testing free.

Poor Eleanor. In a desperate attempt to leave her burdensome household, she may have gone looking for her prince. I know I would have. No one knew of her dating anyone before her pregnancy, and if so, there is not any intel about it that I can find. What we do know of course is that Eleanor found herself a mother-to-be in spite of family and church moral caution and the wholesome example she was meant to portray to the public.

Eleanor Louise had two stories regarding the identification of Ted's father, but neither were ever confirmed. One story was that she was seduced by a man home from the service, a Jack Worthington, and when she became pregnant, he abandoned her. Eleanor said when she tried to track him later, she discovered there was no such person. Her pastor was unable to find the man, and law enforcement later came to the same conclusion.

Another name she gave was William Lloyd Marshall. Some sources say that name was on one of the original birth certificates. There are a few stories and a few birth certificates. "Lloyd" Marshall was an Air Force veteran and salesman.

An auxiliary story is that her violent father was the sperm donor. The family never confirmed nor denied the rumor, which tells me they at the very least didn't know for sure. Otherwise, they would have flatly denied such an unthinkable insinuation. It is not unheard of for the parentified child to be used sexually in the place of the absent parent. Ted, when in prison, still believed his grandfather was his biological father. How he was aware of that possibility I don't know for certain, but I have a good hunch that I will share in the coming chapters.

In the era of 1940, it was a dreadful shame to be pregnant and unmarried, and was absolutely humiliating for the entire family. Eleanor must have been beside herself in her circumstances. Some say the father of the baby took her to a doctor and she got a prescription in an attempt to induce miscarriage. Another source indicates there was a failed abortion attempt. Who knows what really happened; regardless, Eleanor was still left expecting an out-of-wedlock baby in lonely shame.

In the same situation, what would you have done?

The bottom line was that an unplanned baby in that era was excruciatingly inconvenient, and mothers often resented their situation if not openly, at least secretly. Those developing little ones, *even before birth*, would have been impacted neurologically and psychologically by the mother's depressive stress. As growing children they would have felt it even more so, even if they could not articulate what was wrong. Often, many children in these situations came to the conclusion that somehow *they* were what was wrong.

As they grow, little kids can often sense among the unspoken thoughts of the adults around them that something isn't right and typically conclude it's probably them. In midcentury America, as determined as adults were to raise a happy, well-adjusted child to adulthood, the blight of illegitimacy never cleared entirely. For his or her lifetime, the child all too often bore the identity, even if silently and invisibly, of being an embarrassment.

Alternatively, children that thrive out of illegitimacy are the fortunate ones that are told the truth right from the beginning so it becomes part of their personal story. This is most commonly done these days, and the youngsters do much better than the little lost souls of yesteryear. These kids now end up appreciating being kept and loved, and everyone benefits.

At the same time, with each child there is always that nagging little question of who is my dad? Who is my mom? Who are my parents? Sometimes the family does not know, does not want to know, has lost track, or would like to know but are unable to find out.

In American families of the forties, a child born out of wedlock was *absolutely not* an option. It was common for pregnancies to be hidden for as long as possible, if not entirely, and to have a good face-saving explanation, or lie if necessary, if the "bastard child" was discovered by outsiders. Yet these babies came along, and the dirty family laundry needed to be very safely guarded.

How Laundry Secrets travel:

I tell a secret to one person that I trust will not tell. That person tells my secret to one person that they trust will not tell. That person tells my secret to someone that they trust will not tell. Pretty soon the whole town knows what they are not supposed to know and so they don't say anything. Nobody wants to be the one to spill the beans. That was the way it was everywhere in the Western Hemisphere then, and maybe Eastern too, but that information is not in my area of expertise.

Many of us can relate to situations like this happening in our own families. My mother lived in the proverbial small town where everybody knows everyone else's business. Like Louise, my mother got pregnant and was abandoned by the father. Unlike Louise, my mother had her baby right there in River City's small local hospital and everyone knew. What else was different for my mother was that the father of her baby continued to live in this Norman Rockwell town. If he saw my pregnant mother or my mother and her newborn on the street, he would cross to the other side. His family knew, my mother's family knew, the entire town knew. The children that he later had with his wife didn't know, though.

Half a century later, my aunt and I saw to it that the beans got spilled, and my brother was able to meet his adult half siblings a few years before he died of a brain aneurysm. Before then, they did not even know about his existence. How's that for small town secrecy? It can be pulled off in amazing fashion. This story pales in comparison to Louise and Ted's, but I want to establish that the lesser traumas, even when coupled with ongoing affection, still leave permanent lesions on a child's perception of his or her significance. None of us have to go very far in any direction to recall a similar family story.

In a variety of ways, when any of the big behavioral and lifestyle *no no's* occurred, these families were stigmatized by the community. Any unfixable disgraces would have necessarily been "hidden" behind closed doors, or at least as many of said humiliations as possible. Inside the Cowell house, there was concealed secrecy and in public view, the dark secrets were cloaked by bright optimism.

The space in the middle of all that secrecy screams, "EVERYBODY KNOWS."

The impact of these elements on Eleanor and her unborn baby must have been relentlessly intense. The fear of the community finding out this new shameful dimension of the pregnancy likely hung heavy about her and the family, thickening both the atmosphere and the amniotic fluid.

Many studies look at the effect of maternal stress during pregnancy. The expecting mother's exposure to chronic stressors are linked to significant alterations in the child's limbic system and neurodevelopment. The limbic system specifically is markedly impacted, bringing about certain issues such as an increased risk of mixed handedness, mood disorders, ADHD, speech delays, and poor emotional adjustment in the child. All of these conditions applied to Ted. I don't know about ADHD (Attention Deficit Hyperactivity Disorder), but the boy was disruptive in the classroom, required little sleep, and was full of mischief. In a kinder world, his hyperactive tendencies might have been better channeled into being a life-saving trauma surgeon or medic.

Eleanor could not escape the stress of hiding her condition from the public, nor could she escape the stress of sharing her secret with those who "had" to know. The family being active church goers meant that Eleanor had to inform their congregational pastor and his wife. She did and was promptly removed from her role as youth leader, as well as ostracized from the church. Her and her family's shame continued unabated, and now *two outsiders* knew the secret.

Behind Closed Doors

There are mixed stories about Eleanor's father. His family who knew him best reported he was a violent alcoholic, had an explosive temper, was verbally abusive, sexist, and tortured small animals. He was a wife beater and even abused his own children. One daughter claimed he pushed her down some stairs because she slept until 9am and was not awake completing her chores. I would have been thrown down some stairs, too, since I am not an early riser.

The household braced when he would come through the door, never knowing what mood he would be in on any given day. One of the daughters tried to hide every time she heard her father coming through the door. I think the father might have benefited from ECT, but I digress. Eleanor Louise, decades later, rather than applying her typical glossy veneer, quipped to journalist Myra McPhee for Vanity Fair May 1989 issue that "He had a temper" and "did beat up my mother sometimes." Ted was quoted as saying his mother and her father "were both strong-minded." Michaud and Aynesworth. 1983.

With the father's arbitrary mood changes, Teddy was learning the entitled element of surprise. It makes sense to me that Ted would associate, naturalize, and eventually develop a taste for violence toward women with this man that he "felt close to" and "identified with." Michaud and Aynesworth 1983.

Alternatively, non-family sources deny all accusations against Samuel Cowell, saying they never saw any of this behavior and that they thought the grandfather was a wonderful man. Either they said that because they lived across town and couldn't hear his tirades, or they were trying to keep the bean bags intact. My thoughts are, if the grandfather was the fine man reported by some community members, Louise would have *never* said otherwise. The only reason I think she would have falsely admitted to his abuse would have been to distance the origin of Ted's behavior away from her *own* Tacoma household. Many of us would want to do that if we were in her shoes.

Although it was known outside the home that the father was an abusive man, it was still kept within the family *as if* a well kept secret. Again, via neighborhood news communications, others surmised what was going on behind closed doors because they heard the shouting, knew of the mother's psychiatric hospitalizations, and saw when the youngsters were left to manage the household.

We often elect to "not know" what we know. Meanwhile, we find a family with a mentally ill mother, an abusive father, an unwed pregnant daughter, and two other daughters that we know little about. Not only that, but they were fairly open to their community because of their church activities and nursery landscaping business.

Now imagine if you will that the dad abuses the mentally ill mom, so the mom cannot always take care of the household, which is at least to some degree left up to the kids. Dad has a business to run, cats to fling, and comes through the door raging at times. Then he leaves violent detective magazines lying around the property among the African violets. And maybe, just maybe, the father has crept into his daughter's room at night. I submit that this scenario is the environment that created the Louise and Ted we came to know.

More personal and family chaos continued to erupt, but by that time Eleanor Louise was already adept at the skills of burying all of her *would rather not's* into a steel box of compartmentalization and denial. In that case, she got good at putting heartache out of sight, pulling that blind and locking that door.

So constitutionally strong was she that, instead of being forlorn, she faced adversity with rigid optimism. She was to get better and better at cheerful detachment as the years went by, especially in the face of disappointing traumatic realities. She cracked a wee bit here and there, but never bent or broke. Softness, in her mind, was risky. Vulnerability, likewise, was risky.

Considering Eleanor's father, a misfire we can bring about as parents is when our guidance manifests as setting unrealistic expectations for our children. When an accomplishment is achieved, it is criticized or, rather than praising the achievement for itself, the bar is doubled in height. That, coupled with labeling the child as one who can do no wrong, is an impossible combination. Eleanor was upheld as the gold standard example for her younger sisters. Apparently the father was harsh with the younger sisters but loved Eleanor.

She was so competent and responsible, which added to any expectations that *Eleanor can do it*. This assignment of unreasonable expectations and unquestioning praise is exhausting for the youngsters at home and sets them up for failure when they are outside of the nest encountering real responsibilities and outcomes.

Similar to this was Adolf Hitler's experience as a little one. It is difficult to imagine *The Fuhrer* as a boy. When angry, he apparently did resemble a toddler throwing tantrums. A narcissist like him cannot surpass the emotional maturity of a toddler, so I guess it makes sense that he was, at one time, a child.

Hitler's father was not usually home and according to his mother, Adolf could do no wrong, was a wonderful child, and would one day accomplish marvelous things. He was different in this way from Louise because it was implied little Adolf would be effortlessly successful. He wasn't expected to apply himself to inglorious chores or studies, so he failed at pretty much everything in the ordinary realms of life. In a situation like this the child questions: *Am I good, bad, or otherwise? Am I competent, incompetent or otherwise? Apparently it doesn't matter, at least for me, because I am innately awesome.* This brings about psychopathic narcissism at its atomic level.

Hitler reached his position of infamy because of his grandiose entitled ravings that influenced desperate German citizens. These are the elements—a domineering, emotionally unrealistic mother and absent father—that formed Adolf's character.

Alternatively, Eleanor had a dominating father and disabled mother. One thing Eleanor Louise never did was shirk *any* of her duties. With fearless determination, she threw her energy into positive activities, excelled at all she endeavored, and very much deserved to be rescued from that house. Meanwhile, her belly was growing.

Chapter Four

Exiled from Dignity

Eleanor's family decided she would spend the final months of her pregnancy hundreds of miles from Philadelphia at The Elizabeth Lund Home for Unwed Mothers in Burlington, Vermont. The Home had previously been called The Home for Friendless Women. Burlington natives referred to it darkly at times as "Lizzy Lund's Home for Naughty Ladies". The home name was changed once again to "Lund Family Center" some years later, and then more recently to "The Lund."

To this day, The Lund is a thriving home serving vulnerable and marginalized individuals and families. They offer services for pregnant women, infants, adoption services, treatment programs, child care for adoptees, outreach to families and many other admirable benefits. Many such services were available upon Louise's arrival at The Lund Home.

In spite of Eleanor Louise being banned from the church, the pastor's wife generously offered to drive her to the Elizabeth Lund Home. Eleanor being in the company of a seemingly morally untainted driver would have been of no help no matter how kind her driver might have been. Perseverating angst likely vibrated through the mother and in turn pushed down into that steel box where she hid her feelings, her unborn child bathing in those stress-ridden developmental ingredients. That might have been an uncomfortable 382 mile drive for both of them, if not all three of them.

Since anonymity was paramount at this home, each pregnant mother was given the last name "Lund." The home had a bowl full of wedding bands that each girl could select from to wear on her ring finger if planning to go into town. The girls must have found it disconcerting to be *yet another* pregnant 'Lund' woman in town. Burlington Vermont's population at that time was about 30,000. Hopefully the young women could move about *somewhat* unnoticed and not be persecuted. Yes, some of those girls did face persecution. It was not unusual for the expectant mothers to be subjected to sneering, lewd comments, children throwing eggs–which hurt, by the way, and leave a slimy, degrading mess.

The women and girls at the Lund Home were from all walks of life, from PhD candidates to girls as young as twelve, from broken families to intact families, impoverished to wealthy families, and everything in between. There was no demographic. Pregnancy is no respecter of persons.

Contraception was not available to young women for the most part in that era. Abortion was illegal and very dangerous. Furthermore, teens and young adults have a mentality of 'it won't happen to me' and so could be somewhat careless. Birth control was entirely up to the woman, as was care of the baby for its lifetime. Home staff at these institutions could be quite opinionated and judgmental of women giving birth to bastard children. Birth control, to them, was 'controlling yourself.'

Counseling of the mothers varied in homes like this, from wise guidance in some to shaming manipulations in others. Mothers came from up to 3000 miles away to give birth in secrecy. Families sometimes told the curious that their daughter was away for a period of time to visit an aunt. or that she was studying abroad.

In homes for unwed mothers, birthing and aftercare went according to the wishes and safety of the mothers, as well as the wellbeing of the child.

Whether the mother wanted to keep the child, was undecided, or wanted to give the baby up for adoption, the needs of the mother and child were discussed and arrangements were made accordingly. After the birth of the babies in some homes, the mothers could observe their baby through the nursery glass window. Sometimes they were allowed to hold the baby for a few minutes each day. If the child was adopted by a family, the mother was allowed to spend an hour and dress the baby for departure to his or her new home.

Imagine the unrelenting shame and fear of discovery that at some level would be forever with Eleanor Louise after spending time in a place like that. Nonetheless, there she was. In the home records that she allowed to be released, it was indicated that Eleanor, although always polite, did not interact much with the other mothers there. Compartmentalizing? Denying to herself that this was actually happening to her? Ashamed and determined to get back to her "real" life soon? Perhaps those were some of her thoughts.

According to the Home's records, Eleanor's aloofness bothered some of the mothers more than others. Apparently the more emotionally secure mothers felt comfortable with her, but others thought she had a superior air. This dynamic of course is expected in any group where strong person-alities come together, and especially ones under such strain.

Regarding preservation of self-esteem for the mothers, the medical field of the day was no help whatsoever but rather a disgraceful hin-drance. Ominously, medical practitioners in those days, most of them men, defined appropriate behavior for young women. Doctors and psychiatrists diagnosed out of wedlock birth as tangible evidence of the *social deviance* and *pathology of the mother*. Psychiatrists pointed to illegitimate births as a sign of the mothers psychological *neurosis*.

Doctors characterized unwed mothers as *psychiatric problems* and as *victims of severe emotional and mental disturbance*. This was the entire social and *cultural* aura surrounding Eleanor and the pregnancy. There was no escaping it for many young women unless, of course, they lied to their community and abandoned their child. I wonder if Eleanor still dreamed of figuring out a way to go to college.

But rule out college for now, Eleanor. Thanks to the medical professional powers that be, you have social labels of psychiatric proportions: social deviance, pathology, emotional and mental disturbance to boot. She, as well as too many others, had this additional cross to bear at the Home for Unwed Mothers. And their babies were yet to be born.

The Lund Home was clean, safe and confidential, but the air had to have been somewhat dense at times with the heavy angst of ambivalence felt by all of the women clustered there. Each young woman had to wrestle with questions such as *do I keep the baby, or leave it here for adoption? If I take it home with me, what will people say? Will a potential husband ever want me now? What if somebody finds out? Will I be able to get a job?* When it comes down to mother-infant bonding in this impossible situation, clean, private and safe was not enough. Social and cultural barriers *unavoidably* impacted the intended charity and good will in the facilities.

While awaiting the birth of the infant, the mothers were assigned duties such as cleaning, food preparation, sewing, and other tasks that came with maintaining the facility. After the birth of the child, some mothers would stay an additional period of time and work to cover any extra expenses incurred due to perhaps a difficult birth or other complications.

In Homes back then, birth was a rather lonely experience. Mothers labored in the maternity room, where they were told to keep quiet, and then taken alone into the sterile delivery room. They were shaved and given an enema, then placed in the lithotomy position where she lay on her back with her feet either flat on the surface, placed in stirrups, or held by attendants. If the baby was coming before the doctor arrived, the attendants held the legs together to prevent what they would call precipitous birth..

After the birth, the mothers were separated from their babies "to prevent infection." Even with healthy births, after birth care was typically for ten days and women were not allowed to get out of bed. Their babies were brought to them for short periods of time unless the mother preferred to not see the child at all.

Eleanor was at the Lund for an entire month before giving birth to a healthy baby boy. She extended her stay, perhaps because she needed to wait for transportation back to Philadelphia or need to work to cover some infant expenses. We will have to wait until 2045 for the answer to that one. The bulk of Eleanor's records are still sealed, as they are unavailable for 99 years from the admission of the pregnant woman. So the records, if they still exist, will become legally available in the fall of 2045. For us social development researchers, it may shed more helpful light on what Louise and Ted's process was like while there.

Eleanor had long made up her mind to plow through the birth, leave the baby at the home to be adopted out, and get back to her efficient life. A loving landing for the little one into the arms of doting parents would have healed his bumpy start from being abandoned, but things went otherwise for the child.

I probably shouldn't do this, but I cannot help myself. I am going to tell you about the wolf children of Midnapore. This story shows how early environmental forces *do* shape us, regardless of our genetic code.

In 1912, the Reverend J.A.L. Singh set out for the jungles of India to share his belief in Christianity with various outlying tribes. During his travels he was told by locals of the remote village of Midnapore of a 'ghost' that they were hoping he could dispense on their behalf. Hoping to win them to his Christian endeavors he agreed to look into this.

The villagers took him about 30 miles away from Midnapore to a magnificent white ant mound about the size of a two story building. I would like to have seen that. There were about seven tunnels in the ant hill that led to a huge cavern in the center of the mound. While the group was watching, a wolf poked its head out of one of the tunnel holes and made a run for the forest. Another wolf followed and then a few others, and *then* a naked girl about eight years of age with a beach ball size of matted hair and sharp eyes came out on all fours. Following her was a smaller version of herself, a second little girl no more than two years old. She was also on all fours. I would sure like to know the story of how they got there. I have some hunches.

After receiving many scratches and bites, the village people were able to cage the assumed "ghosts," who were growling and snapping out of fear. The charitable Reverend took the girls into his and his wife's care since the couple were administrators for an orphanage. As you can picture, these two foundlings were amazingly different from any of the others at the home.

At first the girls were unable to stand because their hip joints had lost their flexibility, so they walked or ran on all fours. Their night vision was outstanding and much better than their day vision, and just as remarkable was their extraordinary sense of smell and hearing. They did not sleep after midnight and preferred moving about in the dark. They did not like to be touched by anyone other than by each other. Apparently they also preferred raw vegetables and raw meat, and did not care to play any more than a wolf would. Their genetic codes as human beings were still intact, but epigenetically they had been *influenced* by their surroundings.

Only the pastor himself ever told the story, so it is considered by some to be a hoax. If these children truly walked and ran on all fours and didn't talk, though, we know something was up. The youngest girl still had an open language window so could have learned language, but she died a year later from disease. According to the US Library of Congress manuscripts division, the oldest child possibly suffered from Rett Syndrome, which causes impaired language, diminished coordination, and sleeping problems among other things. If that were the case, I wonder if they were abandoned because of the care requirements of the two in 1918 rural India. We'll never know.

As far as wolves raising children, there's also the still heavily debated story of Romulus and Remus, the feral boys that legend says were the founders of Rome. Physiologically, children can be impacted at the hands of their *human* parents as well. Think about the physical deformities of children raised in the confinement of a low ceiling attic, or infants left in their cribs for extended periods who develop flat heads. Our environment shapes us, neurologically and physically.

In the natural order of things, the newborn infant is instinctually desperate for the security of their mother, no matter what. If that's not possible, they will imprint on any consistent caregiver that bonds with them, which is what happened with the Midnapore girls. Babies' hands have a secure grip that winds around your finger right from the start, and there is a reason for that–they want to imprint. Having a finger to grip out of the womb was unfortunately not how it turned out for Ted.

The neurological system of the child begins as soon as the sperm collides with the egg and cells start separating. Once begun, the system develops rapidly at first and then carries on moderately until the person reaches about 25 years of age. From the onset of teen years until about the 25 year milestone, we consider the brain to be adolescent. Yes, really. Lots of things make sense now, no? That's why marriages that are most successful and last the longest are between couples who did not marry until they were almost 30.

We're going to dive into some neurobiology here, but hang in there–if I can do it, you can do it. We are looking at the making of a murderer, so if you want to know how in the world he happened, well, you have to understand his brain from the very start. The brilliant neuroscientists of the world will likely be jumping up and down after reading this and saying, *but there is SO much more than that! And it's much more complicated!* But when push comes to shove, we are drawing with the big crayons and so can only cover the essentials.

During the development of the fetal brain, nerve cells branch out and connect with other nerve cells to form messenger highways. If some of these linking pathways are not being used, they atrophy, shrivel, and disappear, which is called pruning. Branching and pruning are the gist of what happens in the fetal brain that will either allow the child to form healthy affectional attachment or not.

With branching comes the "lighting up" of certain genetic tendencies. First nerve cells have to connect with each other, then they resonate and respond to the environment accordingly. For example, an organism's genetic code may be loaded equally toward psychopathy or non-psychopathy. If negative influences during development occur that cause those psychopathic-oriented genes to resonate, or light up, we will have a child who is extremely vulnerable to psychopathic traits. The genetic makeup is influenced during fetal development and continues to be tampered with throughout the first several years of life by the youngster's experiences in their environment. The genetic code is not altered, but how it is *expressed* is. What wires together fires together. This process in scientific terms is known as epigenetics.

Here is another example. If my family had a genetic vulnerability toward diabetes, and my mother lived off sugary sodas and chips throughout her pregnancy, I would have been adversely affected. The epigenetic crew overseeing my construction would have made sure I was geared up for diabetes myself since that was the environmental influence I was built to adapt to. The organism automatically imprints upon its environment and develops accordingly. Again, the genetic code has not been tampered with, but how it expresses itself has.

One might surmise that the newborn sponge is not making any impressions, but we now know otherwise. Remember that branching and pruning are actively happening even though we cannot observe it. Think about how ducklings imprint upon the first being they see. And ducklings are not human infants; they are, well, birdbrains. Consider the detrimental implications if there is no one for a child to imprint upon, or if the imprinted figure is rejecting at worst or neutral at best.

With this new information, let's go back to our 1940's foundling at the Home for Unwed Mothers in Burlington, Vermont.

After giving birth to the boy, Eleanor Louise did not intend to keep him and signed release papers for the baby to be put up for adoption. Shortly after, Louise returned to her home in Philadelphia without him. Snip. When a child was signed over for release, as I understand it, the mother had a period of time to rethink her decision and choose to keep her child.

Also, adoptive parents were given thirty days with the baby to see if it was a good fit, sort of like parole. If they opted to do so, the refusing parents could return the child to the home.

During an orphaned baby's stay at such facilities, the child was referred to by a number rather than a name. I attempted to verify The Lund as to how they identified the babies but did not receive a reply. At the facilities where numbers were assigned to the babies, it was done in order to actually *deter* bonding since the orphaned infants were to be adopted out elsewhere. When we think about it, not all mothers would have named a child they were passing off to someone else anyway, and new parents would want to select a name themselves.

In such cases, another identification system was necessary. I don't know how orphanages numbered their infants. I wonder for instance, what happened with the number once a child was adopted. Was #242 now up for reassignment to a new orphan, just like a cellphone number is after somebody dies?

I once read an account of an orphaned girl who was labeled Baby #12. She was never adopted so grew up in the orphanage, her name being Twelve.

Orphans were objectified by being numbered. This is why prison inmates are given numbers–to dehumanize them in order to relate to them as objects.

Federal Prison inmates have a several digit register number. The first digits are unique to each inmate, whereas the last digits are based on the federal sentencing court's location. I don't know what Ted's opening identification in the Home for Friendless Women was, but his closing number on Florida State Prison Death Row was #A069 063.

The emotionally distancing orphanage experience is important to talk about a bit more. How we relate to others is obviously based on how we perceive them and how they perceive us. With this in mind, how we interact with them accordingly just makes sense. Consider the orphanage worker's infant care experience.

An orphanage worker's care of Baby#? would be competent, but unavoidably a bit less emotionally compassionate than the care of little "Rixyn Thomas" that lives with and is adored by both parents *outside* the orphanage. The feeling is just different.

Try it out for yourself. How would you interact with a little one in that era that was prejudicially labeled as representing humiliation, disgrace, and a psychiatrically and morally questionable mother? Your interaction would likely be a bit hesitant due to the bias of degradation, as opposed to your reaction to the child outside your place of work that is joyously welcomed by one and all, and everyone wants to know his name.

The disappointing reality that the impression of the little one influenced interactions with him as a baby is inescapable. It drastically impacts the child that develops in the petri lab of ambivalence, of marginalization, and unfortunately at times of outright distaste (environment is downloading . . . prune unused files . . .).

Caregiver employees, even the most empathetic, would have *deliberately* avoided bonding with the infants since they were to be adopted out for their *new parents* to bond with. When I worked as a newborn nursery nurse, it was not the nurse's role to bond with the babies; the children were taken to the parents for connection to be established between *them* and their new infant.

Individuals that work at the humane society often avoid bonding with the animals for the same reason. If they bond with the kitten, they end up taking it home. That is how bonding affects us.

Ted's beginning was precarious and as we look back, we can foresee his end in many ways. In the era of Post World War II America, the daily routine in an orphanage was quite regimented, with schedules guiding the daily workings like many health, education, and other public facility settings of the day. Even prisons.

In these Homes, the babies were merchandise to be maintained and processed. Freshly born and scrubbed babies ended up tucked snugly into a bassinet, warm, full, and dry. They stayed that way until the clock, not the newborn, signaled the next reliable and regimented round of strangers. Although the caregivers were adequate, they were aloof strangers. In some orphanages crying was ignored, as it was thought it would spoil the child to offer 'excessive' soothing and comfort beyond basic care. What happens when a newborn is in the distress of emotional and social deprivation is tragic. Their ability or even desire to connect with humans is steadily diminished, if not exhausted or erased . . . this was Ted's experience.

Once separated at birth from the mother's body and the familiar sounds and smells experienced in utero, the new environment is entirely foreign to the newborn. The sensations of bath, clothing, blankets, and bassinet are nowhere near the familiar liquid conveying mother's smell, heartbeat, belly gurgling, and voice. The shock of expulsion from familiarity can be more easily borne if a mother's smell, voice, and caress offer consistent reassurance amongst the strange new textures and sounds. Smell is the sense most strongly associated with memory and so is crucial to mother infant bonding. Sound is a close second, and human touch must accompany all of it. But the reassuring familiarity of a mother, for orphans, was not existent for long, if at all.

The mortality rate was about 30-40% even in the best homes at that time. When babies are not held, talked to, and responded to in the manner they crave, they all too frequently die. This time in history was *before* broad understanding of the Science of Attachment and Bonding. We understand now that efficiency sans affection, although well-meaning, is not complete enough care.

Various studies have been done to measure the harmfulness of clinical-only care of institutionalized infants in midcentury America. The oft relayed studies in Sociology classes, such as these two to follow, alarm the students and anyone said students cannot help but share the shocking information with.

#1

In 1944, (Ted was born in 1946) forty newborn babies were split into two groups. The first group received normal affectionate care (the control group) and the other was the experiment. The babies in the experimental group had a special facility where their basic needs (ie. being changed, fed, burped, etc.) were met. However, caregivers were instructed not to touch, speak to, or look at the baby more than needed. No communicating with the babies, no extended interactions, just fill the basic needs and keep the place sanitary. The researchers were studying to see what language the infants would naturally speak. Yes, really.

But the experiment had to be halted after four months. By that point, half of those babies in the experimental group had died.

Two more died after being brought into a better place. The very few who remained alive grew up psychologically damaged or mentally disturbed. No physical cause of death was noted, as the babies were all healthy. The scientists noticed that shortly before each death, the baby would stop vocalizing or trying to engage the caregiver. Then they stopped moving, crying, or changing expressions. Finally, they died.

Meanwhile, the control group had no deaths at all; the babies thrived.

#2

In the 1960's, a similar experiment was conducted, this time with newborn monkeys due to child protection laws. The result? Same thing. The control group was fine, but the monkeys deprived of responsive affection died or became mentally damaged for life.

> **"I don't like being locked up like some kind of animal,**
> **I don't know any man that does."**
>
> **~Ted**

In the home where Eleanor Louise left him, Baby Boy #? languished mentally, physically, and emotionally–not for three days or three weeks, but three *months*. Recall that in the examples above, approximately fifteen to twenty babies had *died by 4 months.* Ted was not immediately scooped up by an adoring couple. He remained in the bassinet unadopted. I have no idea what the average length of stay was for an infant awaiting adoption, but there was one influencing factor. Money.

Orphans aren't cheap. Couples wanting to adopt a baby in the 1940's were required to pay fees: two payments of $150 each for "adoption services," $4.50 for probate fees, and $1 to the city clerk for a certified copy of the birth certificate. Our current economy comparison would be over $4000.00. This was reasonable considering the cost of care and housing of the child for an indefinite period of time before adoption.

Bonding is a physical phenomenon that must happen between parent, adoptive or not, and child. It is a physical connection that is crucial for the infant and the parent. I have had clients that had delayed bonding with their child for various reasons, especially if it was a traumatic birth or an overseas adoption. What is different about these parents is they WANT to bond with their child and persist until the connection is in place.

On the other hand, when parent-infant bonding does not occur or cannot occur over an extended period of time, the child will be affected neurologically and psychologically to various degrees. This *depends upon* the length of time of emotional deprivation, the infant's experiences such as injury, illness, or neglect during that time, and the temperament of the child. *Imprinting is filling that database* all along the way.

This is how organisms formulate, sustain, and replicate. Otherwise, faulty attachment development, if not resulting in death, can mutate into the kind of detachment that brings monsters about.

Chapter Five

Daddy's Little Boy

Next stop, the city of brotherly love . . .

Meanwhile, back at the Philadelphia house during Ted's three months in residential care, the family made some decisions. Did Eleanor love her baby after all and prevail upon her father to let her keep the little boy? Did her teenage sisters ask for him and promise to play with him and help? Did Ted's grandmother recover from her bouts with illness well enough to want to raise him? Did his grandfather want another male in the family? Or did he want to raise the child he assumed was his son?

We will never know, but for whatever reason, the grandfather made an executive decision and sent Eleanor to retrieve the baby and bring him to the family house. She was the obvious choice to fetch the baby–Ted *was* and would always be Eleanor's consequence. I wonder if the pastor's wife also made the trip to take her to retrieve the baby boy and bring him back to Pennsylvania.

The plan was to say the grandparents were the parents of a late life baby, making Eleanor and the other girls his sisters. Many families opted to use a similar plan during that period of time. Certainly some in the community didn't buy the story, but it couldn't be proven and remained at *whisper-behind-the-hand Laundry Secret level.*

So, at Elizabeth Lund's Home for Unwed Mothers, the still not attached to anyone three month old Lund Boy #? was to encounter his next introduction to how life is done. He was handled by yet another female stranger, because Eleanor by this time *was* a stranger, and a conflicted one at that, and baby #? was shunted a long distance to a new group of individuals.

As it had been for his mother all her life, the household atmosphere continued to be disorganized, and it was for the infant as well. However, for the time being, the growing child was at least no longer Baby Boy #? but had been given a name.

Theodore Robert Cowell

In the post-World War II world, photos and diary entries were not plentiful, especially among busy families. Parents tended to only document the really big and exciting changes in their child, and even then not so much. The first years of life are typically not as full of news as the later years since a developing child is not undergoing momentous transformations each day that are photo or journal worthy. Many folks did not even have cameras back then and if so, film and developing were not free.

Try to track down any of your family's photos and letters from the 40's and 50's, and you will not find tons of them. They were busy building the future.

These sturdy post-war humans chose to look at the bright side in order to put the shoulder to the wheel. When a hard time came along, they took their situations in stride and certainly did not pull out the polaroid. When crises occurred they tended to dismiss the bump as not all that important, forget about it as soon as possible, or for sure not talk about it. *All will be well. Let's not make mountains out of molehills. Take first things first.* That is what made them, in their eyes at least, the Greatest Generation.

Each household member was busy living their daily lives and were certainly not cataloging each other's development. That behavior is done more these days, especially with our phones readily at hand to capture every moment–well, the fun ones anyway–and post them on social media for the world to see. That was not so in the mid-century period of our history.

I can find little information on his first three years at the Philadelphia house other than random descriptions of him as a cute little towhead scampering around the greenhouse behind the father. The lack of available information regarding the little boy's first years in Philadelphia does not surprise me. For all of humanity, the first years after the wars were spent digging out of the world's conflicts and moving into the future.

When Ted reminisced about his first years of life in Philadelphia while in prison, he romanticized (in Ted fashion) that his aunts "fussed over" him, his grandmother "doted on" him, and he was "very fond of" his grandfather, but when describing those first few years, he never mentioned his mother. A toddler in a grownup household is rather like an adorable puppy: always underfoot and requiring a lot of work. The little one is either capturing everyone's attention, or free roaming and getting very quiet in a back room. As he did what toddlers do, he was aware of the people around him, yet when describing those first years did not mention his relationship with Eleanor.

Remember, however, she was still in a position of household management and possibly even working part time outside of the home as well. Eleanor would have been very busy seeing to a family of six, including herself, and only at the tender age of 22 years old. It makes sense to me that the young woman, being occupied with adult responsibilities, naturally left Teddy in the care of her parents and sisters much of the time.

Shifting among family members was the norm for Ted, but the little guy, like all children, needed to learn who he was and where he fit in life. He had who he thought were the *sisters, mother,* and *father* at the Philadelphia house to orient himself. Regrettably, he was oriented by disorganized relationships, silent tensions, uncertainty of the future, and the strain of being passed from one female to another—*you tend to him now; I'm off to school; read him a story; I have homework; I have laundry to do; I need to go lie down . . .* Consistent inconsistency kept attachment strings still *undeveloped* in the child. What is that saying? "A rolling stone gathers no moss."

"I couldn't get a hold of the things I needed to get a hold of."

~Ted

Like Father, Like Son

Relatives say that Samual Cowell was so mean and peculiar that when growing up, his own brothers wanted to kill him. He was the oldest brother and apparently terrorized the younger ones.

His extended family did not invite him, his wife, his daughters, or Teddy to family events because the man was so belligerent. Despite this, Teddy wanted to be like him. Considering pruning, imprinting, and genetic vulnerability, the boy was being shaped in the wrong direction like crazy.

What we do know for sure is that little Teddy and the father were the only males among several discounted *but unfortunately necessary* females that were there to meet the men's needs. Ted said one of the only memories of his grandfather that was not a warm one toward him was when Teddy left the chicken coop door open and the father got angry, setting him back on his heels. That, and the memory of seeing the father strangle chickens and pull their heads off. If young Teddy began any bonding at all, it was with that man who the boy perceived as necessarily aggressive toward animals and women.

Preschoolers learn faster than the rest of us. Remember that wide open window. They naturally have to learn as much as they can early on in order to survive in their environment. They are imprinting so quickly—they gulp down their observations, even when they don't have the words to describe what they are experiencing. No chewing of the information so to speak, just a big swallow that is mysteriously but undeniably metabolized into their mindset.

Ted claimed he was treated well by Samuel Cowell, that is if we can believe that since so much of his life turned out to be the opposite of what he claimed. Either way, if Ted was fond of the man of the house, seeing Samuel terrorize the women would have made the little guy think that the women must be really bad to deserve such treatment. They must need to be controlled and punished, *and* therefore it must be acceptable to *abuse them* because it is necessary to *subdue them.*

We have the instinctive ability to intuit the unspoken. Even if the family attempted to hide these behaviors from Teddy, a perceptive little one (which he was) with survival antennae up at all times would have still interpreted the *Thou Shalt Not be Aware* atmosphere. He would have absorbed any acts such as flinches, raised voices, cowering, harsh whispering, or shooing him out of the room. When trying to conceal incidents as they occur, the curiosity of little children is piqued with scary mystery and raises their antennae for the sake of self protection.

Samuel treated animals brutally, beat his wife sometimes, had alcoholic rages, and, while it has never been proven, possibly had an incestuous relationship with Eleanor Louise. Such a home life affected the little preschooler's developing limbic system profoundly and permanently. *Are we safe? Am I safe? Wow, he likes hurting people; he could really hurt me. He is really scary. I want him to like me. I'll try to be like him so he'll like me.*

Although there was a strong bond with the father whom he shadowed, any tirades and beatings would have rattled the little guy to the soul. All of this was awash in the young child's brain even if Ted didn't have clear memories of all the trauma later in life. The father deeply established for him an unspoken basic foundation of *"this is how life is done."*

Trauma bonding is when someone to whom we are bonded, or *attempting* to bond with, traumatizes us. Affection versus violence among the individuals alternates so as to form a solid Yin Yang, which is a balanced dualism. The aggressor decides to act with a violent Yin or a gentle Yang, and their choice of treatment is at *their personal whim*, usually unpredictable, and certainly not preventable. If someone has a video camera running or you have company, however, then you can be confident that the aggressor will be on their best behavior.

We do our best to please the bully whenever and however possible in order to prevent another frightening ordeal. Courtesy, charm, submission, or whatever we can come up with is utilized to keep the waters as smooth as possible. If such tools do not work, then the only option is stay out of sight during the unpreventable storm.

Identification with the Aggressor is what developed as Teddy began to emulate Samuel's brutish behaviors. It makes sense if we think of what it takes to survive in the world. A singular individual, especially a *young* singular individual, cannot survive on their own. Air, water, food, safety, and human companionship are absolutely required. The other human, the older or sadistic human, must be fond of you or at least find you useful to them in some way so that they want to look after you, keep you around, or abuse you less.

Little children reach out because they have to reach out for sustenance in order to survive. When in a vulnerable setting, the weak one must do all in their power to remain intact within the group by connecting to that which is strong. Eleanor had to learn this, too. How the powerful one relates to the others is noted even in an infantile, nonverbal way. This is done at a very primal level of which we are just barely aware. Little ones certainly do not have words for it, and their memories are dependent upon words to describe the memory, so recollections can be a bit of a blur. But somehow the lesson is learned somewhere in our bones and we respond accordingly. That is how we survive.

People say that the identification with the aggressor defense mechanism is unconscious, but I think it's a decision we make at the edge of consciousness for the sake of protecting ourselves. We may not be very proud of it at first, but when in dire straits we are able to talk ourselves into it.

This identification with or imitation of another is done so as to understand and establish what and who is acceptable and gets to stay in the group and who and what *is* not acceptable and does not get to stay. Or, it establishes who gets picked on and who does not. If you perhaps allow yourself to be tormented, you might get to stay. If you object, you might get it even worse or you might have to leave. If you don't get to stay, where will you go? If you are not acceptable, who else would want you? That is when the vulnerable may come to the conclusion that *I had better be pleasing to this guy in order to be accepted by him so I can remain in the setting where the bedding, food, and water are.*

Since we all love to be admired, to be considered to be an example for others to follow, the aggressor is going to like it if the weak one is obviously trying to be like him. When it's the *little* weak one, it's satisfying for the bully to see them take on his qualities because by doing so, it is validating as to how influential he or she is. Walking around in daddy's shoes, pretending to be talking on mommy's phone—we all think it's adorable and love to see it happen.

The two roles of imitated and imitator make a great combo until the weaker one is no longer weak but has become a contender, a perceived or real threat to the former powerful one's *sole* right to dominate. That's often when the two who are now equals square off and lock horns. It's biology.

On the other hand, if the father was not only a brute to the women and girls but also directly abusive to Teddy, the little one would think that he needed to be more like the powerful abuser in order to not be controlled and dominated. The little kid loses either way, so Teddy's impressions of how to be powerful with women came about by being in the presence of and imprinting upon this violent man that set that very example.

Being a bright little kid, he easily learned to charm with courtesy and endear himself to perceived authority by imitating in order to be admired by the one in charge. Right from the permanently molding start, Ted did this to survive. To whatever extent all of those incidents occurred, they were the little boy's introduction to interpersonal relationships and social hierarchy.

We have all learned at least to some degree to be astute to threats. Ted was saturated in it while filling that open window, learning rapidly *how life is done* those first four or so years. By five years of age, our personalities are pretty much rock solid. After that it's simply a matter of how to motor that personality as effectively as possible. Learning how to protect and direct our continuously downloading selves is what we are learning for the rest of our developmental years.

We do not spontaneously after years of unremarkable Norman Rockwell experiences suddenly begin heinous crime. We experience shaping incidences, even if at the time they are not recognized or understood in relation to their directing factors. When we look back on our lives, though, we can usually identify them. Serious recurring experiences occurred in Eleanor Louise's upbringing and Ted's early years of life. We only have pieces of such information, but they are disturbing pieces, and enough in my opinion to explain the finished products of both Jekyll & Hyde Ted and Area 51 Louise.

Chapter Six

Daddy's Installation Process

. . . Installing . . . .

Sex and violence were part of the curriculum included in Ted's primary training ground, and he took it in because that is what little ones do. What fascinates me is that he signed some of the angry letters he wrote from prison to his wife Carole as "Sam." Using his grandfather's first name shows another indication as to how much he wanted to emulate his grandfather. I don't know the subject of his anger in those specific letters, but his vexed tone is an example of Ted's association and emulation of the man's ferocity.

Another example of identification with the aggressor is **Stockholm Syndrome**, where a person is or at least feels captive in some way by a more powerful person or group with no hope of escape. The captive eventually inches over to being in emotional accord with the perceived authority, ultimately supporting the captor in anticipation of receiving safety, reinforcement, or promotion and therefore a better chance of survival. We see this often in cults or churches if a member objects to the group's authority figures is then disciplined in some way, or if a member decides to leave the group is shunned or persecuted by the group, and sometimes even rejected by their family. With some groups, a requirement of membership is to be estranged from family.

The original incident that coined the name Stockholm Syndrome was the kidnapping of Patty Hearst, a newspaper heiress, by the Symbionese Liberation Army in 1974. She was with the group when they committed several crimes. Patty was found and arrested nineteen months after her kidnapping. She relayed that she had been raped repeatedly and threatened with her life from the time they abducted her. The shift can happen very fast, and Patty is an extreme example of that. Cult conversions happen the same way, but over a varied period of time depending on how desperately a captive wants to leave their former lifestyle and how much threat occurs if they don't join forces with the captor.

When opting to integrate with whatever group that we are for some reason stuck with, at a very deep level that we are not or at least are barely aware of. We think to ourselves, *I don't want anything to do with this*, but that doesn't get us anywhere because we genuinely are or at least feel trapped. In an innate act of survival, we slowly begin to consider *their* perspective in order to possibly gain safety or, at least in the most domineering examples, suffer less abuse.

The captive, when in horrifically abusive situations, may even begin to feel sorry for, if not admire or idolize, the captor(s) and their cause. In the case of prolonged threat, captives often convince themselves that there is some good, necessity, or purpose for this to be happening to them in order to save themselves *psychologically*. This happened with the Manson phenomenon. Charlie did not overtly threaten any new acquaintances. Instead he gave them new names, new identities of belonging to his 'family', and convinced his followers that *society* was threatening them.

The metamorphosis of empathy continues to happen until we reach the place where we actually *see* the captor's point and more or less join the other side. In some cases the new recruit is the most zealous of all because the rationale is that if I am going to join ranks with something so awful,

I must REALLY believe in the cause. We have all heard the saying, *if I don't make it into Heaven, I want a really high rank in Hell.*

So Teddy, more than ready to imitate the violent acts he witnessed daily, began placing knives in his sister's bed, and no one said a word. It seems to me they dared not comment for some reason. In the spirit of Stockholm Syndrome, I wonder if the father put him up to it as something conspiratorially funny or an initiation of some sort between the two of them. It's just a guess on my part, but that would explain a few things. How a child that small could have the idea and then physically maneuver the scene is beyond me.

This is likely why Ted had a penchant for scaring girls and always owned a number of knives later in life. Don't assume because your uncle Davis is a knife collector that he is Ted Bundy. Ted was not a knife collector; he was a stealer, concealer, and user of the weapons for destructive purposes. A Freudian-oriented reader might even detect the symbolic incestuousness of Ted placing sharp instruments into the bed with his *sister*. Such behavior was not welcomed by her and it was aggressively entitled deliberate conduct by him in an effort to imitate the father. Even if he did not think up scaring her at that age all on his own, he did it and he liked it.

"I just liked to kill. I wanted to kill."

~Ted

When Julia told the others what had happened and nobody addressed it, it would have been interpreted by Teddy as more or less allowed. Unaddressed misbehavior is loosely interpreted as permission. Kids love that and will take it as far as they can run with it until the adults lower the boom. When that happens, the child's mind says to itself, *but why didn't you say anything before . . .?* Grownups in Ted's household seemed to have allowed him free behavioral reign, never trying to end it at all. The Phila-delphia household lifestyle during his first years taught him the following:

**"Women are possessions. Beings which are subservient,
more often than not, to males. Women are merchandise . . .
like a Porsche or potted plant."**

~Ted

Had I been present during the interview when Bundy made the above statement, I would have wanted to ask, "When and where did you get that awareness? When did you *first* get that impression?" Had he given a candid answer, I think the reply would have indicated that it had been very early on in his life. He did not learn it later when he moved to Tacoma, as Louise was dominant in his home there. My thoughts are that this conclusion was already settled in Ted's solidifying mind before he left the Philadelphia household. The origin of this concept was in his grandfather's house.

Ted's three year old entitlement was possibly because he was becoming like the *father,* which gave him position or rank in the household. Even at the age of three and a half, he was pretty much deputized. I think Louise all her life saw Ted as non-opposable. Based upon the principles of Stockholm Syndrome, avoiding opposing an aggressor is instinctive. It seems Ted in turn also did not oppose Louise, or at least he did not oppose her openly. In her home, she was the authority figure, so Ted had to join forces with her as he had his grandfather. I picture them bound together tight with a boulder between their smiling selves.

It probably worked in the little guy's favor that he was a cute little blonde headed boy. He learned to charm the ladies early in order to be readily forgiven and keep his hierarchical spot secure in the bedding and food chain department. At that age with nowhere else to go, we might have done so too. His learning to keep in the good graces of women and assuage authority for his own benefit kicked in right off the bat.

Louise conveyed during one of the rare glimpses of any possible flaws in her family that her father had said Ted was conceived in Hell. If *that* was the impression given by the father, the young child had even more to overcome, especially since this alleged declaration came from the man that was his idol. On the other hand, young Ted might have taken a bit of pride in the bad guy image. He was evolving into a little version of the ominous, omnipotent, and omnipresent father.

Now back to little Teddy's continuous human attachment failures. There may be some questions from the reader as to why secrecy and coverups even matter to a child, especially when the incidence is so small. In Ted's day, everyone thought that the secrecy did not matter.

Emotional and Behavioral Developmental Science of today is showing otherwise. As I stated before, a child's character is pretty firmly formed by the age of five. The farther past that age a child gets, the more solid and permanent character and behavior patterns become. We all have met preschoolers that demonstrate definite personality traits and behaviors by the age of five, because every year before that was comprised of events that made them who they are. The three months in the orphanage had serious impacts on Ted's sense of self in relation to, or in his case *not to*, others. Hour after day after week after month, only Ted's basic needs were met and nothing more. The newly forming child's brain was downloading what? All of this time of detachment. The limbic system is not capable of denial and will respond according to its programming. It will always be convinced that every foundational experience did occur and that each one was profound.

Besides the limbic system, the other developing system we need to think about is the traumatized brain when bonding is unsuccessful. Emotional, neglectful, and other abuse causes physiological damage to the central nervous system. If the baby, young child, and growing teen has the love and company of his parents, he will grow up with a solid sense of identity and significance. If he does not have these things, there is a likelihood that his craving for this essential affectionate care will *increase*. In that case, the child constantly seeks reassuring attention, and is likely *more prone to hate* those who fail, or seem to fail, to provide it.

In a household where the child's identity and his relationship to those around him is being hidden because of shame, the message is interpreted loud and clear. He's yours, not mine, yours.

We have all been acquainted with stories of the young child that unfortunately does not get enough to eat at home so hangs out at the neighbors', steals from the store, or takes a classmate's lunch. When it's affectional starvation, which is likely to be the case with that young child, too, neglect presents itself in needy attempts to be seen, acknowledged, cared about, and fundamentally protected by a social group.

When that is not available or enough, he will manipulate or steal in other ways than manipulating. Manipulating is in fact a form of stealing. When we manipulate another, it is getting them to give us an outcome they would not have provided for us otherwise. Manipulation is covertly used when we would get a "no" if we asked.

When the neglected child exhausts all interpersonal attempts, the result is either withdrawal or *predation*. They are left with becoming their *own* element, not requiring emotional connection to others or even desiring it. These directions of attachment or detachment are established depending on the child's temperament and environmental influences. Becoming oneself is not a light switch; it's a process, a growth pattern that evolves as the little one experiences all of the enjoyments and vicissitudes of early life.

Louise, Ted, and all the rest of us have different temperaments. Some of us are easy going and independent while some of us are more sensitive and reactive. We are just born with various temperaments, and these can differ widely even in the same family. The shaping that comes along with socialization has further influence. Indeed, even identical twins vary from each other based on their singular experiences with their separate environments. We are that malleable.

When a child is not responded to in the necessary affectional life giving way, they will try and try again, hoping for emotional nourishment. Some of us need more reassurance and are more reactive to perceived let downs than others. When feeling continuously unsuccessful, our anger can build and we might act out negatively in order to be seen and responded to. We all want to feel like we have enough worth and agency in life and that we *matter* to other humans, and some people require more direct responses to feel this way. Not all of us have the same reassurance needs.

> **"Society wants to believe it can identify evil people . . .**
> **the thing of it is that some people are just psychologically**
> **less ready for failure than others."**
>
> **~Ted**

Unfortunately when a child acts out negatively, it brings negative attention, but at least the child is receiving *some* attention. Sometimes even the negative acting out is overlooked, dismissed, or even denied, as it was in Ted's case. Although naughtiness is being overlooked by some, it is still necessary for the little one to learn to move about *as though he is benign*, endearing himself to the authority figures among his counterparts.

Getting on the good side of the boss can eradicate undesirable behavior. At least with the Boss. The detaching child begins to act in the expected ways and perform necessary roles, but they suffer deepening loneliness when it comes to connection to other human beings. Their personal self, which includes the naughty parts, has not been tended and wisely guided. Ted's knife incidents never addressed by the adults in the house could have been interpreted by the child as *I can do no wrong, so even my bad parts must be good*. That would make a lasting moral and identity imprint on any child, and it undoubtedly did on the central player of our story.

The 1993 Edition of Time/Life hardcover True Crime displays a picture of Eleanor Louise, the father and little Teddy at the beach. What interests me is that the photograph appears to depict a crowded beach and summery fun. A picture speaks a thousand words. Both Ted and the father were looking serious here. If they were laughing or smiling I wouldn't be so intrigued, but they are not so it catches my eye. Louise is looking the other way while tending to her hair. Her looking the other way and tending to her appearance seems to support my thoughts on Ted being neglected, but this is only one picture so I have to leave it there.

Chapter Seven

Don't Fit Anywhere

. . . Square peg in a round hole

"When I was a little kid and I felt I didn't fit in, I compared it to a planet drifting out in space that didn't have a sun to orbit around. It's cold and lonely when you drift through empty space. You either have to find a sun to orbit around or you have to turn yourself into a sun and have others orbit around you. It may be all pretend but it's profoundly important that you do it."

~Ted

It was not too long after the knife games that Ted was once again uprooted from familiarity by, let's see–how did Psychiatrists describe unwed mothers back in the day? Oh, right–a *psychologically disturbed woman.*

To her credit, in a house where chaos and abuse is familiarity, it's of course best one be uprooted. Had Eleanor stayed in Philadelphia with little Teddy, it would have been at the risk of confirming the suspicion that she had an illegitimate child. There would be no escaping it then. By this time, Eleanor had developed coping mechanisms by being in charge of her surroundings and no longer wanted to compete for management of those surroundings with her father. In a situation such as this, she knew it would be best to get out of town. And so they did. Eleanor would become the alpha that Teddy would be forced to identify with.

It had been deeply instilled in Teddy's four year old mind that his grandparents were his parents, his two aunts and Eleanor his sisters. This upheaval of what he perceived as his family structure was a further disorganizing rupture to his already distorted sense of relationships, detached and dysfunctional as they were. Ted, when harkening back to his early years, described the family as being dysfunctional. That statement was also a stain leaking through the perfect family portrait. Of course all of our families are dysfunctional somewhere along the line. Where it's a problem is when it's denied and left unaddressed.

Perfect and dysfunctional home lives aside, Eleanor was gathering herself and Teddy up to move from (some family said to escape from) the father's household. Teddy's awkward connecting-to-humans attempts so far were failing *any* longevity at all. This little stone was still bare, hardening daily and not settled or certain enough to resonate with caregivers in a reciprocal way.

Eleanor and Teddy, who was then about four years old, moved across the North American continent from Philadelphia to the West Coast. Another arduous journey to parts unknown with a woman the little boy did not necessarily feel safe with and was likely only *precariously* attached to. This woman was taking him away from his house and family *as he knew it.*

He had to have had a confused loss of the familiarity of the father, the mother, and the sisters, and in all his life was *never* told the Philadelphia house relative's true relationship to him or how to perceive them. He was left to solve that mysterious Story Problem later in life, as were the rest of us. In fairness, I don't know how I would have told young ted about his origins had it been mine to tell.

Eleanor changed her name to Eleanor Louise Nelson and started to go by Louise, and she changed Teddy's name. **Theodore Robert Nelson.** Their Cowell surname was gone.

Now he was Theodore Robert Nelson and was still not getting a settling in of himself as to who he was and where he belonged. Instead, life was still continuously shaking up his snow globe. Why the name changes? Avoiding suspicions of incest? Distancing herself as far as possible from her Philadelphia life? Again the little boy's always concealed and fragmenting identity was challenged with yet *another* name coupled with the uncertainties and awkwardness associated with the entire family situation. Ah, Louise.

Little Teddy went from number, to new name, to new name, and now *sister* Eleanor to Louise, *all* in order for the child to be hidden from *humiliating* discovery. A child can feel those feelings but not know what or why they are happening. He can see and hear the concerned or, even worse, disapproving look and the anxious clearing of the throat by an adult. Although attempting to avoid tactlessness in the kindest circles, many adults unavoidably fall into this trap because we are people, after all. He saw all and heard all, but the secrets were never explained to him. *So what kind of freak am I? They let me get away with murder because I can act so cute, but nothing is being explained to me.* Not to be overlooked is that this little organism had been exposed to all of these reactions from people in his world from the start, so for him it was his defining world and self image.

"I didn't know right from wrong."

~Ted

By this time Teddy would have had a good handle on the right and wrong *notions* of truth and lies, and was definitely questioning inconsistencies in the actions of adults. We are not supposed to tell lies, and we are supposed to be good, but there was something askew that he could not sort out, and the caregivers were not talking about it. Louise was just glazing over whatever it was, with smiles, courtesy, and instruction for Teddy to behave well. I would really like to have come across indications that somewhere in these years he was receiving comfort, reassurance, and at least some answers to his questions, but I have not been able to find any sign of it.

Eleanor's aunt in Tacoma, Washington sponsored the trip. The expense would not have been a frivolous expenditure. This aunt and uncle were conservative, well ordered folks. The Tacoma uncle was a professor and an established professional concert pianist. The couple's life was stable and they were well respected publicly. Her paternal aunt and uncle successfully rescued Eleanor and her boy from the Philadelphia household and they moved into their home.

Louise and Ted lived with these supportive relatives long enough to make some permanent and positive imprints on Ted. Later in life, he described his enjoyable experiences with them. The aunt and uncle had a son close to Ted in age with whom he would remain familiar for years.

Ted said he admired his Tacoma uncle because he had money, was a university music teacher, and taught Ted about classical music. He said he liked his aunt because she came from money, was refined, and had breakfast in bed. He described them almost as though they were luxury cars and honored places to park. Bundy's detachment was likely the reason he described them in this resume-like manner.

In their home, the little boy discovered a taste of predictability and dignity. His uncle, Dr. John Cowell, was the youngest of seven siblings when growing up in Philadelphia, with the oldest child being Louise's father. As a boy Dr. Cowell was a music prodigy and his parents nurtured his talent. He became a renowned composer and concert pianist, as well as a respected professor and educator.

Dr. Cowell performed in the symphony halls of New York, Europe and Seattle and composed music for the Seattle Ballet Academy, Seattle Symphony, and many other ensembles. He earned his music composition degree from Yale and a doctor of arts degree from the University of Washington. He was also dean of music at Cornish School of Music and Allied Arts, so Ted had an exemplary example of well-earned distinction from his Uncle John whose family respectfully referred to as Uncle Jack.

Following the first imprint years of uncertainty at best, a new and different formative layer of social upper class and calm intelligence was discovered that young Teddy absorbed gladly and emulated distinctively whenever possible throughout his life. Of note, as with the years in Philadelphia, he said nothing about his mother during their time at her aunt and uncle's home either.

Later in life young Ted asked his uncle if he would adopt him, but the uncle refused. I have wondered if, due to the uncle's understanding of Ted's illegitimacy and suspicion that he was a product of incest, he did not want to become more than necessarily associated with Ted or Louise. Further, he *was Louise's child*.

The Tacoma aunt and uncle had less reason to hide information regarding the Philadelphia relatives from Ted due to their cross-country distance from the older brother Samuel Cowell and his clan. They may have even felt a bit of noble relief by attempting to give Louise and Teddy a fresh start, so they would have been more likely to describe the situation honestly to Ted for that reason.

The aunt and uncle decided not to tell Ted the truth, however. Louise, as his mother, was obligated to explain to Ted his origins, not the aunt or uncle. It was really none of their business to divulge anything. Yet, likely due to a natural human need to distance unpleasant emotional exchange and preservation of privacy and family name, they shared the difficult information with their son *only* rather than Ted himself. Or perhaps they never told their son of Ted's beginnings and instead he overheard conversations between his parents through the door. Who knows.

But somehow their son, Ted's cousin, knew and was apparently unable to keep it to himself. Youngsters are more likely than adults to divulge secrets, even painful ones. The boldness of youth causes delight in knowing *the* mysterious information and being able to inform the uninformed.

The cousin revealed to Ted his illegitimacy at the age of 13 and must have shared more of the story with Ted as time went by. If I were Ted, I know I would have been prying my cousin for more information. The father in Philadelphia had been a disastrous example of maleness for the little boy. Ted said his grandfather was warm to him and yet one of his Tacoma neighbors said that when Bundy was in his teens, he told the neighbor kids that his grandfather liked to beat him and call him a bastard and that was where his speech impediment came from.

He also told one of the neighbor boys that his grandfather raped his mother, so his grandfather was in fact his father. At the same time, Ted said his mother *never told him how he came about.* I wonder if Ted's cousin also told him this other information, which made him an *incestuous* bastard. No matter what rumors Ted spread to the neighbors, Louise stubbornly kept his father's identity from him. She likely did so to protect him, but ended up leaving Ted wide open to lifelong shame and humiliation.

Back to four year old Teddy. Having settled into a calm predictable environment with his uncle and aunt in Tacoma, the little guy found his new holding environment was dissolving as well. Noticing a pattern here? As the still preschool aged child's fate would have it, Louise met a gentle, somewhat passive man (it's likely that she felt she could control him rather than how it was with her father, and she could). Louise had established membership in a new church, where she and Johnny Bundy met at one of the church's functions. They were married within the year.

This next relational rupture occurred when Louise and Ted moved from the uncle's lovely home to an isolated rural house with his new financially limited "Dad." Unlike the classy uncle, Johnny was a cook. Not *even* a chef. This would bug Ted forever. To his credit Johnny was classy enough to adopt Ted, granting yet *another* name to the little lost boy, which eventually became his infamous surname.

Theodore Robert Bundy. This name stuck.

He called Johnny "Dad," which would have been straightforward for the five year old, even if resented, but he was still left confused addressing the woman he thought was his sister as "Mom." Ted said that for a period of time he thought his real dad had died. I wonder if that was before the incest suggestion came up in his teens.

Neighbors said Johnny was mousey and strict and that Louise expected him to 'raise' the children. I think how Louise's father expected the women to tend to the household while he dominated them. In this new power dynamic, if Louise was the boss and gentle Johnny was the underling, that would have driven Teddy absolutely crazy following the misogynous template that had been instilled in him at the Philadelphia house.

But Johnny was the new male in the household now and roles would not be arranged by Teddy. Louise, Johnny, and Ted lived in the country house for about a year. Ted said the nearest kids were a boy a half mile away and another boy a mile and a half away. It doesn't seem likely that they played together all that often given the distance, and even if it was as much as weekly, that left Teddy alone for days at a time with Louise, who didn't have a car and was focused on her new husband and their first pregnancy together.

That first pregnancy for the couple sadly resulted in a miscarriage. A miscarriage for a mom often brings humiliation, a sense of inadequacy, and grief . . . more emotions for stalwart Louise to cram down. Meanwhile Teddy was trying to find out where *he*, the little former deputy, fit in his new family. Displaced, displaced, and displaced again left the child floundering in yet another setting. But that was soon to change as well. Give that snow globe another shake.

The family's next move was to Tacoma proper. They relocated to a house in town with a bustling neighborhood and other children. He said years later regarding this move that he was hopeful and hungry for friends. But by this time, his blunted sense of self, insecurities, distorted socialization skills, and overall awkwardness made it difficult for the secure "*I know who I am and who I come from*" children to connect with him. His being the secret thorn in the flesh continued to be his *lifelong* identity.

Ted never quite fit in, according to neighbors and according to himself. When he moved to the new neighborhood in Tacoma among other children, he suffered a speech impediment, about which the other kids teased him of course. You might refer back to speech problems occurring in unattached children. He also blamed his grandfather for it. As if that were not enough, he was also left handed. Recall that mixed handedness is a frequent-but-not-always outcome of prenatal stress. Also, being a South Paw in those days was considered unfortunate at best, which established yet another social demerit against him.

Making friends and fitting in was still not going well at all for Ted, and given his already stunted ability to attach to others, he began to show his reactive anger and resentment. Other kids clearly had a mom and a dad from which they came into the world. This little boy had no idea where he came from or who he was. And no one was explaining it to him. He *had* to have asked his mom, at least in the beginning until he learned not to.

By this time, young Teddy's animosity began to flair toward other youngsters. He was punished by his teacher in the second grade when he was playing marbles with a classmate, became angry, and hit the other child. Ted, as an adult in Utah State Prison remarked. "I don't know what was the matter, I only hit him twice." He added that he didn't like that teacher because of what he described as her *arbitrary punishment*. Ted could not tolerate ambiguity at all by second grade, and he had no more insight as a man in his 40's having been convicted of and imprisoned for aggravated kidnapping than he had as a child. He was and remained stunted—permanently stalled at the emotional level of a preschooler.

As if this avalanche of derailments was not enough, Louise gave birth to more children, four in all. As the years went by and he gained new siblings, Ted described feeling more and more distanced. Louise busied herself with excellent homemaking and devoted mothering of the children, but Ted felt disconnected from everyone. Recall how the child is treated or how they *perceive* being treated becomes their identity reference. While clean clothes and cupcakes are more than enough for the more bonded kids, for the emotionally stunted child, it may as well be cardboard.

Ted said he was mixed with resentment and confusion when seeing his mother show generous love and affection toward the younger siblings but when he would seek it, he said he would be brushed aside and told to play outside. Or at least that is *how he interpreted it*. The new family hierarchy was so different from his powerful grandfather that kept those women in line. Now it was Louise that made the household rules, and Johnny was content to follow her directives.

In fairness to Louise, who was molded early into homemaking responsibilities, she likely filled her time with housework because she unavoidably had a natural, unshakable unsettledness toward Ted. It might have been her way to cope with Ted because that very ambivalence toward him had to be *hidden*. Furthermore, her eldest son was possibly beginning to more and more resemble her father, and Louise noticing his social awkwardness among others very possibly weighed her down with more than she could metabolize. So she put a sunshine sticker on Ted, hoped for the best, and continued on to the next household task or to take care of the younger children. Of course, in every family, the littlest ones require most of the attention, so Ted was no longer a caregiving priority.

Ted never fit in anywhere, from his hidden birth to family disconnects and rotating authority figures. He was always without choice and filled with an unexplained sense of shame. These changes in relationships and why he didn't fit was endlessly obfuscated by his mother's ambiguous acts toward him. Despite all the confusion he faced, his concerns seemed to be met with an underlying agreement:

Do not ever, my child, ask for clarification.

Chapter Eight

They Walk Among Us

. . . Psycho Sociopaths at home, at work, at play

I have a parenting story.

There was a set of grandparents that had been asked by their adult children to pick up their two granddaughters from an evening function at the girls' grade school. The grandparents agreed. Come evening, they promptly forgot. Their granddaughters waited alone in the dark outside of the school. The girls, being stranded, had to figure out what to do. There was a building across the street with lights on and cars out front, so they went over to use the phone. It was a bar. They called the grandparents who were horrified that they forgot and immediately came to get them.

Well, the grandparents got in trouble with the parents of the two girls for forgetting, but I don't believe they should have. Obviously all adults in the girls' family had influenced the girls to problem solve in a safe, responsible way, which they did. Before the wonderful Rockwell all turned out well spin at the end, we all get a bit sick reading this story because of how it *could* have gone, but that's just life. No one did anything wrong here, and those girls and their parents have a fun family story to tell at reunions when lovingly teasing the grandparents.

Achingly, not everyone gets this outcome. Not because *they did anything wrong*, but because of the kind of men in this book. That's why I'm writing this for us.

The parenting that brought about the seriously disturbed characters in our story is the flip side of that sweet coin. For example, in little Charlie Manson's case, he was simply tossed out onto the sidewalk to seek his fortune. That little boy whose birth certificate name was "No Name Maddox" didn't know who his father might be since his mother was a 16 year old prostitute. His mother left Charlie with various folks for periods of time in exchange for alcohol, food, rent, etc. It was the red light district after all.

Things got worse when Charlie's mother, along with her brother Luther, was arrested for armed robbery. Charlie was eight years old at the time and already on a downward slide. He only went further down hill from there. While his mother was in prison, she first left him with her sister and then he was shifted to other relatives. By the time his mother got out, he was already well embarked on his life of crime.

Charlie's mother next found herself a husband that was a circus worker. He was not father material as he could not keep a job or stay sober. Worse, when Charlie clashed with the man, his mother took her husband's side and had Charlie sent to a Catholic boarding school for wayward boys. He ran away from the school, but his mother sent him back. He ran away again and with other boys, started to steal cars among other things, and ended up in a variety of reform schools, juvenile detention centers, and state jails.

So reader, don't worry about *your* parenting.

The point of no return always has a beginning. It just so happens that illegitimacy and being passed from one "home" to another during infancy and childhood is *very common* among psychopaths. I will add to that–a child can be emotionally shunted about even though housed with the same family. Parents and siblings, for example, can be chronically otherwise occupied or even disconnect themselves for personal reasons. Louise and Johnny had four children aside from Ted who needed their attention. According to Ted, he always felt like he was getting in the way. Sadly, parents can often be unaware of the detachment and loneliness within their developing child.

A high incidence of delinquency and depression are consistently found to occur following *disrupted* affectional bonds during early childhood. We have a ready understanding of delinquency and depression, but to explain further, getting to the point of psychopathy itself is jumping off point of the delinquency continuum. It's not that psychopaths don't get depressed–they do–but it's not because they don't want to be psychopaths. Psychopaths actually think their lifestyle is working quite well for them, and when it doesn't they will see to it that it does, and then once again their behavior will continue to make the people around them, the *rest of us*, stressed, anxious and depressed.

Before I move along, this would be a good time to clarify some terms. Antisocial Personality Disorder is the umbrella term used when *formally diagnosing* an extremely socially disturbed individual. Sociopath and Psychopath are *informal* terms used frequently and interchangeably by most of us for these psychologically disordered criminals. When referring to a serial killer, we don't usually hear folks describing them as having an Antisocial Personality Disorder.

Instead, sociopath or psychopath is used by non-clinical observers. I have my own term that is certainly not official but I believe describes the disordered individual. Not all narcissists are psychopaths but all, or at least most psychopaths *are* narcissists, so here or there I will refer to them as "narcopaths." It works for me as a reminder that it's the narcissism that they *cannot hide for long* that alerts us to their jeopardous inclinations.

To further clarify, I think of a sociopath as not quite as bad as the baddest of the bad: the psychopath. Sociopaths are more like sloppy criminals and score lower on the antisocial personality scales than the psychopaths who are more calculating, sly, and exquisitely difficult to detect. Sociopaths tend to display themselves pretty obviously Like Jack Nicholson's character in the movie *One Flew Over the Cuckoo's Nest* (1975). Psychopaths like Louise Fletcher's character as Nurse Ratched make everyone miserable *undetectably*. I detected her psychopathic tendencies early on since I myself was a head nurse in a small hospital psych ward, and I watched her like a hawk for the entire film.

Now I will scare you to death, but only for a minute.

Let me introduce you to a grownup psychopath. You likely know one since they are plentiful. It is estimated that at least 1 in every 100 people is a psychopath. You can relax. Most psychopaths don't even know they are psychopaths and certainly don't go around killing people. They are the calloused, disregarding types that you know not to trust too far, usually because they have already gotten one over on you or someone you care about.

We can see this in Nurse Ratched's psychopathic behavior. Her callous disregard is obvious to a fault, but that is mainly what we see. We do not see her trying to impress or snow anyone, to brag or manipulate. She did not have to because she *already* had all of the patients at her mercy. Unable to escape her, they tried their best to protect themselves from her cruelty and *she reveled in it*.

Narcopaths are conniving risk takers not interested in being subject to rules like the rest of us. They tend to brag and manipulate others in order to get what they want. They are parasitic in that they expect others to take care of the things they would rather not do, like support themselves, and want to have help with, well, everything. They only do work for themselves when people they want to impress are watching or in order to build their nice guy credits back up. In other words, they have no qualms about living off the efforts of other people. They don't have empathy, anxiety, or remorse. And, no surprise, they have difficulties maintaining close relationships.

Just for grins, let's all take Lynham's Child Psychopathy Scale (1997)

There are lots of "He's, His's and Him's" in these following descriptions because psychopaths are predominantly male. Women are catching up though, and when it comes to narcissistic personality disorder it is pretty much 50-50 male/female. Women are socialized to be more empathetic than men so are not typically nurtured into cruel behavior or are they biologically equipped for it. Usually I selected this scale because Ted, other than having an impressively extensive vocabulary, was pretty much 12 years old in his cognitive depth, pre-adolescent in his coping ability, and preschool level in his emotions throughout his life. If that is not apparent to you now, it will be after we explore more of his history. You may want to come back and review this scale later. The random comments set in between asterisks are mine. Keep in mind there are no right or wrong answers.

1. Is he a warm and kind person? *if so, it's too often fake*

2. Is he easily frustrated?

3. Does he make close friendships with other people? *if so, it's for personal gain*

4. Does he try to blame other people for things that he has done?

5. Is he open and straightforward? *but he appears to be very sincere*

6. Does he try to be the center of attention? *Does he show off to get people to pay attention to him or pretend to be a victim for special attention?*

7. Does he stay away from scary things and places?

8. Does he try to act charming in order to get his way? *Beware of charm. It's not your friend. Charm is *always* disingenuous and always for the purpose of winning us over.*

9. Does he think about what he wants to do with the rest of his life? *but he might tell you what he's going to do when, or what he could have done if not for . . .*

10. Are his moods unpredictable? *Do his feelings change often and quickly?*

11. Will he usually tell a lie if he thinks he can get away with it?

12. Is he easily bored?

13. Does he show his feelings openly?

14. Does he try to see how much he can get away with?

15. Is he protective of people who are close to him? *yes, that is if someone is watching or he is trying build some credit*

16. Does he try to take advantage of other people?

17. Does he give, lend, and share things?

18. Is he considerate and thoughtful of other people? *You are probably getting the idea now*

19. When he starts working on something, does he stick with it?

20. Is he mean to other people?

21. Do his feelings come and go quickly?

22. Does he use his head before doing or saying something?

23. Is he reliable and dependable?

24. Does he have a hard time waiting for things he wants?

25. Does he usually pay back what he borrows?

26. Does he plan things ahead?

27. Does he usually feel guilty after doing something wrong?

28. Does he do dangerous things for the fun of it?

29. Can he be trusted?

*In a nutshell, he has an unemotional callous disregard of others, and leads a parasitic lifestyle, getting others to do what he does not really care to do to meet *his* whims.*

How did you score as a kid? Everyone will have some points, it's just that the more of these elements we have, the more attention we need to pay to how and if they are being addressed.

Meanwhile, any psychologically trained scholar is going to be concerned since we do not DIAGNOSE anyone under 18 years of age with Antisocial Personality Disorder (psychopathy, sociopathy) but rather Oppositional Defiant or Conduct Disorder. That is because if caught soon enough and well channeled, there is still hope for the child.

At the same time these are the elements that *do* begin to be evident in children that have been impacted by developmental trauma. If not picked up on and channeled in healthy directions, they culminate in very scary adults that we *do* diagnose with Antisocial Personality Disorder and refer to informally as psychopaths.

How does this happen? Think of Little Charlie at the ages of one, two, three, and four living the Red Light District life. His preoccupied mother frantically tried to make ends meet with men coming and going. These men were not people with either the young mother or the child's best interests at heart. His housing was likely a little apartment not kept up because of mom needing to be out all night to earn money or as a result of her alcohol abuse. The air in that cramped space probably smelled like stale cigarettes, alcohol, and sweaty men.

The entire Red Light community was dangerous. He was left with random babysitters and sometimes no babysitter while she entertained Johns regularly. Sometimes she brought them home with her. Too often, "No Name Maddox" was abandoned with unsafe company, and more often completely left alone to figure out life by his own little devices. *Who am I? Do I matter to anyone? I'm hungry, I'm scared. Where's my mother? Are you my mother? The people around my life are sketchy, so this must be how one does life. Now I'm in reform school. Again.* Eventually these kids give up and toughen.

Finally, at the age of nine, Charlie burned down his school.

Delinquent behavior with detached kids starts early. The kinds of experiences children have seriously affect whether they can *expect* to find a stable base while *developing* behavior. The level of competence they learn in initiating and sustaining rewarding *reciprocal relationships* is crucial. Whatever pattern that they *start off with* tends to persist. Think about it. Charlie's preschool setting was crime and neglect.

When Charlie was being emotionally deprived, his detachment increased and angry resentment built up from being overlooked. We often have a feeling of weakness when powerless and a feeling of strength when angry. So, in order for these youngsters to feel powerful and in control, they use their anger to manipulate weaker souls that they *can* control. Everyone becomes mere objects to them since they increasingly have no idea how to safely trust and effectively relate to living beings other than through domination.

Of course, the child does not understand this and cannot articulate what's happening even though it is happening. This is the crux of many a serial murderer, including Bundy, Dahmer, Manson, and Gacy to name a few.

Think of both Ted and "No Name Maddox" when considering and reviewing the following: if the attachment base is disorganized and unstable, separation anxiety occurs within the child. *Will you take care of me? If not, how do I obtain care?* This is called anxious dependance. If anxious dependance and disorganized attachment continues beyond normal developmental landmarks, *arrested development* occurs where one *remains* insecure. Attachment instability brings about a child that reacts with angry uncertainty. If developmental trauma is not resolved, the angry uncertainty evolves to angry resignation or rage, and then we have an angry adolescent, then crazy adult Charlie or cruising-under-the-radar Ted.

For an individual to be most successful in gaining autonomous maturity, the child must have *at least one safe, affectionate, and consistent* attachment figure *throughout* his or her developmental years. This research is pervasive and continues to demonstrate that insecure attachment contributes to anxiety, as well as difficulty managing emotions and interacting well with peers; this gets the developing child that needs to accomplish social maturity nowhere except frustrated and angry.

The youngsters that don't even have kind old codgers across the street to show them some kindness are less likely to break out of their self-protective concern because they haven't experienced the parent as a consistent source of affectionate reassurance. Instead what develops is mistrust and anger toward authority figures. They never form trusting attachment to others but instead look at others as having weaknesses that can be exploited as though toys or pawns. They increasingly obsess about having power and dominance over others—this is such a good example of Charlie's formation and outcome.

Manson was a bit of a Tasmanian devil toward anyone perceived by him to be in a leadership position. HE was to be the leader, and don't you forget it. Ted by comparison was polite with his mother and anyone else he perceived as an authority figure, but make no mistake, he had an ongoing rebellion simmering beneath that *very thin* veneer, and the courtesy was a con in order to make his sadist self invisible so he could creep about unsuspectedly. Sorry to say but *over* politeness IS a red flag. Louise had feigned courtesy, too. It will help to remember as we go that Louise was not well attached in her original relational constellation either, so consider her detachment level as well. Her lifelong involvement in her home, neighborhood, and church was very task oriented, not obviously relationally attuned.

However psychopaths motor about, the callous disregard in place is because they have given up on attaching to people. How psychopaths think, for example, is like this: the chair or appliance (you or me) is just there for them to use if they want to or not. Early on, these little kids became more interested in non-living things, or helpless smaller things that cannot emotionally hurt them in any way.

Okay, I'm going to belabor my point on attachment, but it's worth belaboring. Remember that the attachment bond between a mother and her child is first formed in the womb. As mentioned earlier, rapid early learning processes continue during the third trimester and the newborn stages of development, in which children instinctively recognize their mothers' smells and voices. Imagine regularly smelling your mother's sweat as a result of stress or hearing the voice of someone yelling at her. Louise certainly experienced the stress from living in a violent household, which means prenatal Ted did as well. Stress hormones are very toxic to the nervous system that links the baby and mother. When it comes to stress hormones, think of the problems that putting rubbing alcohol on your lips for an extended period of time would cause. Prolonged or frequent exposure to stress negatively impacts the mother and the developing human within her. These impacts formulate the directions the child's natural genetic markers will take. Think about how wires and stakes shape the bonsai tree. In the same way, chemicals and hormones influence early wiring direction of the developing human brain.

To put it simply, how the *inner* workings of the fetus processes this chemical stew can be thought of as this: our genetic code of how we are biologically intended (i.e. directions for assembly that we are dealt at conception) holds all of our possibilities that can be molded in various ways(Nature).

Environmental influences (Nurture), including those during the prenatal stage, determine which genes are enhanced, reinforced, turned on, or turned off, indicating the child's genetic predispositions. Whether you live in a high stress environment can determine how the anxiety prone gene is manipulated and may flip that switch. Again, your genetic code is not changed, but the way some of your genes express themselves is influenced.

Closer to our subject matter, if I have genes that are *vulnerable* to the development of psychopathy due to my genetic ancestry, it can go *at least* one of two ways. The direction and degree of direction depends on my environmental influences.

If I am in an environment that manifests extreme violence of any kind and I am awash with toxic stress hormones, I could slant toward callous disregard as a chemically influenced outcome. Remember if mom is awash with cortisol and stress hormones, so are you. In addition, more molding occurs in early childhood via *identifying with the aggressor*. In this situation, the vulnerable prey eventually becomes a predator or at least callous and dismissive, which is something I do think was politely evidenced in Louise.

On the other hand, with the *same genetic predisposition toward psychopathy*, if I am raised in a supportive loving home, my epigenetic slants might be channeled in a totally different direction. Instead of becoming a terrorizing night slasher or dismember-er, I'm more inclined to be guided into the professions of vascular or orthopedic surgeon if extremely bright, or something creative like a chef! Yes, this could really be an outcome. Epigenetically developing tendencies do not need to be eradicated so much as wisely channeled early on in life. Along more statistical lines, top careers of psychopaths include CEO's, Lawyers, Media People, Salespeople, Surgeons, Chefs, (and of course we already knew this) Public Officials.

This is not meant to suggest that your surgeon or chef is a psychopath, although there is a small chance they could be. If so, you can be certain the job they do on your *whatever* will be excellent because a narcissistic psychopath requires self accolades and will likely do a magnificent job to achieve that.

Our environment's interaction with and influence on genetic outcomes is unavoidable and pertains to all of us. It may already be obvious to the reader how some of this information applied to Ted and his mother. Louise is again the important starting point because she was in an *impossible* position from the start as, although involuntarily, the carrier, conduit, and mediator of all things in her and Ted's, as it turned out, ill-fated world.

Erich Fromm, the author of *The Anatomy of Human Destructiveness*, 1973 was a German Jewish Psychologist who escaped the Nazi regime by coming to the United States. He studied at Columbia and Yale and is an expert on human social development. His words reinforce for us a dynamic to be kept in mind throughout the rest of this volume.

"Children in whom develop no affectionate bonds toward their mother do not emerge to break through the shell of desperate narcissism [*me first, look at me, take care of MY needs*]. . . .

If [children] never experience the mother as a love object; they never form any loving attachment to others, but, rather, look at others as if they were inanimate objects, and in keeping, they often show a particular interest in mechanical things."

Preventing this virus starts early. The inoculation combination is affection, attentiveness, accountability, and the teaching of empathy. This does not mean we create snowflakes. Empathy does not mean weakness; it means asking the question that my gramma always asked me when I mistreated someone else: "How would you feel if somebody did that to *you? It wouldn't feel good, would it?*" That is how empathy is developed in a child. However, empathy cannot be installed if the child has been so neglected or mistreated that they are sealed over. Affectionate attentiveness and accountability must come first.

Chapter Nine

Ikea without Directions

. . . Do-it-Yourself In-the-Dark Assembly of Childhood

Although some overlooked the actions of calloused Ted, others pointed out concerns. The next series of alerts that were recorded in his report cards over the course of his elementary school years show how his teachers began to notice a few concerning behaviors, although they framed their remarks discreetly. Each of his report cards were signed by Louise, indicating she had read them.

Kindergarten—Teacher's Comments:

Dear Mr. and Mrs. Bundy,

Theodore has shown satisfactory growth in kindergarten and we feel he is ready to make a successful adjustment to first grade.

Grade 1—Teacher's Comments:

In the areas of social studies and science Teddy contributes good ideas to the planning of the group. He has a good background of experiences from which to draw.

I am so curious about this—what was he sharing?

Grade 2—Teacher's Comments:

. . . Although Teddy wants to be a good boy, he is sometimes boisterous and undependable.

Grade 3—Teacher's Comments:

Teddy is making satisfactory progress in his third grade work. Teddy is not a fluent oral reader but his comprehension is good. *Recall that oral development is often affected by neonatal stress, and or reported grandfather abuse*. Ted's progress this year indicates he is ready for grade 4. *Teddy needs to become a little more mature in his behavior. Ted has tried hard to work and be a good citizen.*

Grade 4—Teacher's Comments:

Teddy contributes worthwhile information . . . and shows enthusiasm in public affairs. He has been interested in reading, especially for information . . . Teddy has made satisfactory progress and is being assigned to fifth grade. *His immature behavior has kept him from doing as good work as I feel he is capable of doing (on the scorecard, he got an N in music).*

Parent's Comments:

I would be interested to know the reason for the N in music and if there is any way I can help correct the difficulty there.

Signed: *Louise C. Bundy.*

We see in these report cards the minor progressive regression in his social behavior. Remember immaturity becomes more problematic in detached kids. How or if Louise and Johnny addressed these concerns is unknown, other than the way she disregarded the teachers comments about Ted's behavior and instead asked how she could correct *the* music difficulty, not *his* music difficulty.

What comes to mind for me is a Ted Tip regarding discipline that was described by his long-time partner Liz in her book *The Phantom Prince (2020)*. When Liz's daughter, Molly, was getting mouthy one day, as children do from time to time, Ted said,

"If the child apologizes and stops behaving that way, we will speak to her again."

The Child.

Does anyone else picture Louise using Ted's approach? If Louise had disciplined Ted in this way, a little kid struggling with identity would be affected by hearing *The Child*. Hopefully Ted came up with that methodology somewhere else on his own and not from his mom.

When it came to report cards, Louise's family of origin philosophy continued here as well: "don't ask, don't tell, and make a positive impression." It appears Johnny passively did the best he could but may have very well allowed, even preferred, Louise to handle Ted's social and moral difficulties. Although, it doesn't seem to me like she ever acknowledged concerns since years later she glowingly referred to Ted when a youngster as "*the best son in the world*" and "*never a problem*." She continued to praise him even when he was on death row, convicted of several murders and facing three death sentences.

Perception management was paramount to Louise and Johnny, and Teddy absorbed it unconsciously. With his mother's meticulous grooming and Johnny's backup, he learned to present himself as a nice kid from a nice family.

A Class Photograph:

There is a school class picture from Ted's 2nd grade year. The children are smiling regular kid smiles and dressed in age appropriate school clothes. Except in the back row there is a little boy in a starched white shirt smiling the biggest smile in the class almost squeezing itself. Scott Rouse, an expert consultant to law enforcement and the United States Military on behavior and body language describes exaggerated expressions as "extra face" used in order to convince others of the mood or thoughts they are having, I think Teddy at the time of this photo was trying desperately to fit somewhere, to be liked and to belong, or at least appear so. His mother had dressed him in order to make a really good impression and not necessarily as a school boy. Both of these elements are examples of perception management. We all do it to some degree, but knowing what we do now, in Bundy's case it has more meaning.

In other photos that are of him as an elementary school child he is looking mischievous, and we might think "oh isn't that cute" if it were not Ted.

As difficulties arose with his behavior, Louise continued her denial and compartmentalizations regarding any wrongdoing of her son. She essentially continued this for all of his life, persistently denying her son's *real* reality—real self—right up to his last living days. I know I'm jumping a bit ahead here, but this very strange occurrence is an example of her resolute disregard of her son's criminal behavior:

A few days prior to his execution, Bundy started confessing to the murders. Journalists Hugh Aynesworth and Stephen Michaud reported in their book *The Only Living Witness* (1983) that they took a tape of Ted's confessions to the Bundy home in Tacoma and played it for Louise and Johnny. They did this with the intent to break through the couple's persistent denial and show to them who their son was.

Listening to her son graphically describe a rape and murder he committed, and how he then drug the girl by one arm into the bushes, Louise moaned and squeaked in distress. When the tape finished playing, the men asked if she or Johnny had any questions.

Neither of them had any questions.

Well, Louise had one question: "Who's for apple pie and ice cream?"

So they had apple pie and ice cream. Imagine the four of them at the table eating the dessert together after hearing such horror . . . it's surreal. Neither Louise or Johnny said a word about what had just transpired, politely thanked the detectives for coming, and never spoke to Michaud or Aynesworth again. The journalists left the house stunned.

Imagine having a parent that does not address misbehavior but instead shifts to task oriented activity. Like writing a response to the teacher asking how one can help correct the music difficulty when the child is clearly disrupting the classroom year after year. Or after setting a neighborhood cat on fire (oh yes, he did-and laughed while doing it) or hitting the neighbor kid with a board (yes, he did that, too). Instead of facing any repercussions he was, what? Called in to wash up for dinner? Your guess is as good as mine.

"What cannot be spoken to the mother cannot be told to the self."

~John Bowlby

With Louise's acts of compartmentalization in mind, it's possible, even likely, that she couldn't talk to her mother and so in turn could not talk with Ted and help him resolve his behavior.

Sandi Hilt, a neighbor that grew up with Ted, described Ted in a documentary as a boy that never fit in. When it came to scouts, sports, and socialization, he did not know how to perform the skills correctly. He said he was embarrassed that he had difficulty learning to skip and had to practice a lot before he mastered it. When referring to his teen years during an interview with Dr. Carlisle, Ted said, "I felt like the teenage boy with acne that nobody wanted around . . . I was hungry for friendships." He says he spent time with "Glenn (Ted's younger brother by at least *five or six* years) and his friends, hoping I could learn from them by watching."

I was invisible to them, not rejected, but as though I wasn't even there." It seems much of Ted's formative identity was too often labeled as invisible, awkwardly inconvenient, and always, always good despite poor behavior. He was always aspiring to be in control of everything like the first father figure in his life, and always watching others to learn how to do so. Fledgling psychopaths have few to no attachment emotions of their own, so they pick up cues on how to look and act from watching others. They watch us closely to learn. There is such a thing as the psychopath stare. You may notice a person that is always looking at you, and if you catch them looking, they don't stop. They keep watching. They keep showing up in your field of vision. Or they will use your statements as their own when talking to someone else. They don't pick up on the social cues that it's rude to stare at or copy others. Mostly because they don't care about social mores and are not about to let such social nonsense stop them from gaining any advantage. Pay attention to that. Imitation is not always the best form of flattery after all.

Failing socialization outside of school, Ted said he was almost precocious inside the classroom because he responded positively to the structure and rules of being in class. He could answer questions confidently, being certain of the information. Remember his teacher's comment that he was very good at gathering and sharing information.

He was successful academically, however confidence was lost in the social setting because he couldn't understand the nuances of friendships and groups. Although he was nice looking and polite, socially he was superficial and limited in high school. He experienced even less interactions with peers as he noticed his guy friends moving on to new activities, dating, and various other social opportunities. Upon arriving home from a day of skiing with them, they would drop him off and head on to their various plans for the evening. Ted said he was never asked to join them.

I wonder if and in what way his fellow students picked up that he had different interests. I think they only brought him along with them on the ski trips because he forged their ski tickets. Regardless, he knew he was different and apparently, at least in this case, his "friends" only hung out with him in order to use him.

Due to Ted's social awkwardness and reported mistreatment of other kids in the neighborhood, he faced the natural consequence of constant deep loneliness. As Bundy continuously spent so much time alone, he discovered the absolutely wondrous and magical power of daydreaming as self-entertainment.

In his custom-created grandiose revelries, he at first fantasized about being Roy Rogers and saving ladies in distress. As time went by, however, Ted's reveries became more violent. His boyhood devolved and his internal screen produced pictures beyond being the hero that solved the crimes. By his early teens, Ted's fantasies featured detectives not being able to solve *his* crimes.

His daydreams preoccupied much of his alone time and were very enjoyable to Ted—more enjoyable than, as we know, his real youngster life which never went so well for him interpersonally. He could create his own successful *inner* world without interference since it occurred only in his ever-growing imagination. Ted himself produced, directed and played the leading role. I think he was smug about that, too.

Throughout his childhood and youth, Ted was taken to church and Scouts regularly, taught socially expected manners, roles of decency, and how to be trustworthy. Learning to perform these skills didn't necessarily help him in his interpersonal relationships as a child, but they ironically served him later in life to make him successful in his interpersonal *presentations* and unfortunately, deadly manipulations.

Ted's disturbingly darker, deadly, and manipulative side presented itself early on in life. Ted told his attorney, John Henry Browne, *The Devil's Defender* (2018) that he would obtain (likely steal) mice from the pet store and "play God" by deciding which of them would live or die. In later years, he said he did this when out hunting for female prey as well. He liked to be able to omnipotently decide the fate of others.

Ted described hovering his hand over the individual mice, deciding which would live or die. If the mouse was to die, he would hold the body in one hand while pulling the tail with the other, eventually yanking the spinal cord out of the living mouse.

Ted was also known for sneaking up from behind and scaring people. Various females in his life said he would do that often and it would scare them to death. He also built "tiger traps," where he would hide stakes down in a hole and cover them with foliage. He did not set these in the jungle, mind you, but in the woods behind a residential neighborhood in the city of Tacoma, in the state of Washington, in the United States of America. One time, a little girl had the length of her leg seriously sliced by stepping into one of those traps.

Ted told Dr. Dorothy Lewis that he never understood why he had taken the direction he took. He said that as a boy he never understood how love worked. How people could tell how another person was feeling and know how to respond in kind. He never understood what attracted people to each other. Bundy's affectional experiences failed time after time so much that he was sealed over *before* he could learn how affection even worked or experience it for himself.

Although completely lost regarding human connection, he did make a few early attempts at what he imagined to be romance. He began spending time with an Asian girl and when introduced to her father, the dad made it clear that she was to ultimately marry an Asian boy, so Ted gave that up.

At 13 years old, Ted developed what he thought to be a crush on a school-mate by the name of Gail. He built up the courage to ask her to go with him for a soda. She refused and then he saw her go with someone else.

For Ted, not knowing how to make sense of himself while in the company of others brought about a growing resentment of absolutely everyone. He had long since lost his deputy status at home, and instead of *the father* ruling the roost, Louise was Sheriff. As a very confused, betrayed, and humiliated teen, his simmering resentment was absolutely beginning to boil.

Louise was to young Bundy another example of a woman being what to him was inappropriately controlling, unlike in the material he had now been obtaining while out creeping the alley trash bins. Those images would have crystalized at least unconsciously the vague imprints of his first mentor, *the father's* ugliest interests and behaviors from years ago and contributed to Ted's fantasy life.

As his private hero fantasizing about girls grew to become more and more time consuming and violent, Ted began a permanent detour, but nobody saw it. He told one source that, when it came to girls, he didn't know what to do about them. This comment is curious to me in that instead of saying "I didn't know how to relate to them," he said, "I didn't know what to do *about them.*"

As though it was up to him to deal with them.

Chapter Ten

Being the Humiliating Family Secret

Some synonyms for illegitimate: illegal, unlawful, illicit, criminal, felonious, unsanctioned, banned, forbidden, barred, prohibited, taboo.

No need to define incestuous. Or maybe we should. Okay, incest is the term used for sexual relations between biological family members. It is a universal taboo, meaning every culture around the globe forbids it, yet it still happens.

Regardless of parentage, which is certainly not the child's fault, how is it our society ever looked at our children as the "humiliating" family secret? Fortunately those days are pretty much over. It is true that every family has its secrets, big and small; however, it is the content of the secret and how we think about it that really counts. It is human nature to hide our weaknesses and foibles if we can. We have more survival chances if we are part of a group and we have better longevity within the group if we are perceived as healthy and solid in body, mind, and spirit.

To be marginalized or never quite welcome in the group to begin with, whether in the family or neighborhood, limits sociability in all other aspects of life. Feeling socially awkward can bring about deep resentments when one is not readily sought out or enjoyed by others. And when one can sense that others know something about them that they don't know, an internal pressure builds.

Many people who were the family secret throughout their developmental years do not grow up murderous, the difference being that they knew they were loved, significant, and part of the family. For many of these individuals, making the inevitable discovery was shattering and confusing, mainly because they didn't understand why they hadn't been told earlier. *So who am I anyway?* In our current culture parents tell these youngsters about their bios whenever it is safe and healthy to do so. These days, 'out of wedlock' children for the most part are brought up knowing who they are and that we are so glad they are here with us.

Although illegitimacy right up until more recently was considered a necessary secret, keeping secrets can affect children's lives, whether the child knows the content of the secret or not. Children are extremely perceptive and become alarmed or anxious if they sense something of a serious nature is being hidden from them. The most damaging scenario, as is sometimes the case, is when the child in the family believes that they are somehow personally responsible for whatever hidden undercurrent is going on in the home. It is most destructive for a detached, awkward, and socially troubled child like Ted.

Hiding secrets within a family can create a false sense of reality in a child. Children learn about the world and who they are within it from the adults in their lives. When eventually told the truth about their origins, either from a relative, sibling, or even by someone outside the family, they feel betrayed and shattered. Kids perceive but don't know what it is they are perceiving, that is, until they do. Then they feel betrayed because they pretty much have been. Ted didn't have a chance.

This is how it happened for Bundy. At age 13, Ted and his moneyed cousin, the son of the uncle that he had lived with when small and admired so much, were talking about their imagined futures. They began to spar as to who between them would be most successful in college and in life. In a competitively reflexive response, the cousin told Ted he would never get anywhere because he was "a bastard."

Ted was horrified. He heard the truth *derisively* from a relative to whom he already felt inferior. Ted really wanted this cousin and his family to like him, but this boy, *his aunt, and his uncle* knew a humiliating secret about him—one that HE *didn't?* That blow psychically demolished his already fractured self.

The story goes that the cousin told Ted the proof was stored up in the attic. After investigating in an attic trunk, Bundy found his Birth Certificate from the Elizabeth Lund Home For Unwed Mothers in Burlington Vermont. In the place of Father, it said, "Unknown." This ripped away any remaining possibilities of attachment for the young adolescent. He had already been stealing, sneaking up and scaring people, picking on smaller beings, and building traps, but this information pushed him over the *next* ledge.

Ted may have thought, or at least I would have, "Is *the secret* too horrible to speak of? Am I too horrible to speak of? I DIDN'T ASK TO BE BORN. I am YOUR fault, not mine. You mean I've been walking around illegitimate all this time, *everybody* knowing but me? Here I've been looking like a stupid idiot before God and everybody. Damn you all."

Others, and of course Ted as well, would have expected that such important information would have already been shared with him by his mother. Instead, Louise left Ted wide open for the worst public humiliations possible. It was another degradation that others knew, several *others knew, but she had never told HIM*. Remember, though, that Louise may not have been sure herself whether her father was Ted's father or a different man. If you were in her shoes, how and when would *you* tell Ted, and how much of the truth would you tell him?

It isn't easy, is it, to find the best way to tell your son . . .

Regarding having confirmed his illegitimacy, Ted told Dr. Carlisle in *I'm Not Guilty* (2017), "It wasn't a big deal like getting bit by a dog or anything." I can imagine being told by his cousin that he was a bastard and the product of incest was a pretty big deal, and it had kindled a teen rage that brought about *his* "felonious" origin. Select any of the synonyms for "illegitimate" at the beginning of the chapter, combine that with Ted's appetite for brutal intrigue and anger, and you will understand what fed his desire to have things in *his* control alone.

Some years later when in Philadelphia for a semester at Temple University. Ted addressed what I think was the original reason for deciding on attending that particular university. He told his grandfather in a letter that he intended to go to law school there, but Temple Law school doesn't admit students without a Bachelor's degree. His real reason was to get a sense of his roots. If he hadn't seen his original Pennsylvania family for 20 years, he may have had many unanswered questions for them. I would have.

We know that during his time in Philadelphia, Ted took a side trip up to Burlington, Vermont. He found the city on Lake Champlain, only 50 miles away from the Canadian Border. He understood The Lund Home was selected for his mother because its distance of nearly 400 miles from Philadelphia further ensured safe anonymity of anyone finding out about *him*.

Ted went to The Lund and said as he approached the building that he imagined his mother walking up the same curved walk so many years before. He found his birth certificate, verifying for himself that Louise *was* his mother, not his sister, and that a father was indeed not named. At twenty years old, those questions were now confirmed: his sister Louise was his mother and his father was *unknown*. Since his teens, he had been telling others that his grandfather had raped his *sister*mother, so he may have been hoping it was not really true and another man's name would be listed on the certificate.

Upon his return to Tacoma, he never asked his mother to explain the betrayal which he had now confirmed. She was a solid wall and he knew not to ask. Not being allowed to ask–not being allowed to *know*–was yet another form of rejection for him. Perhaps he picked up on a feeling emitted from Louise of *nothing we can do about it now*. So he pretended in matter-of-fact *Louise style* that it didn't matter. Ted kept his own murderous secrets hidden behind a cheerful face of innocence. Louise and Ted mirrored this face to each other and to us. Thus, according to mother and son, as always everything was Hunky Dory in the Bundy Family.

Ted *deeply* resented Louise. In his mind she took him away from his Philadelphia family, his aunt and uncle in Tacoma, and then married Johnny with whom she created her own family. I think Ted did not especially want to have anything to do with being part of that new family, or even the human race, even if he had known how. He never understood what reasons underlay love, social interactions, or friendships.

The kid had nothing to connect with. Much of his attachment was pruned off before he ever got out of the orphanage and frazzled more in the Philadelphia house. Tacoma brought about continued social confusion, and over time he abandoned trying to figure out social queues. In spite of love being extended to him by others, he was left with no arms to hug with.

With puberty steadily increasing alongside his humiliation regarding his only partially confirmed origins, Ted was even more at a complete loss when relating to peers. For him, it was more comfortable to be alone with his own thoughts and sexual feelings. Neither his thoughts nor his feelings required other living people, other living souls. It was completely safe because his own fantasies would never reject or scorn his existence.

He often said he loved darkness, the feeling of invisibility. He said when he snuck out at night, he liked to strip off his clothes and run naked through the woods. I would have tripped over logs and got clotheslined by tree branches, but apparently Bundy's night vision was rather good. The Wolf-Girls of the jungles of India saw better in the dark than in the daylight and they preferred night as well. Perhaps the feeling of safety and concealment in the dark was reassuring for the girls. That's certainly why Ted liked it. In Martial Arts training and Military skills development as well, darkness vision acuity is deliberately developed. It's a thing, and Ted had it.

His love of night stalking likely was because he was enjoying being alone and invisible *by choice* for the first time in his life. In this way, he felt in complete control of others and undetected by them. His activities could be concealed in the darkness and instead of feeling lonely or empty, he was excited by it. These were addictive, exciting feelings for the young teenager. And HE was in control, which made it an erotically satisfying passtime for him.

These activities of night stalking and peeping fueled his fantasies for a long period of time. They were so exciting to him that they made regular social life absolutely dull by comparison. Suspected or assumed by many, he may have done something further, beyond spying, imagining, and simply look-ing into women's windows.

When Louise in later years was told of this behavior, she said that she didn't see how that could have been possible since she didn't know how young Ted could have gotten out of the house. Umm, the door? His window?

Her deliberate defensive naiveté was as always predictably formidable. On the other hand, being the mother of five children, most of whom were under ten years of age at that time, she probably slept hard as a rock at night. Her household was spic and span. She took devoted care of every-thing under her roof and was likely ready for a solid night's sleep at the end of each day.

This is a reason why so many serial killers target the young–they don't want to prey upon those who have been wizened by years of caring for others and themselves.

That's why Ed Kemper preyed upon young women, to take them "before they become mom." Sort of an easy nip it in the bud.

Jeffrey Dahmer said for him it was the lust for control, of not having to consider the young men's wishes or chance being rejected. He could keep them as long as he wanted and do with them what he wanted.

Ted's excuse was he wanted to know what a girl looked like as opposed to the adult women that he had been vicariously feasting upon in his magazines or through the neighbor's windows. He said he never saw his younger sister, as his mom locked the door when the girl was bathing. A few days before his execution he told Dr. Dorothy Lewis that he had a sexual relationship with his sister. It sounds like Louise was locking the bathroom door for good reason. I wonder if she talked to the sister or Ted about it. I am thinking not. I picture her locking the door and going to the kitchen to take the cookies out of the oven and turn off the timer, hoping she had covered the necessary bases.

Ted liked young girls, even as a grown-up. He had realized as a young teenager that a child was easier to lure and control than adult women. He started off playing cat and mouse with cats and mice, and things just got worse from there. At some point that was invisible to all of us, Ted took the next step. I think it was here that he deliberately stepped off the final ledge to killing humans.

"You reach that jumping-off point where you begin to wonder if actually doing it will give you something beyond just reading about it or looking at it."

~Ted

Regularly when on his paper route, Ted encountered an eight year old little girl named Ann Marie Burr. Ted said she would follow him around like a puppy. It was never proven that Ted killed this little girl, but he surmised to Dr. Carlisle that *whoever* did it likely arranged with the child that he would come at night to show her something. He came to her and she willingly went with him, trustingly curious as to what he had to show her. Ted suggested that when she was told to undress, she objected and her killer inadvertently strangled her as she struggled to break free.

It is not possible to *inadvertently* strangle someone; it takes strength and time. Ted would have been about fourteen when Ann Marie died. Her body was never found.

Ann's mother wrote to Ted in prison hoping he would explain to her what had happened and where her daughter was. Ted responded volunteering that he was a normal 14 year old boy that did not wander the streets late at night.

We all know otherwise, Ted, because you told us about your night escapades. And we all know nothing about you was normal.

In "The Violent Mind" (2017) Bundy told Dr. Carlisle that when it came to selecting what he referred to as worthy prey, he emphasized choosing the woman. Not an ideal type like "long dark hair parted in the middle," although he did start out with these very similar prototypes and picked them as often as they serendipitously came into his view. What made a selection the ideal woman, according to Bundy, was if she would be considered desirable by his peers. This makes sense because of his social insecurities and the resentment of seeing his "equals" succeeding with women. He did not have the skills or the courage to get to know and be known intimately—*whatever that is*—by a female. That confidence was never built into his emotional intelligence quota.

The illegitimate incestuous bastard as he perceived himself to be, self-taught by trial and error that it was easiest to sneak in unseen and bludgeon at night, or use manners, perceived helplessness and gallantry by day. He honed these skills to gain the trust and isolation of his prey so he could possess them for himself and do what he wanted with *his trophy*. He took his "trophies" like a preadolescent stealing a really nice dirt bike or other treasured object. Each woman was a stolen object desired by his peers, but he possessed her now and could do what he wanted with her for as long as he wanted.

> **"The ultimate possession was, in fact, the taking of the life.**
> **And then . . . the physical possession of the remains."**
>
> ~Ted

Bundy embodied shame and anger. Shame is a feeling when someone *else* is responsible for causing our humiliation. Guilt is a feeling of disgrace that comes about because of something that is *our* responsibility for having occurred. Since Ted's core self concept was one of shame, to his way of thinking, his behaviors were not his fault, but *theirs. I am your fault, not mine. How dare you suggest otherwise.* This unthinkable level of theft, the theft of women, added to his sense of power and significance in place of shameful vacancy.

When Ted enrolled in college, he enjoyed the variety of exotic game in view he could shop, stalk, and potentially possess. He very much liked the campus scene for this reason. Meanwhile, insert here a real attempt at a romance with a *living*, beautiful, smart, rich woman. She was to be his first, at least to him, real girlfriend. Yes, he really did try his hand at an actual relationship. It may not surprise you that she bore some very Freudian similarities to his mother.

Chapter Eleven

SisterEleonorMomLouise

. . . You remind me of my mother

In early adulthood, Ted took his next risk of female relational affiliation. Think *JAWS music here*. He developed what was his first legitimate attempt at a romantic relationship with a beautiful, smart, rich woman who was a bit older than him. They dated for about a year, and I don't know if he ever introduced her to his mother. As the relationship progressed, his underlying terror of being jilted *again* from something he *really wanted* raised its scary head.

Although at first this relationship risk seemed romantically promising, it soon caused Ted's self-mustered confidence to evaporate. The insecurities of his arrested development became nakedly manifest. His girlfriend sensed this profound insecurity which caused her to question Ted's maturity. Remember that disorganized attachment, when untreated, is set in place for a lifetime with these individuals.

At first, the 'woman of his dreams' was in love with Ted. At first. As time went on, she became aware of his lack of goals and *"his bowing manner, always trying to get people to believe that he was humble and that he wouldn't walk on anybody's toes. It was a put on."* She caught whiffs of his entitled unaccountability. *"His actions were to make people feel 'poor Ted, sweet little Ted look at me innocent Ted'"* (Carlisle, 2017). Recognizing his red flags troubled her and she ended the relationship.

Smart woman.

With this rejection, Ted's trauma bond was triggered and he was unable to bear further damage. His demoralized dependence on a rejecting woman, Louise covertly, female classmates overtly, and now his first girlfriend sent him into a silent, seething rage. The tiger had been poked again by a female.

Ted later denied that this perceived outrageous and *public* abandonment by this woman was a catalyst for his crimes, but this is when his vicious killing sprees began publicly in earnest. He headed off to the East Coast to Temple University, and visited the Lund Home, Jersey Shore and relatives for some months. Still profoundly humiliated in his self concept, Ted returned to Washington with murder on his mind.

At the risk of sounding psycho-babble-ish to you, my reader, I am going to give you a Docent tour through Ted's head as I see it.

The killer selects his object of vengeance and method of obtaining, attacking, and disposing of his prey according to his own human frailty and the starting place of his anger. He selects *symbolic* victims, mostly women whom he believes to represent the dominating women (or in Gacy, Dahmer, and Wuornos' lives, men) who he blames for the difficulties in his own life. For Ted, although he often emulated his misogynist grandfather, emotionally distant females were the ones who had mostly dominated him from his first breaths.

When emotionally healthy, we possess the love of our mother. We call her *my* mother. That spot in Bundy's heart, as we know, was empty. The tide was now to turn. He would dominate, and do one better, *possess and destroy* women as he sucked in their last breath.

These killers often do not see themselves as committing crimes per se but rather obtaining revenge. An example of this is Gary Ridgeway, whose mother had been distant and sexually inappropriate with him throughout his childhood and into his adolescence. Gary told law enforcement officers that by getting women off the streets, he thought he was doing them a favor. Ed Kemper said that in order to stop killing coeds, he finally had to kill his raving mother. Charles Manson didn't make any sense at all—he blamed all of society, you and me, for screwing things up. In some ways he had a point.

For Ted, selecting bright coeds as prey is ironic since Louise could have been a bright coed. She never got the chance, however, because she had him. Ted may have been seeking some distorted hero revenge by destroying these women since his mother did not get to be a coed because of him. Now that is some extraordinary dark cognitive dissonance.

On the flip side, another possible reason he continued destroying the young women was because of his perception that Louise was humiliated by his existence. In his mind, this severed his ability for intimacy with women, or anyone, because of her denial and rejection of him, even though his existence was *her* doing. The violent paradox brought about the tragedy of Ted's conclusion that he could only fully possess a woman not through love, but only through bindings, unconsciousness, or death. This way, the smart and beautiful woman could not blow him off, *because she would if she knew him.*

To clarify, the woman that Ted 'fell in love with' in college was not an intimate *relational* attachment. He had nothing to attach with. The last remnants of bonding possibilities were completely gone by the time he was adolescent, if not before then. And so for Ted, an attachment bond would be like trying to kiss without lips. His was a fantasized connection to a smart, beautiful, rich woman who made *him* look good, which made him feel as though he would be perceived by others as *important.*

She was so classy, he described her as Saks compared to his Sears. She elevated him and he felt some significance with her, but only *because* of her. Had she not broken up with him, Ted would have continued to love what she brought to and provided for him. That's as much affection as he could muster, like having a really *really* nice Mercedes.

The girl of his dreams, due to his lack of direction and ambition (other than his ambition to continue being her *boyfriend,* that is), quietly and firmly ended the relationship. He had surely flaunted her about socially as his girlfriend to impress others, so her breaking up with him was publicly humiliating. *Another social mortification brought about by a woman.* Ted never forgave her of this insult. When she rejected him just like *the two girl classmates and his mother* had, he began to rampage full time.

How dare *another* woman abandon and humiliate him as though he were nothing. Ted's concrete-thinking mind perceived this as women expecting him to be perfect or he was not worthy of existence. This, in his mind, reinforced that women are simply merchandise and *they* are the ones not worthy of existence. Black and white thinking is always an impossible mental trap.

Ted was a *benign looking* quagmire that would relentlessly hurt and kill young women and girls. Because of his mother's persistent refusal to tell him who his *father* was, who *she* was, who *Ted* was, he sustained a rejection of his identity. Geez Louise. His life was full of so much painful absurdity that he could not wrap his head around, causing him to experience more confusing degradation. Ted's college girlfriend should have been able to break up with him without drama. Because he perceived that women *needed to be of use and kept subservient*, it brought him, who was *the man failing to be in control*, even more humiliation and fueled his rage.

Ted would be nobody's victim. Ever. He would be the sun (son) to be reckoned with.

Back in the day, there was a song that went something like "I want a girl just like the girl who married dear old dad. She was a pearl and the only girl that daddy ever had, a good old fashioned girl with a heart so true, one who'd love nobody else but you . . ."

Of course with Ted there were knots in the lyrics, but I think the similarity between his rejecting girlfriend and Louise is remarkable. The blended image of the two was likely to influence his 'ideal' woman image, enviable to peers and 'worthy' of selection as his next victim. Ted transitioned from killing mice to Ann Burr to young coeds because he had a sadistic taste for murder and the accompanying adrenaline rush—which of course is addictive. Thrill addiction is rationalized by the killer at that point as *vengeful entitlement.*

After a few years of bloody venting, Ted decided to make things square in his mind. He hoovered that college sweetheart who had broken up with him. He used self accolades of working for a presidential campaign, a governor campaign, various political associations, and a year in law school to assure her how wonderful life would be with him, and she was hopeful and impressed. Ted did in fact suck her back in and even led her to believe they were engaged. She was going to move to Seattle and pay for the parasite's next year at law school.

Bundy thought that she would make a good governor's wife when he became governor. Yes, he had those thoughts, but by this time he had *other* governing interests that he was acting upon. When he was certain he had *complete control* of the relationship, Ted dumped her.

Vengeance is Mine; I will Repay, saith TRB.

Louise said that after Ted left home, they rarely saw him and did not even have his phone number. A former co-worker of Ted's said that she once called Ted's mother to ask if Louise would influence her son to pay back some money he owed her (about $700 in today's economy). Louise said, "He doesn't live here anymore and we're not responsible for anything he does." Periodically there would be a chink in Louise's armor showing personae gaps, but those were always short lived and then she returned to her virtuous character.

"She fed me and paid the bills and never yelled at me."

~Ted

There are only two family photos I can find. One is a photo of a beaming Louise with picture perfect children. The little girls are in taffeta fluff and corsages like their mom, and younger brother is in a suit and bowtie. Ted is in a plaid shirt of the same fabric as his mom's plaid skirt. Louise may have sewed both. Ted has an easy smile here and is leaning in, but there is still a gap between him and the others. The sister in front of him has a disregarding smile. The younger siblings are looking cheerful like mom.

As mentioned before, Ted told a psychiatrist the day before his death that he'd had a sexual relationship with his sister. Looking at family photos, Ted is directly behind the oldest girl in both pictures. Coming up from behind was his go-to approach. Of course in photos, the taller ones are necessarily in the back row. Still I wonder, given her lopsided smile, if she was sensing something from him. Just another observation on my part.

Considering the suspicion of his abduction and murder of eight year old Ann Burr when he was a young teenager and at least two twelve year olds later, Bundy was drawn to young girls as well as young women, which would make him a hebephile. When arrested in Florida, officials found Cheerleader and Majorette magazines in his car. I don't think Ted would have EVER admitted to child murders until he was on his way to the chair, not because he felt guilty or ashamed, but rather knowing what happens in prison to baby rapers. With nothing to lose in the death cell, he played that wild card. It didn't work.

Louise *had* to know things were very wrong with her son. I think she knew he had tipped before they left Philadelphia, but she was unable to save him. She did what she had always done, and I think it's all she knew to do. She excelled at functional business. Ted said she didn't talk to his siblings about personal matters either. I think her emotions were as non-existent as Ted's. It makes sense because she had spent *all* of her developmental years in the Philadelphia house fulfilling her duties and performing good works in order to survive.

Polly Nelson, one of Ted's string of attorneys, flew Louise to New Haven, Connecticut to meet with her and psychiatrist Dr. Dorothy Lewis. Here again were two professionals trying their utmost to break through Louise's denial of Ted's guilt and gather *some* understanding behind Ted's actions. Louise was described as "polite, cautious and tightly controlled . . . impenetrable . . . no break in character, no emotion, just frosting-covered steely reserve."

I watched Louise's testimony on YouTube frame by frame. You might try this yourself when you want to see what expressions televised speakers are showing behind their planned ones. I noticed a definite reaction when she was asked about Ted's first job, which was the paper route that included the residential area of Ann Marie Burr. When asked this, she swallowed before briefly confirming that her son had a paper route. She then quickly put her chin up and went on to refer to his lawn mowing business, expanding a bit by saying it was quite an enterprise. When asked about her own work, she swallowed again when replying, "University of Puget Sound," where the little girl was suspected of being buried. Take a look and see what you think. Maybe she was just thirsty, or nervous, or both.

Another observation I made is that throughout her testimony, even when asked about Ted's impending execution, she does not show any indication of a grief muscle in her forehead. When grief crosses the face, an upside-down horseshoe shaped muscle appears on the forehead, but there is no indication of it on Louise. Her forehead remains smooth throughout the time on the stand, unlike Ted's that is always wrinkling in search of agreement.

Louise looks at her son during her testimony a few times. At one point, she claims that they have a very special relationship and gives him a wink. Ted was a winker. It means nothing. If anything, it's maddening because it implies affection.

Even after Ted's execution, Louise's confusing presentations of family perfection to the outside world was observed in the Bundy home by journalist Myra Macpherson. Myra described the home as a Cleaver perfect household setting. The journalist noted several hundred condolence cards from when Ted was electrocuted were lying on the dining room table's lace cloth. Louise had arranged the cards in rubber-band wrapped piles of fifty. Obsessive compulsive personality trait? Here I go again–I can't seem to help myself.

Almost singing in regard to the hundreds of cards from strangers, Louise said to Myra, "We've made quite a few new friends." What? Her sense of reality when it came to Ted, as always, was nearly catatonic.

During this same interview, she admitted to Myra hesitantly that her dad did have tirades that could be heard down the block, but stated it "wasn't anything" and that "he was never violent with anyone." Then she displayed a hint of dissociation when a little while later during the same conversation she countered with, "My dad *did* beat up on my mother once in a while. But it wasn't frightening to see." It wasn't frightening to see? Or to hear? How about for the little child who wanted to be like that man?

Regarding having retrieved Ted from the Lund Home, she said in hindsight that perhaps she shouldn't have done it. When Myra asked if she would have felt awful giving him up for adoption, she resigned with a "probably." At times, I wonder if Louise's father insisted she retrieve the baby after that period of time because back in the day, a tortuous common reprimand was, "You made your bed, you lie in it." She displayed unchanging ambivalence from beginning to end toward her firstborn.

Louise's conflicting values did not stop there. After divulging the *Thou-Shalt-Not-Divulge* secret regarding the domestic violence in her childhood home, she gave a call to McPherson the next day saying she hadn't slept well because she was really upset at the image of her father that was now 'seeping out.'

Bravo to Myra McPherson for uncovering that important crack in the facade!

Louise was a tight drum. I wonder if she ever allowed herself to flip out. Of course, she would not have done so in public. A robotic persona does not portray affection, even warmth. I pity the child that cannot elicit anything but mechanical efficiency from their mother. Baby chimps that are given fake moms to cling to get sick and even die. Hopefully, as Ted claimed, she showed unbridled love to his siblings. I have a sense that her unbridled love was tending to assignments. I hope I am wrong about that.

When in prison, Ted said his mother sent a Christmas package of cookies.

That's not enough, Louise.

As his mother staunchly defended Ted until the very end, I wondered if she was defending him for his sake or hers. In 1980, when interviewed by the Tacoma News Tribune, she said that Ted Bundy did not go around murdering women and little girls, and that the family had faith that he was innocent and would stand by him. As seen in her testimony videos, she spoke of him glowingly when on the witness stand. Sometimes a privately resented child is given public privilege and praise to over-compensate for the internal resentment the parent holds toward that child. Ted must have hated that feigned praising, except for when it helped him get away with something.

I wonder, too, being completely adrift as far as behavior goes since his wrongdoings were never addressed, if Ted said in his mind, "Oh, I'm so good, am I Mother? Let me show you how BAD I can be." Still, she *never* acknowledged his crimes and praised him persistently right up until his confessions and even prior to his execution. While the reporter was in her home recording the last encounter by phone between the mother and son for history, Louise's last words to Ted were: "You'll always be my precious son."

Edmund Kemper, the coed killer who finished his killing spree by finally killing his absolutely vicious mother, said, "I wanted to love my mother."

Everyone wants to love their mother. That is not always possible or safe, however. As Judith Viorst says in her book *Necessary Losses* (1986), "The child in the burn unit wants to love their mother, even when it's the mother that set them on fire."

Louise and Ted publicly professed lifelong devotion to each other, but there remained an impassable obstacle separating their smiling selves. For Louise, the ruse was needed to ensure a good motherhood and family image. For Ted, it was to represent to the world a good Christian family of origin, *so how can I be bad?* Ted did concede to his rage at his mother even though he could not define what it was about, firmly denying that it had anything to do with his illegitimacy or the sister/mother dilemma. "He doth protest too much," as per the Bard.

Ted, in his tendency for romanticized recollection, told the journalists Michaud and Aynesworth (1989) that his mother taught him the English language and would type his homework papers while he paced and dictated. "I got really good at thinking on my feet." He said he never once got below an A in high school or college and that he attributed that to his mother. Au Contraire, TRB, your college transcripts show B's and incompletes here and there when you were likely distracted by your sadistic activities.

Bowlby's words echo to us in these next paragraphs: *"If it cannot be spoken to the mother, it cannot be told to oneself."*

Ted referred to Louise's beautiful handwriting and extensive vocabulary, but claimed "she never *says* anything." He went on to say that "she never talked with me or the other kids about personal matters." He denied resentment of her, but "there was something in her background that kept her from opening up. A log jam of feeling that she doesn't open up and explain . . . Nothing newsy or gossipy comes from her, she's not a socializing type of person . . . she is not a joiner of women clubs or card games, she doesn't even *think* about doing it . . . We never talked about her childhood." He saw in her school album she was extremely successful in high school. "She was the head of everything . . . She has a lot of character but doesn't project it."

I really think Louise could not confide in her mother either, perhaps due to her mother's illness or because of the father. That log jam came from somewhere.

Ted said he was never good at organized sports. Whenever he was not picked for a team after tryouts, he "was devastated, it was a traumatic source of agony," yet he *"never talked about it with her, never had occasion to, but you'd think there would have been an occasion don't you?"*

I'm sure both Louise and Ted would have liked their bond to be healthy, good, and true, but Ted had long since given up on that. By his teens, Ted had contempt anyway for such cotton candy. Louise had created a robotic ground rule with every living soul of *"don't even go there."* Her church peers would have never inquired of her regarding Ted because it sounds like she kept them as arms-length acquaintances rather than confidants.

By the time of testosterone onset in his early teens, Ted had heard of his illegitimacy and the assumed incestuous nature of it. When it came to girls his age, to add to his sense of embarrassment, he had been rejected by two girls. In my opinion, I think he selected his first murder to be an 8 year old girl because she might have symbolized the former two classmates' rebuffs. This rejection-revenge timeline makes sense to me. We do not know what similar person-on-person crimes he was responsible for between the ages of 14 and 22, but we do know he was continuously training by skulking around the neighborhoods at night.

Ted's mother didn't see anything wrong with him. Starting with the incidents that occurred with the knives and his sleeping aunt to reports from teachers and law enforcement during his adolescence, Louise always insisted there were no problems in his childhood. Wow, even TV mom June Cleaver was alert to mishaps and insisted on honesty and consequences with her boys.

Marilyn Feldman, PhD from Brooklyn, New York administered psychological tests on Bundy in 1986. She observed, "He lacks any core experience of care and nurturance or early emotional sustenance. . . . Severe rejection experiences have seriously warped his personality development and led to deep denial or repression of any basic needs for affection. Severe early deprivation has led to a poor ability to relate to or understand other people."

BINGO. Exactly what we've been talking about. I love coming across assessments from supreme primary professional sources.

Hugh Aynesworth reported in *Conversations with a Killer* that Ted had a moment with Louise when he was home on bail from Colorado. He said Louise's face became dark and serious and Ted knew she was going to tell him something, so he changed the subject. He left the house saying he had other things on his mind. I suspect what was on his mind was, "NOW you want to tell me? NOW you want to talk about it? Too late, Mother. That ship has long since sailed."

This is the crux of what made Bundy who he was. It is important information for us to digest in order to prevent or interrupt any detected formations of such confused, disconnected, and angry young individuals. This is not to say that we are looking for a TRB under every rock, nor should we, but understanding how people like him come about is crucial.

Just as we are not looking for another Ted, we are not looking for a Louise under every rock, either. Any of us that have done our share of misled parenting can get a bit tense looking at this information. An important thing to keep in mind is that we all make mistakes sometimes because to err is human. In fact, I would argue that, in order to be a good parent, we must screw up from time to time so that our children are resilient enough to survive a boss from hell or solve their own problems when there's no one around to rescue them.

Louise never stood a chance to raise Ted this way, given her upbringing, yet she persevered with relentless hope that everything would turn out okay. In a kinder world, I think she would have been a gladiator. Well, that wouldn't be too kind, would it? Still, I picture her answering the Halloween door with a bowl of candy for the trick-or-treaters, dressed in a Russell Crowe gladiator costume. The kids would have absolutely loved it.

Chapter Twelve

Daddy Dearest

. . . who the hell are you?

An unmarried pregnant woman in mid-century America needed to have a really good story as to how her "unacceptable" condition came about. Louise had it well covered because she not only had one story; she had two. She first said that Ted's father was Jack Worthington, a sailor that seduced and then abandoned her. When researchers first tried to validate the possible connection, they could find no such person. To Louise's credit, she possessed the sustained determination to preserve personal and family dignity in the face of cultural stigma, which should be respectfully appreciated. In more recent years, however, Bundy researcher Kevin Sullivan, author of *The Enigma of Ted Bundy (2020)* was able to find three John Worthington's that would have fit the appropriate age parameter in Philadelphia at the time of Louise's pregnancy.

Another possible father suggested by Louise was William Lloyd Marshall, a salesman and an Air Force veteran. Perhaps in an attempt to protect Lloyd, she gave the false name of Jack Worthington. The second name was in fact a real person who you will meet in the next few paragraphs. Regardless of whether Marshall was the father or someone else, this was still another man not stepping to fatherhood, but cowardly leaving mother and baby to be held in shame and dishonor in the eyes of their family and community.

Here is an alleged quote about William Lloyd Marshall from his great niece:

"He was married twice, which his family didn't take kindly to, and there's something about a child in his history that another family member raised. I believe he didn't hold a job too long and borrowed money on a regular basis before he moved away. Needless to say he was a black sheep."

*This is from a Bundy researchers' blog, THEODOREROBERTCOW-ELLNELSONBUNDY.WORDPRESS.COM The name of the great niece is not included with the quote.

To whatever degree psychopathy genetics contributed to Ted, Marshall may have left some of his black sheep genes with Teddy if he was indeed the father.

Google provides many images of anyone in Ted's constellation. When looking at many of Ted's photos, he is postured as described by his college girlfriend as appearing humble, unassuming, even somewhat pitiful. These pictures catch him with shoulders forward, chest in, and chin down, depicting him in his presentation stature of: "It's just me, I'm safe," while he was surveying prey like a falcon.

When looking at photos of young Ted, graduating Ted, and adult Ted, it is easy to see his postural tendency as described by her. In the only photo of William Lloyd Marshall, his body frame is held strikingly the same. Having reportedly served in the military, I would expect to see Marshall standing with a more chest out, chin up posture. Perhaps this photo was taken before the war. See what you think.

In the photo of Ted and his grandfather together at the beach , the resemblance here is remarkable as well. Look at the sinewy arms of the father, just like Ted's spring-loaded musculature.

In spite of trying my best to learn about Sam Cowell's developmental years, I have come up with nothing. His temper could have been the result of a head trauma. Brain injuries can result in episodic dyscontrol in the form of rage. If this was the reason for Cowell's anger, the injury would have occurred in early childhood since we do have stories of his tendencies to act out on his younger brothers to the point that they wanted to kill him. What troubles me about this theory is the father's reported sadistic behaviors, which are different to a fit of temper.

Thoughts cross my mind of how Samuel Cowell, perhaps like most men, wanted a son, and that is why he had Louise go collect the baby. He likely assumed Ted *was* his son. Although Louise may have known her father was a possibility, she may have also known there was another possibility.

If that were so, she was likely equally ashamed about that. Imagine having to tell *anyone* that the pregnancy could have been caused by your father, and if not your father, *another* man. If the family assumed it was Sam and left it at that, would Louise want to introduce another possibility to them, making matters worse? As if they could be made worse. Whoever he was, no wonder she kept it to herself.

Louise's worst nightmare: *Your father might be my father who is actually your grandfather. If it is not him, it would be this other man, but I will not tell you. I cannot bear to think of it myself.*

We now know Louise had no reason to worry about the former option. DNA testing done by Dr. Dorothy Lewis and reported that Ted was not a product of incest. I do not know where that laboratory test result is or if it still exists. If it does exist and his genome was ever sequenced and downloaded to *23 and Me*, people would be having strokes when he showed up in their family tree.

It is often the case that a youngster will strongly resemble a grandparent. The not-so-grand father was not a direct genetic contributor, but he did in other ways, as the grandfather, add to the chromosomal pool that became Bundy. The grandfather certainly had some psychopathic traits of his own to pass forward.

So, the mystery has remained as to who Theodore Robert Cowell Nelson Bundy's biological father was, and the question will apparently remain forever unanswered. As grandson Hunter pointed out over Thanksgiving dinner, "No one is going to step forward now."

Research is clear that many serial killers come from a broken home with a domineering mother and absent father. Ted had various father figures, but none early on that he bonded with or respected other than the grandfather that was his main male imprinting influence for the first four years of his life. The next male figure, his uncle whom he admired, was also short lived. He never did connect with Johnny—he was always contemptuous of Johnny.

Johnny was not an interpersonally involved father according to Ted. When trying out for sports, he said Johnny never tossed the ball around in the yard with him. To be fair, Johnny was not an athlete, but rather duty oriented like Louise for the most part. The sense I get from reading about Johnny is that he was similar to a personal assistant. I certainly don't know, but I hope he hugged and chased and tossed the siblings laughing into the air now and then. Maybe he did.

Ted was disengaged and disconnected from father figures one after the other. Whether we think of them as good or bad, they were still imprinting consecutively onto the little boy. Louise's actions also imprinted the following message on young Ted's mind: *I don't get to have a father because she keeps taking me away from them. And then she brings home this guy.*

Colliding Innocent Worlds

Johnny, by all accounts, did his best to father Ted, still Ted did not appreciate him. Rather than adopt Johnny's family loyalty, Ted, like his previous father figures, also failed in the Dad department. His wife Carole that he was married to while on death row wanted to have his child, and he accommodated by use of the visitor area bathroom. Cynically minded as I am regarding him, I think he utilized fatherhood as another endeavor to garner sympathy. Rosa was born under the unfair pretenses that she would only know her father as the man she and her mother visited in prison.

For little Rosa, *Ted* was her Daddy Dearest. She adored him, and it should have been safe for her to adore him. Her mother believed in Bundy's innocence wholeheartedly and had every expectation that all would be cleared up, he would be released, and they would be a happy family. She should have been able to think that.

The little sweet girl and her mother had no earthly idea and, much like Molly and Liz, *idolized* the Ted that he presented to them. Ever the actor, he was the man on stage characterizing innocence to *all of them*. Meanwhile he was heartlessly duping them right along with everyone else.

But law enforcement and prison guards had seen for themselves the off-stage Ted enough times that they understood he was a chameleon. All they could do was present the evidence, find more evidence, and do their jobs. It was not their job to convince the people that loved Ted as to who he *also* was. Even if it was their job to lift the veil, his loved ones wouldn't have believed them.

We want what we *want* to be true, to be true.

Which person was he? They could not grasp that he was both.

The mind splitter came when his loved ones had to ask: "He REALLY DID THAT?"

We cannot hold dueling realities in our mind, so we pick one. It can take forever to find any way to blend those realities because they usually *do not blend*. Or, after much therapy, we can pick a final conception, because both are there. Everyone who believed in Ted had to deal with ongoing confusion and crazy making. I suppose Ted, when in rationalization mode may have thought, "Well life, what do you think you've been trying to do to me? *How does it feel to not know who I am?*" And then, as justified in his own self-centered mind, he continued to exact more revenge.

His betrayal of the women who loyally stuck by him is sinister enough . . . but the little girls. His adoring little girls. A parent cannot imagine how much to tell a grieving young child when they are also in shock regarding what they cannot understand in this situation. At four years old, Rosa's understanding was minimal. Molly on the other hand was already old enough to know he was twisted, although she certainly did not want him to be.

We do not know how Carole guided her daughter through this. I'm sure she was in shock. My impression of Carole is that she did not, like Louise, close the door as to the *who, what, and why* of Ted. I don't agree with Louise's approach, but do empathize with her impossible dilemma. At the same time, I honestly do not know how I would have handled it in Louise's place, in her generation.

In Carole's situation I would want to have a therapist guide me through this nightmare and one to help my child as well. In my hypothetical world, I would want the therapy to be provided intermittently and ongoing. By that I mean initial therapy for the shock and recovery period of time, and then seeing someone regularly while we try to come to grips with our new reality. Then, after weeks, months, or years, we can hopefully feel like our trauma has been folded up and put away. For now. Then, after another while as life goes along, questions and realizations bubble back to the surface now and then, which can't be helped. Thoughts occur to us further down the road that we hadn't pondered or considered regarding the trauma.

When that occurs, more gentle processing needs to take place. No digging, only handling what has presented itself and the questions around that realization. When sorted to satisfaction, then some more time may go by of living and enjoying life until the next realization surfaces. We repeat the cycle with no rigid time frame or determined number of sessions. Recovery and review is determined by the wellbeing of the individual.

Liz's daughter Molly has grown to be a classy woman with a solid thread of wisdom woven through her mind in spite of those early years with Ted. Rosa is completely off grid. She needs to be respectfully allowed to privately enjoy the life of her choosing. My guess is that her name was changed in order to protect her. Her mother, being a smart woman, likely had Rosa in therapy to sort whatever information was digestible for the little girl, and the therapy likely continued as Rosa grew. She may still see a therapist from time to time, but I don't know. It makes sense to me that as the little girl grew up, as little girls will do, she inquired of her mom and her older step brother about Ted, who were both snowed and then betrayed by Mr. Bait-n-Switch.

I would like to know more about where Rosa is today, but it is important to let the out of sight souls like her live the peaceful, private lives they prefer. I have also made attempts to contact Ted's siblings who have remained mostly off-record, but I have not been successful. Certainly in their shoes, I would not want to talk with anyone either. I would want people like me to go away and leave me alone. Everyone left in Ted's wake simply wants the nightmare–and us–to go away. Having said that, it's true that had a sibling or family member agreed to talk to me, I would have been there in a New York minute. We need to learn all we can from this subject matter, but the survivors get to choose if they talk or not.

Chapter Thirteen

The Cleavers

Sandi Hilt, a childhood friend of Ted's who I have mentioned before, was interviewed for "The Ted Bundy Tapes" (2019), a Netflix Documentary. She said the Bundy's could not have been more Beaver Cleaver if they'd tried. Visitors to their home commented that it looked like it was out of a 1950's movie set. Table cloths, matching sofas, polished knick knacks, gleaming surfaces, pie and coffee served on affordable china.

In those days, many houses were kept clean and tidy like that. Well, for some of us not necessarily *that* tidy. The fact that the Bundy home was very 50's even in the 80's suggests to me that Louise took very good care of things she and Johnny obtained during their decades together. Sandi said in the neighborhood there was a definite difference between the "haves" and "have nots," the Bundy's being in the "have nots" category. Despite this, Louise made sure that what they had was well tended to and presentable.

Apparently Johnny Bundy was Mr. Fixit, and if he didn't buy it, he created or restored it. He maintained the same job for decades and was devoted to supporting his family. Louise chose well. She also worked outside the home part time, but her household came first. These were honorable characteristics in both of them.

Whereas TV mom June Cleaver was terminally worried and always hovered mother eagle fashion over her boys, Louise was terminally optimistically firm about the absolute best public perception of her son. All along the way, the modus operandi of the family was Emmy Award worthy:

concealment of anything questionable. Ted's identity and personality were depersonalized his entire life, and so he concealed himself masterfully. He even said his self concept was concealment.

What differed also from the Cleavers, at least when it came to parenting Ted, was persistent skewed or lacking accountability. Not being held accountable or responsible in the television family's home was absolutely unacceptable. This Cleaver value was evident in every episode, here is one example in this episode of *Leave it to Beaver* (Oct. 2, 1958). The Beav unexpectedly won a contest and prize for a poem that his dad had urgently written on his behalf at the last minute. The parents did not pretend that Beaver had written it himself and did not allow the boy to accept the misappropriated accolades.

Mr. Cleaver confessed to the Principal that he in fact had written the verse in order to help his son get it in on time. Beaver confessed to his teacher that he waited too long to do the assignment, so his dad helped him. The teacher had him write it over again from his own imagination. This scene, of course, is really cute and makes us all warm and fuzzy inside when we see it.

However, it was not so in Ted's world. He had zero accountability in the *seeable* history, except the time he was punished when his mother caught him masturbating at age 11. From report card concerns to stolen items, one-sided fights, injuring small animals and other children, forgery, attempted auto theft, and burglary, the parents HAD to be aware of his actions. Can you *imagine* what Ward and June would have done if their children were caught doing that stuff?

Accountability is the rudimentary feature of good character. When accountability is not installed in the hard drive, or if it is selective responsibility only, then there is a glitch in the system. We are all selectively accountable to some degree, but when the selectivity is pervasive, deceitful, and always allowed, there is a problem.

Accountability is also important because it is an outward reflection of investment in the life of someone else. There is a photo of Louise embracing Ted's Boy Scout Shirt. I wonder if he was ever warmly embraced or was it reserved for his meticulously tended belongings. He described being brushed out the door to play when his siblings were getting affectionate attention. We know he was detached early. We know that he said his mom paid all the bills and never yelled at him. We also know her sisters described her as having a temper like her dad. Ted's childhood cohorts said they had rarely if ever entered his home. One young visitor that entered the home asked about Ted, as his bedroom door was closed, and his mother said he had chicken pox. Neighbors described Johnny as gentle, but Louise as gruff and in charge.

In fairness, any of us that have actually been in charge of a hectic household have certainly done our percentage of yelling, or at least commanding, since that's sometimes the only way anyone actually hears us. What is missing here are both hugs from mom to show love and the switch to show discipline. That's how it was done in those days—the switch, I mean. Properly applied, it was considered corrective, not abusive.

A story from my own upbringing is that one day my brother and I were in trouble for something. I don't remember what. He was about eight years old and I was about six. We were sent down into the basement to select which stick of kindling we would get our swats with. We did our best to select what looked like the most sting-free piece. When we were ready, my brother said to me, "Carol, if you go first you will get it over faster." I fell for it, got my three swats and he was right. I did get it over faster.

These days instead, we think in terms of, well, Leave it to Beaver accountability. The Bundy's didn't seem to do that either, though.

When Johnny met Louise, he did not ask about her and Teddy's background. His history with them began when he and Louise met. Perhaps that was Louise's requirement. In the same position, it might have also been mine. It seems Johnny preferred Louise to steer the ship. Johnny, like many of the rest of us, liked life to be Cleaver-like: simple, fuzzy, and manageable with no riddles. Yet the poor guy had married a riddler and was raising her Chinese Finger Trap.

Ted had contempt for what he considered Johnny's lack of depth and antagonized him regularly. He would do this until his stepfather, certainly feeling disrespected—and we should keep in mind feeling disrespected is a trigger for violence—would swat Ted. Acquaintances said Johnny at times whacked his stepson with a belt, at which I picture Ted smirking with disdain. So there were times after all when at least Johnny would give him a comeuppance.

Unfortunately, it's not possible to steer someone aright when they are already long adrift.

The Cleaver series representation of the *rascal personality*, as we recall with a smile, was Wally's friend Eddie Haskell. He comes to mind as a character that's a good example of an individual who was genetically vulnerable in childhood to Conduct Disorder. If not corrected long before adolescence, this can gel into Antisocial Personality Disorder, which is the umbrella term, as you remember, for both sociopathy and psychopathy.

Throughout the series, the character Eddy is definitely leaning into a consistent pattern of unemotional callous disregard, being mentored by his similar-in-character father. Remember nature versus nurture. In spite of Eddie's swaggering con artist behaviors, every once in a while, we see a soft side of him that, when Eddie realizes it is showing, he is always determined to hide. Much to Eddie's chagrin, the Cleavers see the soft leak in him. In an environment other than the Cleaver's home influence of warm accountability, things could have really gone south for Eddie in a hurry. Fortunately "Leave it to Beaver" was a wonderful fictional comedy, so I am going to leave Eddie's outcome at happily ever after.

Ted's emotional and moral life from the time of his conception was progressively untethered. During those early months, he was not readily absorbed into a warm, welcoming family with his best interests at heart. Instead, right off the bat he was a number, having been abandoned for adoption. Oh and then months later, on second thought, retrieved. Whereas daily schedule at the orphanage was emotionally vacant and regimented, alternatively life was emotionally chaotic at the Philadelphia house. Then lifestyle was predictable and classy at uncle's, then awkward and lonely in Tacoma with Johnny. I think that Ted's natural born temperament was one innately needing more reassurance than a more naturally confident child. That is a guess at best.

Awaiting longed for significance and losing his hope of ever receiving it, Ted developed cunning to hopefully gain some relevance, or at least relevance in his own mind. As he said, he had to become his own Sun. He couldn't grasp the fact that we are all connected, and so he could never quite plug in. He was so hungry and angry about that craving for significance that he would do anything, unfortunately *anything*, to be noticed and reckoned with. Publicly, he was an All American Boy, but secretly he was a raptor. His costuming was so perfect he was never noticed, at least, until he was. And his parents were not aware that something was rotten in the state of Denmark?

Ted's younger siblings, in contrast, benefitted from landing directly into loving arms and tended to from the start. Richard, the youngest boy, is the only sibling that has come forward to describe his childhood years with Ted. Richard talked of, at the age of 14, being sent home early from a visit with Ted in Utah and feeling so disappointed by the abrupt ending to his vacation with his big brother. He so loved the times he got to spend with Ted, but his big brother reassured him to go home, promising him he had a new bike that he would ship to him.

The kid should have been able to enjoy camping with his big brother. What we know now is that Ted would have been familiar with that camping site based on his explorations for other purposes. His little brother, of course, was *mercifully* none the wiser.

While at the airport for the trip back home to Tacoma, Rich described seeing a *horribly dark look* on Ted's face while he was looking out the window. Ted didn't know someone was looking at him. It was a profound enough change in Ted's countenance that Richard remembered it vividly into his adulthood. That is the only indicator of the *other side* of Ted that Richard himself can think of. Had Richard talked with his parents about it, I'm sure it would have been dismissed. Unfortunately, Ted's behavior was always dismissed, meaning *Ted* was always dismissed. In a frustrated, narcissistic rage, I think he said to life, "Discount me? Dismiss me? How dare you. Well what about THIS?"

Richard was blindsided by his relational link to Bundy soon after he returned from the trip. When Ted was arrested in Utah and charged with aggravated kidnapping, it was broadcasted on national TV. Imagine when young Richard heard the news—on the news—that Ted was his *half brother*. What a shock it must have been for him. How did the police and reporters even learn that Ted was sired by a father other than Johnny?

The news media was blatantly informing the world and Ted's siblings of the step-nature of his relationship to them, and *even then* it was not discussed within the Tacoma household. Any answers were up to Ted, his siblings, the world, and us to find for ourselves. Whether the answers were accurate or not did not seem to matter. Louise allowed this taunting mystery that plagued Ted since his birth *to continue for all of his life and all of his siblings' lives.*

Richard angrily resents the betrayal his idolized big brother brought about. In a family with compartmentalized, deeply plumbed secrets that "*don't* exist," the participants themselves were blinded by the keepers of the classified information that "*didn't* exist." Mind blowing, isn't it? The secret was on a need-to-know basis and no one needed to know, so the entire family continued to *live* with it every day without fully knowing what or who "it" is.

However, in some other ways, Ted seems to have been a father figure to young Richard and perhaps a few of the other siblings as well. It sounds like Ted kept Richard under his big brother wings at times. Richard said he stayed with him on weekends when Ted lived in Seattle and when Ted went home to the family house, it was mainly to see Richard. I wonder if Richard, being the smallest and quite a bit younger than Ted, was at the same emotional maturity level as his emotionally stunted adult brother.

Richard's other brother, Glen, who was the middle brother, had possibly already outgrown Ted in social interaction acumen and peer activity participation. Remember Ted saying he would watch Glen and his friends to learn how to act. I do not know how Glen reacted when he found out about Ted's illegitimacy, [but based on his interactions with Ted growing up, it probably didn't surprise him.]

Another childhood friend, when told of Ted's illegitimacy, said that it all came together for him. He had seen angry outbursts from Ted that were exaggerated and inappropriate. This tells me he noticed things about Bundy that didn't make sense until he learned of his illegitimacy. So many factors indicate that problems seen remained unidentified because young Ted's identity was fundamentally hidden, forbidden, off limits. It seems Ted was a bit of a ghost.

What a way to grow up.

Chapter Fourteen

Con Artist Playing House

... All in the Family

Throughout his early adult years of clandestine murder, mayhem, and false identities, Ted was loved and supported by Liz. They met at a popular local tavern in the University District of Seattle and she fell completely in love with him. They would be *together* for several years. She paid some of his first year law school tuition and he ate meals at her house. She paid for a lot of things. Ted loved that she came from a wealthy family. Liz was happy to cover expenses much of the time because she believed Ted was going somewhere, and she believed he would be taking her and her daughter Molly into the promised future with him.

Here we see another example of the parasitic lifestyle. Although he kept his own place elsewhere, Liz provided Ted with much of his daily home needs. Being very conservative with his *own* expenses, he knew that if he was rarely at his apartment, his own utility costs would be low. This left his own place available for practicing his established hobby in private whenever it was convenient for him. How did he get away with taking advantage of Liz like that? I will tell you.

First of all, his narcissism convinced him that *of course she will take care of me.* I'm ME, I deserve this, and she is lucky to have me. Remember what the well cared for Bundy said when referring to his mother: "She fed me and paid all the bills and never yelled at me." His narcissism never allowed him to tolerate being yelled at or to bear criticism because he assumed control in every situation. He felt rather proud of how he was able to dazzle Liz and secure her devotion to him as a replacement for Louise. Unlike Louise, however, Liz *did* yell at him sometimes. Bravo Liz!

At the same time, I think her warmth and emotional concern for him puzzled, if not troubled, Ted given the motorized emotions he was familiar with growing up. But her loyalty was right up his alley.

In her book, *The Phantom Prince* (2020) Liz describes her time with Ted. How she was taken in by him, mistreated by him, left him, then drawn back in by him. She and Molly should have been able to adore him. While she and Molly loved him devotedly, however, the leech benefited from them year after year.

This is a good time to talk about *Love Bombing*. It is a dynamic that occurs when a person wants to capture the love and devotion of someone else. "Hook, line, and sinker," as they say. Some advice often given to young adults is, "Marry someone that you know loves you more than you love them." Immediate dominance of the relationship is *guaranteed* in that arrangement. Guaranteed to ensure less heartache. Well, less heartache for the one that loves less, that is. For the completely heartless it's even easier.

Love Bombing is what Ted used a few years later to win back his college girlfriend after she broke up with him. He used self accolades and future faking as juicy bait. *I have accomplished all this, am involved in these important things, these public figures rely on me, this is what I will do next, and we will have a nice life together.* "I am such a prize now" is the message he presented to his ex, and she swallowed it up and agreed to marry him. With his mission accomplished and being quite pleased with himself, Mr. "I will make you pay" Machiavellian dumped her.

You may be wondering, why didn't he kill her? It wasn't because he knew that he would have to dodge being the number one suspect since their 'engagement' was public. As slippery as he could be, that was not the reason. He wanted her to be *publicly humiliated* as he felt she had done to him. As you recall, narcopaths will sometimes only punish the object of their rage by keeping them alive so they can bombard their victims with guilt, saying, *"See what you made me do? It's your fault, not mine."*

When Liz walked into the Sandpiper Tavern the night they met, she caught sight of Ted and fell instantly in love. He knew it. They danced and talked all evening. She said that in her mind, she was already planning the wedding and naming the children. He knew that, too. When it was time to leave, she asked if he would take her home as she felt too impaired to drive.

That first evening, when they arrived at Liz's apartment, he continued the *capture and retain* method of Love Bombing. He knew he liked her just fine, but she was absolutely mad about him. If she rejected him, it wouldn't be that much of a loss as it would someone he *really* wanted.

Liz had told Ted about her young daughter, Molly, while they were out earlier that evening. Molly was asleep on the living room sofa, so Ted gallantly offered to sleep on top of the bed in his clothes, which she did as well, as she said she was too impaired to do otherwise. Ted did not even try to kiss her. That won a lot of *safety and respect* points with her, even though she might have wished like crazy that he would kiss her.

In her blurred sleep, Liz noticed during the night that Ted was looking at the items on her dresser (he was always shopping) and then she dropped back to sleep. When Liz woke up in the morning, she heard sounds in the house and remembered that he had stayed the night. She found Ted and Molly in the kitchen making breakfast together.

That was like opium to the young single mom. He had her at "Hi I'm Ted," reeled her in more by not trying to have sex with her, and *really* sealed the deal by making breakfast for her and her little girl.

Now would be a good time to discuss the halo *effect and confirmation bias*. The halo effect is when we really really like someone and believe everything about them is good simply because we *want* it to be true. Confirmation bias occurs when we really want something to be true and seek examples that confirm that belief. We do it all the time without realizing, and when the reality of the substance of the individual is revealed, we can have an extremely difficult time absorbing it. Ted used this natural tendency to his advantage.

With these two loving souls, Ted was closer to having his own adoring family than he ever had been in his life. Unfortunately, he was already seared beyond repair by that point. He was *such* a good actor and entertainer. They absolutely adored him and would have loved him forever had he not been . . . Bundy.

Entering this relationship was Ted's likely attempt at securing a *Family Man personae* for himself that he was in control of, could rely upon, would support him monetarily, and make him look like a good person. The relationship made him appear normal and wanted by desirable people. Foundational. He didn't think Liz fit the role of a governor's wife . . . but for a foundational appearance, the lovely young mom and daughter would do nicely.

A serial killer (I can't remember which one, so sorry pal, I can't credit you) sagely described "the necessity of building a foundation," meaning one must have a personae that appears as wholesome and traditional as possible. A family, a job, and a community position all deflect suspicion. *He's such a nice guy! We know his family! They come to our barbecues! He has served the community for years! If it wasn't for him . . .!*

All part of "The Foundation."

When Ted first took Liz to meet his family, Johnny welcomed her with pleasant conversation and Louise was formally kind. I picture Johnny's role as being pleasant and interacting in order to put the guest at ease while Louise mashed the potatoes and directed the kids to set the table properly. After leaving his parent's house, Ted assured Liz that they liked her. Years later, when Louise learned Liz had informed police of her concerns about Ted, Louise said something like: "She was a pretty mixed up gal."

During a time when Liz and Ted were briefly engaged, or at least Liz thought they were, they went to dinner again at his parent's house. Liz waited for him to tell his parents about their plans. Instead of Liz and Ted excitedly telling the family together, Ted and his mother excused themselves to another room. After a while, they came back to the table and Louise hugged Liz, saying she wished them happiness. I wonder if Liz felt like she was being hugged by a really soft robot.

You may have sensed it, and you are right. Ted told Liz as they left that his parents thought he should finish law school before they got married. Who knows what he told his mother, but this was a way for the disappointing decision coming from someone other than *him*. Louise was still steering Ted's ship. He let his mother take responsibility for his flaccid accountability. Another day, when Liz and Ted were window shopping together, they passed a jewelry store and Liz suggested they go in and look at rings. She looked at rings while Ted looked at watch bands.

Everyone in Ted's world was compartmentalized according to use, and he assigned roles to them based on his perceived necessities, regarding each relationship as a tool to be used for *his own* advantage. Such compartmentalization had been successful throughout his developmental years, so he carried these practiced abilities into adulthood with remarkable skill.

Meanwhile in Ted's mind, Liz and Molly would conveniently work as part of his appearing like a normal, even admirable, person. However, *this* "Family Man" was too loose of a cannon and not capable of maintaining relationships anywhere near intimate enough to prevent him from committing murder after murder. His sadistic appetite was too entrenched. Ted's relationship with Liz was problematic, of course, as he was frequently unreliable due to his alternate life that kept him occupied elsewhere, which of course frustrated her to no end.

This is an example of another maddening phase of love bombing. Once Ted was secure in the knowledge that Liz and Molly were completely dedicated to him, he got lazy about it, even disappointing. He would for a while, that is, until Liz would demand some respect. Whenever Liz became frustrated with him to no avail, she would begin talking about ending their relationship. In response, Ted would run the vacuum, do the dishes, cook a meal, make some future fake promises, and whatever else he needed to do in order to keep her in his sway. Random reward is the strongest form of addiction formation, and it becomes a pattern in relationships. Once the relationship is secured again, one gets lazy again, and when the partner gets ticked, love bombing once again solves the problem. Ted was *so* good at it. If you have a love bomber in your life, make a run for it if you can do so safely.

Later in their relationship, Ted blew his top when Liz briefly broke up with him and went out with someone else. To clarify, this was *ego*, not heartbreak. Refusing to be jilted, Ted showed up uninvited one night when Liz was out with friends. He loitered on the periphery of the room, watching her while looking both sad and angry. Remember the creepiness of the psychopath stalky stare—they don't know when to quit. Liz wasn't having it and made him leave.

But then he showed up at her place later dropping bombs of how much he loved her and that he had screwed up. He professed that he couldn't live without her. The truth is it would have *inconvenienced him* to lose her because then he would have to find a new host, a new supplier.

Liz and Molly should have been able to plan on the future he was promising them. Hoping it would be different this time, Liz reconsidered. Because he was so fun and quirky and could easily make them laugh, he won her back with the dark art of love bombing.

Ted, by this time, had blown his halo effect, so now he had to rely on her confirmation bias of assuming the best each time he dropped a love bomb.

Love bombing, seducing, or placating with gifts is common to the manipulator's cycle. They will splurge to obtain or get back good graces, but often they will give gifts that have cost them nothing. They will even give accessories that they have taken as trophies from their victims in order to see the reminder of their prowess each time it is worn.

For the Christian reader, manipulation and murder is displayed front and center in the opening pages of the Bible. Eve was charmed right out of the gate to enjoy the purported benefits of the fruit, which according to Genesis brought death itself to the human race, not to mention painful childbirth and hard work. And it didn't stop there. One step down in the family line, her son Cain killed his brother Abel. Cain can be thought of as, well, after Satan that is, the first Biblical psychopath. There are several of them in the Good Book of course, and that could be an interesting Bible Study. I would call it "Psychopaths of the Bible."

Anyway, the story goes that God wanted the brothers each to bring him a sacrifice, or what we would think of as a *gift* to show their love and gratitude. Well, God liked Abel's gift best as it was exactly what God had asked for. Cain's gift was not at all appreciated, so as sibling rivalry would have it, jealousy raised it's ugly head and Cain killed his brother. God tracked down Cain and asked where Abel was, and the first human psychopath answered, "Am I my brother's keeper?"

Since God does not suffer mocker's gladly, he put a mark on Cain to warn others of the murder. I wish God did that with criminals today; it would save us a lot of grief. I suppose there are reasons why he doesn't.

Abel's gift was a sacrificial lamb which being dead, was non sustainable so ultimately *cost* Abel something, not to mention cost the lamb its life. Unlike Abel, there is no indication as to what Cain's sub-standard gift was other than something from the 'fruit of the field'. Maybe the Serpent convinced him to give a zucchini as a sacrifice. I don't know.

As if his disrespect of Liz was not enough, Ted's relationship with Molly was terribly worse and secretly indecent, according to adult Molly. She described Ted as not following rules like other grownups, and often his quirky ideas were really fun. But unforgivably, sometimes his conduct was heinous.

At first, whenever it was convenient and for good perception management, Ted treated Molly well. None the wiser to his true character, Molly absolutely fell in love with him. There is a photo taken with Molly from *The Phantom Prince*. It would not surprise me if Bundy had combed little Molly's hair and put the bows in. As we now know, he loved to primp himself and the bodies of his victims. He might have been more usefully channeled into fashion and design. Wow, can you imagine the *BUNDY* or *TRB* American brand . . . Ew. If Ralph Lauren reads this, he might faint.

Adult Molly said of her pictures taken in Ted's arms although she was smiling she did not like the way Ted was touching her. Liz, of course, did not see. However, she did see times when he would pick Molly up by the crotch, and she made him stop.

In *The Phantom Prince (2020)* Molly has other examples, *very serious examples,* that indicate that when it came to a female, age was not a deterrent for Ted. In their book, Molly describes being home alone with Ted. Once, he suggested they play a hide and seek game. When looking for him, she found the freaking mutant under a blanket, naked with a purple erection. Then, when reading one of *his* favorite story books (Uncle Wiggles) to Molly, he ejaculated, leaving the little girl confused in a wet bed. The child had NO idea what was happening. She describes his foul behavior as *so confusing* since she loved him, but she could sense it was wrong.

Let's pause for a minute and take some breaths.

Liz was not aware of Molly's experiences, and the little girl did not want to ruin all of the *wonderful* parts of their family life. Love is blind after all, and secrets are kept often to protect the ones we love. He was that good at acting the part, and they loved him that much.

They love bomb the children in the relationship too.

In order to remain in Liz's good graces as a family man, he had new acts to learn. He told Dr. Carlisle that, with such an empty identity, he needed to see how others acted in order to learn each of the "roles."

Like an actor, *with lots of practice you get really good at it*. He had school, scouts, church, and home life to teach him the rules of good citizenship. So, with time, he adopted various amusing or endearing characters appropriate in each setting. His personality disconnect was so complete, he could do a seamless slip in and out of whatever role was required of him at the time. Shapeshifting, he could sink into the required characterization.

When daydreaming and fantasy become so intense and frequent, individuals can become rather unaware of everything around them. We have all had intense daydreams that space us out at times, or have finished a book but still are mentally absorbed into the story even as we move through our day. Screen actors can deeply dissociate into a role. In fact, some actors will sustain the character throughout their daily life and relationships for an extended period of time to hone the role. It's called Method Acting.

Alternatively, when deep into imagination we become absent. Sandi Hilt, when describing Bundy as a youngster, said he not only didn't fit, but that *he just wasn't there*. Had I the opportunity to ask her, I would have wanted some examples of that. Liz also said there were times when Ted was spaced out, not even there. For an extreme example, she said there was a time when she and Ted were having sex and he put his hands around her throat. Terrified, it took her awhile to bring him out of it.

There was no real attachment ability in Ted to prevent full immersion into imaginary roles and exploits. Unlike Dissociative Identity Disorder (DID), formerly Multiple Personality Disorder (MPD), where neither personality (or role) within the individual knows about the other, Ted said he was able to fully recall activities he was involved in when he allowed the "entity" (as he called the *other Ted*) to be in control, stalking, hunting and butchering women. He said he had a clear, detailed memory of each of his "projects."

His detached personality tells me that when strangling Liz, he was going for it. He had murderous thoughts about her, too. Another time he plugged the vent of the fireplace and when the house started rapidly filling with smoke, he left the house saying he was going to get a fan. He did not come back. She was able to get to a window and air, and saved her own life and maybe Molly's too. I don't know if the little girl was there. I'll bet when the phone call came and it was *Liz* rather than the fire department or coroner that Ted was a bit puzzled.

He had told others that he worried about Liz because at times she threatened suicide. Having established that idea in others' minds, had she died, he could have easily suggested (brokenheartedly, maybe even with dry tears) that her smoke inhalation death was a suicide. Or thinking that she was suicidal at times, *they* may have suggested that to Bundy with great concern. But *who would want to die that way?* Louise's words come to mind: *She was a pretty mixed up gal.*

Ted worked his perception management with Liz, although she began to see inconsistencies and downright betrayal, and she called him on it. He also finessed anyone else he wanted to be in good favor with so that he could use their generosity or have their undying support when he needed it. Ted had become the puppet master, pulling all the strings.

Chapter Fifteen

Porn Pomp and Politics

. . . The Devil made me do it

Pornography has been around since before King David watched Bathsheba bathe on her rooftop (Peeping!). God settled that mis-step of the Old Testament monarch sternly, but the king did get to keep Bathsheba. I don't know much about Hebrew porn proclivities other than, despite God's efforts, they could be quite hedonistic. On the other hand, they were quite war-like under King David's command, but he said God told him to do it. God-blamed wars happened during the Medieval Inquisition era too so the Hebrews weren't the only ones.

A squint worthy look into Hebrew history gives us the impressive profile of King Solomon. His daddy dearest was King David mentioned above. When becoming King, Solomon asked God for wisdom, and boy did he ever get it. The Old Testament Book of Proverbs is chock full of the best advice ever, and he was considered, at least by his contemporaries, the wisest man that ever lived. Even Jesus vouched for him on this account.

As often happens when at the pinnacle of success, Solomon didn't follow his own advice. At that level of power, people don't think they have to follow the advice the rest of us do and so begin to deteriorate. Solomon started on a downhill slide and ended up with a harem of 700 wives and 300 concubines.

Being no slouch intellectually, Solomon had an amazing way of expressing himself poetically on papyrus. He wrote The Song of Songs, which is an erotic composition–at least by Old Testament standards–describing the intimate lovemaking of a bride and bridegroom. To find its way into the Bible is a bit of a surprise, but go look it up. You'll find it between the books of Ecclesiastes and Isaiah.

Solomon's sonnet is tucked discreetly out of direct sight, but the Greeks and Romans were more conspicuous. They set the porn bar really high with nude body sculptures everywhere depicting not only bronze and marble lust, but naked brutality as well. The Renaissance followed the lead by expanding the art form onto canvas and in color.

Song of Solomon aside, for those concerned about pornography on the church population, I think you might relate to this:

The parable tells us, "If an unclean spirit goes out of a man, it passes through waterless places, seeking rest, and does not find it. Then it says, 'I will return to my house from which I came; and when it comes it finds it unoccupied, swept and put in order. Then it goes and takes along with it seven other spirits more wicked than itself, and they go in and live there; and the last state of that man becomes worse than the first." Mt.12:43-45 (NAS)

Lots of well meaning speakers could and do enthusiastically build admonitions off of this one.

I will take a crack at it because this parable is what comes to mind when I think of the conditions that brought about Bundy.

Here goes:

I think of Ted's sense of himself *feeling* abandoned and empty, and so he moved elsewhere looking for relevance. Then I picture Louise sweeping, tidying up his no longer occupied room. Had she been my neighbor, I could have learned some great housekeeping tips from her.

Back to the parable:

Young Ted, having sought a grounding fulfillment of himself elsewhere, didn't find it, and returned to his starting place empty handed. With no change in his now swept clean but still disembodied world, he takes up seven other spirits more evil than himself and now "me" has become a powerful "we." *And the last state of that man becomes worse than the first.*

Was King David repentant here, or afraid he'd get caught? Is the title I would give to Posterazzi's painting of David, bent over with head in hands after watching Basheba.

For Ted, peeping and violent porn were pastimes which developed into a method of expressing his furious lust for revenge. Well, at first he may have rationalized revenge but then somewhere along the line, and I think it was early on, he murdered because he craved it. The fact that he compared himself with other males and normaled the porn addiction process is inappropriate. Other young men may dabble at viewing brutal eroticism but are typically horrified by it and do not embark on a vocation of sexual violence.

Furthermore, most boys are emotionally connected with others, are involved in school, sports, social activities, and enjoy the affection of their friends and families. Off to baseball practice, skateboarding with friends, home for supper, gaming with friends, texting with friends, *getting a sit down accountability conversation when necessary and making appropriate restitution.*

What is different with Ted is that he had not formed anything more than feigned surface attachments with *real* humans. As we know, Ted's connectors went blunt early on. Warmth and even civility from him were acts since he didn't have the developed capacity for relationships in the way that we experience them—with compassion, empathy, and emotional reciprocity. He knew how to play the romance role, but when off-stage, all that was left of him was *not* pretty. Since nature abhors a vacuum, it *will* fill.

Let's have a word about pornography addiction. Like any other addiction, porn is progressive, requiring more stimulation as time goes by. As the material gets seedier, amorous contact with regular people or partaking in non-violent sex becomes rather ineffective. So as you might surmise, porn is a relationship wrecker. Another important fact to consider is that as with alcohol, drugs, gambling, etc., the enslavement *progresses* even when the individual is not using. My first thoughts when hearing about the Chi Omega rampage was exactly that. The addiction had progressed while Ted was in prison.

Ted claimed pornography didn't make him kill. He wanted to do it. He liked doing it. Ted said that he at first associated pornography with his grandfather when he was little. This would have made it okay in his mind since his grandfather was the youngster's first role model. Ted dove into raw detective stories in order to feed his fantasies. The reveries were imaginary and therefore *false* human connections. His imagination made him feel in charge and formidable like he remembered his grandfather. It's important to recall that the more distant the memory, the more we glorify the remembered.

Early shocking impressions are lasting. For example, as an adult, here I am exploring this subject matter in my own way. Ted, having said he was influenced by his grandfather's pornography, brings up for me a memory of finding a pile of detective magazines behind my Grampa's recliner rocker when I was about three and a half years old. Immediately absorbed, I remember wondering, "why are people doing this?" Gramma discovered me pouring over the spread of images on the floor and scooped them up immediately. She told me to never look at those things again, and I never saw them again. I have no doubt Grampa got an earful.

There is not a youngster alive that at some point didn't trip over some nasty magazines. The pornography exposure I am referring to here is not as was described in Ted's final interview. We are not talking about a group of giggly neighborhood boys that come across a Playboy magazine somewhere, become addicted to porn, and grow up to be serial killers, as Ted implied in his interview with Dr. James Dobson. In that interview, Dr. Dobson *so* wanted to establish a reason, a *preventable* reason for Ted's murderous sadism. He also wanted to establish some sort of reason and closure for all of the families, and, since it *was* his job, see Ted's soul saved.

In Dobson's statement to the press after the interview concluded, he said that Ted expressed remorse and that Bundy had wept and accepted Christ as his Savior. Watch the prison interview. Ted was wiping at a dry face. How actors and psychopaths, all psychopaths being actors, fake cry is by wiping as though a tear is on the dry part of the face, and allowing any welling up mustered in either eye to be visible and not cleared off. If it spills over, they let it run down the face and don't wipe it off. There you go, that's how it's done. If you did not already know, Ted did take a theatre course while at Temple University.

Ted, in addition to the fake tear during the interview with Dr. Dobson, did a sideways swipe at remorse by distantly saying he *hoped people would believe his expression of sorrow and remorse,* but didn't actually make one. That is like saying I hope people will believe my apology. Okay, we are waiting . . .

What was lacking from the start for Ted, as you now know, was a sense of belonging, of being emotionally connected and included with people. Craven emptiness was there instead and was easily filled with the wrong stuff, graphic ideas as *methods* of deriving what for him was pleasure.

Ted absolutely craved relevance, significance, and importance. Instructor for The Behavior Panel YouTube channel, Mark Bowman, is a human behavior expert and consultant for some members of the G7. Being a

Brit by birth, Mark refers to the instinct for significance in human beings as seeking "stay-tus," or what we yankees on our side of the Atlantic pronounce as "status." We all require feeling a sense of worth, belonging, and significance among our fellow human beings. It's absolutely crucial for survival.

Seeking status is not healthy when the narcissist is pressing down, submerging the heads of the other swimmers to lift himself up so he can get the air. Feeling like an insignificant vessel so to speak, Ted filled the gaping space with that which made *him* feel alive, important, enviable, powerful, and effective since those things weren't happening for him in his personal reality elsewhere.

Ted spent long hours in his room from the time he was a young boy listening to the radio, and continued following talk shows and speeches into adulthood. He liked thinking up his own questions and answers on the subject of the hour, but it was more than that. He said hearing the people having conversations with each other was comforting for him. He was socially lonely, even in his own home.

The only interpersonal, non-murderous jobs that were thrilling for Bundy were his positions as a campaign worker. He boastfully told others that he served as a Nelson Rockefeller Presidential Campaign delegate, Art Fletcher's driver and bodyguard during Fletcher's run for Lieutenant Governor, and Campaign Aid for Dan Evans, for whom Ted trailed opponent Rossellini, recording interviews surreptitiously and distributing the intel to Evans' campaign team.

Ted loved rubbing shoulders with and getting the back-slapping appreciation of political leaders. He fit in so well to the political setting because so much of it is a performance. He was always making a good impression whenever and wherever possible. Such leadership power was something he sorely coveted for himself and would never have. At least not in the political world of influence.

Bundy was even seen among the crowd at the Governor's Ball. He was not interacting with anyone in particular but chatted it up with many and was pleased at seeing *himself in the elite setting. He* seemed to consider the lovely young woman with dark hair parted in the middle that was standing nearby.

When not on the influential government platform, he was increasingly obsessed with rape and murder, stalking, voyeurism, and it filled his free time, filled his head space and colored all his other thoughts, education, and pseudo-social life. It became the goal of his education to enrich and expand his fantasy library and create opportunities to further build his homicidal skills and to further enact them. Meanwhile, he had all these influential public figures for solid references.

Ted had been so successful throughout life at stealing objects and getting away with it that he continued to be quite cavalier with his night time forays. He, even in hot weather, dressed in black pants and black turtlenecks at night to be better concealed. I don't know if he was always wearing a ski mask, but likely so since he had one in his predatory gear when arrested. He became a professional of night-time stalking, having himself a uniform and the necessary tools, and he took personal pride in it.

Whenever possible, he found day jobs to support and ensure the viability of this criminal fixation. To improve his genre expertise, he studied psychology, law, worked with the Crime Prevention Advisory Counsel as Assistant Director, and developed a compilation on rape prevention (yes, really), which gave him access to rape scene investigations. Bundy volunteered at a Crisis Line and was partnered with the crime writer Ann Rule. She innocently shared her detective articles with him. She should have been able to do so. Rule said her partnering with him was coincidental, that it just so happened. I think he picked her in order to glean whatever he could learn from her expertise and simply pretended that their meeting was accidental.

Ted was always conniving his next crime opportunity and strategizing the best ways of avoiding detection. Meanwhile, he had to juggle impressing the impressive as often as possible. After a murder, when returning to his civilized—although artificial—self, he said the horror, disbelief, and regret he experienced was not from what he had *done*, but because of the terror that he could get *caught*. And what would people that he so very much wanted to *impress* think of him if they found out his true identity? A public figure, upon realizing Ted's crimes, said in disbelief: "He was one of *us.*" *Bundy* had slithered himself in there among the elite and made himself right at home.

Narcissistic psychopaths want to impress people and win them over in order to more easily manipulate them. They are always working to improve their character resume in order to have credible personal references when accused of any wrongdoing (ie: Dan Evans, Ralph Monroe, Ann Rule, Art Fletcher, Nelson Rockefeller . . .).

An article in the newspaper featured Mr. Rising Star himself right in there next to Senator Henry Jackson.

Having felt successful alongside the successful, his grandiosity bloated and he was determined to get more powerful. This way, he could become more easily invisible to the ones that could do him the most damage and he could continue his crimes with impunity.

Ted was now as serious as a heart attack. Here is his own declaration of his intended embarkment on his intentional murderous career. When he applied to University of Utah Law School, his application letter is amazing now in retrospect, actually telling the truth about his *criminal intention* pertaining to his reason for studying law:

"*. . . I could go on at great length to explain that the practice of law is a life-long goal, or that I do not have great expectations that a law degree is a guarantee of wealth and prestige. The important factor, however, is that law fulfills a functional need which my daily routine has forced me to recognize.*

I apply to law school because this institution will give me the tools to become a more effective actor in the social role I have defined for myself."

T.R.B.

WOW. See how dark intentions do leak? Here it was in bold print and invisible to the uninitiated and certainly unsuspecting eye.

And then, having been accepted into this law school, off he drove in his Volkswagen Beetle to start classes and continue with his chosen career.

.

Chapter Sixteen

Whiffs of Psychopathy

. . . *Psychopathy for Dummies*

"When you can smell and taste their last breath . . . When you feel the last bit of breath leaving their body, you're looking into their eyes. A person in that situation is God!"

~Ted

Psychopathy in its adult form can be described as a personality disorder. Remember full-on personality disorders are on the same unfixable level as mental retardation, or intellectual Disabilities. So don't get your hopes up.

Robert Hare, PhD, is a rock star of psychopathy. To be clear, he's not a psychopath, but is an expert at sniffing out the miscreants on our behalf. He sums up what we should watch out for:

"Psychopaths are social predators who charm, manipulate and ruthlessly plow their way through life, leaving behind a broad trail of broken hearts, shattered expectations, and empty wallets. Completely lacking in conscience and in feelings for others they selfishly take what they want and do as they please, violating social norms and expectations without the slightest sense of guilt or regret." (Hare, 1993:xi)

Given those glaring traits, one would think we would see psychopaths a mile off. But they have been learning all of their lives how to act in various situations. They are uber good performers, playing at being humane in order to manipulate us, so we miss the signs. They use charm to put us at ease so we trust them, get us to 'want' to do what they are asking, then plow forward with their own well-being in mind.

I think about manipulation as getting someone to do something they would not otherwise do and making them think it was *their* idea. We need to teach future generations how to spot manipulation as religiously as we do the Golden Rule.

The good thing is, psychopathy is not contagious. Well it kind of is if we are being raised by human animals and live in an environment that requires our adherence to their malevolent ways. Identification with the aggressor for the sake of survival happens in this setting, so it is a learned behavior rather than inborn. If already predisposed to the condition genetically, we learn it really fast and it sticks.

As far as inheriting psychopathy, we sort of *do* have to watch out for that. Nature, or how we're built biologically, versus nurture, or how we're raised socially, affect our development pretty much equally. When a child's environment affects the function of his or her genes, which is known as epigenetics, a child's natural tendency toward certain behaviors is skewed. If psychopathic traits run in that child's family, we need to be mindful about the environment in which they grow up. Those babies are going to act up in the future unless someone deliberately teaches them empathy and accountability to combat their predisposition toward psychopathy.

Much also depends on the temperament and natural resilience of the child, as well as the degree of environmental influences he or she has experienced. The *persistence* of the influences impacts the child.

Pregnancy is when the first onslaught of environmental stressors impact the developing child. During the third trimester, when the baby is nearly ready to pop out, he or she is already taking in the environment. I like to think of the first several months *following* birth as the fourth trimester because the child is still in a pivotal stage of development. Bundy spent his third and fourth trimesters in an environment of human abandonment.

Psychopathy always starts in early childhood. Unless it's caused by a bump on the head, that is, or a tumor in the wrong spot on the brain. One serial criminal was suddenly committing crimes out of nowhere, *really out of nowhere*, and was appropriately convicted. When doctors discovered that he had a tumor in said wrong spot, they removed it. Certain that the tumor was the reason for the criminal behavior, he was released from prison and he returned to good citizenry. He remained difficulty-free for years until guess what started happening again because guess what started growing again.

In Louise's case, her environment growing up seemed cruelly inflexible, which would have been a crucible that required exquisite denial and compartmentalization as her survival mechanisms. She naturally passed these coping styles to Ted. Louise probably didn't sit him down at the kitchen table and say to him, *"No matter what difficulty happens, minimize or forget about it and always deny that it was negative in any way,"* or maybe she did. At any rate, that very message was passed to Ted, which he internalized in some primal way and followed true north until the end of his life.

On the same thread, the core innate features of psychopathy are emotional detachment and callous disregard. Detachment and disregard begin early and persist in various ways based on any rejection the individual perceives. Louise exemplified these features herself in a softer, safer way.

Callous disregard does not sit well in the neighborhood or school, so in order to socially survive, the organism must learn to pretend. They learn how to use charm, bluff confidence or humility, feign empathy, talk a good talk, and adapt to the setting in order to get what they want. We see that with Louise in many ways. Although an impressive student, being the head of clubs and projects is not the same as having a group of friends. It is often lonely at the top. As Bundy implied, her pinnacle was administrative rather than relational.

Ted withdrew into himself by comparison and was exquisitely insecure. He said he felt like the kid with acne that no one wanted around and that mom would brush him off. Like his mom, the structured school setting was his place to shine. Yet he was socially lonely. When alone, which is much of the youngster's time when they don't fit in with socially comfortable others, they create that inner life of fantasized (delicious to the perpetrator) *successes* to review and practice within their mind and enjoy.

Both their outer and inner lives are artificial. These entities learn from their experiences and can readily apply them in whatever setting they find themselves. It doesn't mean they enjoy or seek out others. An example of group setting behavior that would have been interesting for me to observe either Ted or Louise in is this: According to some, if you yawn when with a non-empathetic individual, they don't *have* to yawn back as it is not contagious for them.

Lots of yawn studies comment on the phenomenon of *yawn contagion.* The jury is still out, but so far it looks like the contagion happens mostly among higher order species like us (assuming we are higher order), as well as apes and even some non-primate mammals. Yawn contagion relates to stimulating alertness when vulnerable, like at bedtime and when first waking, or when bored. Researchers believe the yawning is mainly for the purpose of being alert to potential threats. In experiments in regard to yawning causing increased alertness, there was an improved ability of the yawn-er post yawn to find the dangerous creatures in pictures. The hypothesis was that in a group setting, we need to keep each other alert for danger, and yawning together helps.

Empathy comes in when we are more likely to participate in the behavior for the sake of the group, especially in groups we are akin to in some way. As you may have already surmised, the psychopath doesn't care about the group. I'm not sure how valid the empathy yawning correlation is myself, but the studies continue. One thing for sure, I am certain that during these last few paragraphs you have been doing your share of yawning. At least I hope you have.

Greg Hartley, a retired army interrogator and Resistance to Interrogation instructor admonishes behaviorists, saying, "The organism will do what has made the organism successful." Always. So as psychopaths practice their craft, they learn what works and stick to it. Trial and error, apply what was learned, and repeat. Like all narcissists, psychopaths even become rather predictable–which is part of what criminal profiling is about.

Because the essence of Ted's individual self evaporated early on, learning necessary roles and patterns based on prior successes, mastering the skills, and appearing socially smooth were his approaches to life. One of his core mottos was, "Before any more women reject me, I'll reject them, and they won't see it coming." And no one saw it because he became so successful at it.

When it comes to encountering a Bundy, a Kemper, or a Ridgeway, seeing the real organism shining right through their cover would be ideal, but most of the time all we see is what is presented to us. We should not have to sort whether the presentation is authentic or artificial, and so we don't scrutinize what we see but usually take it at face value. When in doubt, we give the benefit of the doubt, and that is what the predator banks on.

Still, the psychopath's callous and remorseless impulsivity leaks through if we experience enough of life with them and are paying attention. Louise was compelled by her need to display only the best of herself and her family. Liz was distracted by love and hoped things would get better. Psychopaths like Ted do not spend too much of themselves in any one place with any one person for that reason.

No one gets *that* close for *that* long. The folks in their lives can sense a barrier but typically attribute it to something else such as introversion, insecurity, arrogance, confidence, high intelligence, or a mixture of any of those traits.

Liz said Ted would take lots of naps during the day. Being a creature of the night, he would need daytime sleep. At Florida State University, other students at the same boarding house where Ted rented a space said his room was absolutely silent during the day, and they could only see light from the fuzz of the tv screen seen through the crack under his door at night. The only times they saw him was when he was either coming or going.

Psychopaths keep their lives as compartmentalized as possible, so our time with them is usually limited to only what they will allow. But enough time spent with such an individual will portray shortcomings of character if we listen to our gut and watch. Liz saw increasing signs such as finding a bag of women's clothes in his house. When she asked about it, he told her the clothes belonged to his cleaning lady. She was also puzzled by a bowl of random keys at his place. Think souvenirs or keys to buildings and apartments he had stolen. In his car, Liz found a chopping cleaver, but Ted did fancy himself a chef (ooo and remember, top careers for psychopaths are chefs, attorneys, and public officials). She also found a hatchet he said he needed for "cutting wood," a knife, and other items that she thought of as unnecessary tools to keep in an automobile. Regardless of Ted's gaslighting, the discovery caused Liz's antenna to shoot up given the terrifying murders happening in the Pacific Northwest during that time.

Bravely, Liz called the police to express concerns about the things she *had* noticed and the worries about her boyfriend *in spite of second guessing herself.* Even when in doubt, report, and let the experts determine validity.

Unfortunately in this case, the experts thought it wasn't likely that a law student with what they thought was a clean record was responsible for such crimes, so they did not pursue the lead Liz gave them right away. Investigators know that individuals don't just drop out of the sky and start a pattern of murdering. There is always a string of crimes leading up to what's happening currently. Since they found no priors, they dismissed him as a suspect. But thanks to Liz's call, Ted did remain on their list.

"Which one do they pick? Do they pick the law student with no criminal background, who was probably even known by some of the prosecutors working the case? Or are they going to go after the types, you know, the guys in the files . . . the real weirdos?"

~ Ted

You *were* a real weirdo, Ted.

What was not picked up on by law enforcement was Ted's expunged juvenile record of ski ticket forgery, attempted auto theft, and burglary charges. I called the Archives department in Seattle to ask if there was any way for law enforcement to sniff out a juvenile record, but there isn't. When expunged, those records are gone forever. Zip, zero, nada.

Nonetheless, Ted's parents *had* to know about those charges and suspicions, but if the crimes were suspected and not proven, it would have been consistent with their pattern to have dismissed the charges as nonsense. Had they *only* spoken up.

When our children do something stupid, we want to give positive concessions, but Ted's youth *was* sketchy and these crimes were not stupid. Likely the most difficult thing for a parent would be admitting concerns of that nature for fear the child would be wrongfully accused, put away, and never have a chance to be the socially beneficial individual they desired for them to become.

Fortunately "pretty mixed up gal" Liz followed up on her concerns even though she was not certain, and she continued to second guess herself right up to the last segment of Ted's life. Even when she knew beyond doubt, Liz still could not believe it, but she was forced to believe it because the truth was plain as day.

It is not that easy to smoke out a psychopath that has honed their skills so well. It is especially difficult when the individual is considered nice looking, bright, and presents himself *as though* he were socially respectable and accomplished. These elements, when authentic, are coveted and admired in our culture. Ted's act was so good, which is why no one believed Bundy could possibly be a murderer.

If Ted had been homely, he would not have gotten away with so much for so long. First of all, girls would not have trusted him as easily or wanted to help him. Secondly, if he had been of lower intelligence, he may have blundered early on, not being able to as effectively execute his crimes, clean up evidence, or articulate suspicions away. Nor would he have been able to pass himself off as a college graduate and pose as a law student because he would not have gotten that far.

Ed Kemper was more intelligent than Bundy and also targeted bright college women. He was not easy to suspect, either. He hung out with law enforcement at their local pub where they met to talk about their work day. They knew him as "Big Ed." He was not necessarily considered by them as one of the guys; instead, he was more of a harmless pest. But he was still considered harmless.

Ed knew not to ask too many questions since law enforcement officers know that perpetrators like to insert themselves into the crime scene and investigation in order to learn the details. He rarely asked questions but always listened. Since he was familiar to the guys and never raised suspicion, he surprised them when he turned himself in after killing the real object of his rage, his mother.

Ed's monster image was a little easier to believe once he stood up because of his size. He is an imposing 6ft 9in and weighs over 300lbs. He intimidatingly measures head and shoulders above those around him. Yet lovely coeds hopped in his car because he was sitting when driving. Had he been towering outside the car, I think they would have hesitated longer before asking if they could hitch a ride.

Another dynamic that keeps these individuals invisible for so long is that the folks who interact with them usually do not know or talk to *each other*, so they do not pick up on the antisocial leaks that add up. No comparison of notes takes place, so to speak—something else the perpetrator arranges and keeps in place as fastidiously as possible.

In a small town, the gossip chain keeps pretty much any curious listener advised. A community knows if little Billy Marshall's home life is not the best, even if it appears to be perfect. They see he is alone a lot, does not have many friends (if any), and is a bit of a bully. They noticed when young Billy Marshall was mean to the pets in the neighborhood, and they are aware when teenage Billy Marshall gets caught sneaking off with Brian Kelly's iPad but talks his way out of repercussions.

Talking with the parents of detached kids does not get all that far because often the parents are also detached from the child, for their own reasons, or they have their own narcissistic traits guarding the gate.

In a large city or in suburban living, people lose touch and are politely occupied with their own business. In crowded areas, we don't remember the strangers around us or notice who should or should not be there. Another factor in place during Bundy's rampaging time was that police jurisdictions did not communicate with each other, much less participate in inter-state information exchange. Of course Ted knew that from the intel he gathered when working for the crime commission. Abduct in one county, dispose of the object in another. Abduct in one state, leave to animal interference in another.

Susan Rancort's disappearance, along with most of the others, was not addressed right away because her disappearance involved separate police jurisdictions. Possible evidence was lost because of that.

It was thanks to Liz Kendall that the first inter-state information exchanges regarding serial crimes occurred. Utah did not know about Ted's crimes in the PNW. A friend of Liz's who lived in Utah told Liz that the crimes started happening down there at the exact time they *stopped* happening in the PNW. Liz knew Ted was going to University of Utah Law School. She called the Utah police to tell them of her concerns about Bundy and they blew her off. She called her dad who lived in Utah and asked if he would call them, thinking Salt Lake City would be more likely to believe a man. He told her no, that she needed to realize she could ruin Ted's career.

Sheesh.

Thanks, Dad.

She could have ruined his fake career for sure and saved many lives.

Next, she called Seattle police and informed them of what she had learned about the Utah crimes. As Ted moved on to hunting in Colorado, law enforcement there did not know about the Utah crimes nor the PNW string of missing girls. Until they did. Out of desperation, the territoriality between police jurisdictions dissolved, which led to increasing evidence implicating Ted in crimes in Washington, Utah, Colorado, and ultimately in other states. From then on, they were all on each other's speed dial so to speak, and intercommunication became informal practice between those agencies.

It was not until a decade later that ViCAP (Violent Crime Apprehension Program) was established formally by the FBI. ViCAP facilitates communication and coordination between law enforcement agencies throughout the country. ViCAP intersects with InterPol currently, which is a network consisting of 194 countries fighting crime internationally.

With the worldwide saturation of the internet, tracking criminals has become more and more effective through these networks. Different jurisdictions and precincts now refer to one another as partners in these situations.

Although once disconnected agencies and states now communicate with each other on a broad scale, the rest of us have not been adept at exchanging alarming information among ourselves. If we are not occupied by spending time with family, friends, or neighbors, many of us love to play games on the internet or check social media so we do not get bored. We are becoming more increasingly connected online instead of in person.

People do not talk over the back fence anymore, but are e-connected with acquaintances not only near but far. And that is not going to go away. With less direct community interaction, we are less likely to share the repeated worrisome behaviors of an individual with others.

As we consider the neighborhood approach, this is an example of what happens when we do have concerns in our modern age. If I am troubled over the actions of little Joey Morris (sorry to the real Joey Morris's out there), who do I talk to about it? His teacher? His parents? His neighbors? Not that easy, is it? We hesitate communicating because we want to respect the youngster's right to privacy, we are unsure of his family's reaction, or we worry about the consequences if we're wrong. We may even think to ourselves, "Who am I to accuse or insinuate?"

Personally, I have approached law enforcement or school counselors in order to go on record about concerns regarding individuals that have in some way come across my awareness. That way if they are tagged for something, there is an alert on record as to a frightening behavior that has been reported.

If no other concerning mischief occurs, no loss, because my concern is not utilized unless more infractions do occur. That may seem like a grain of salt in the ocean, but on occasion it makes all the difference in getting the needed help. That to me is worth it. My preference would be that redacted records become visible if someone is a violent crime suspect. There must be a good reason why that is not an option that I don't know about.

It's the lack of interconnectedness of all the folks who know the psychopath that ensures the anonymity of the predator. Although school shooters are not always budding psychopaths, they are clear examples of this phenomenon. When looking back on the warning signs of the pending slaughter, many of their peers claimed overhearing them say something about the attack, others saw them post threats on social media, and occasionally someone else was aware of questionable packages being delivered to their houses. Yet no one said a thing because they didn't want to believe it could actually happen.

An example of how we don't see what we don't want to see is a disturbing account of a boy killing his teacher in a classroom in front of his disbelieving school mates. He had been telling his peers how much he hated this teacher and wanted to kill her for some time. His classmates did the internal eye roll, not expecting that he meant it or would ever *really* stab their teacher. Until he did. He had shown students his knife before class that day, and they still said nothing. Once class had begun, he pulled out his knife in front of his classmates, walked up behind their teacher, and stabbed her. They probably still could not believe it.

Disturbed children *do* leak their darkness before they reach this point, and we need to believe it when they do. Unfortunately, by the time parents are concerned enough to take action, they are sometimes a bit afraid of their kid and not as likely to confront them. They sometimes also deny the possibility of dark activities and hope for the best.

Given the information to which she was privy, I wonder if Louise was ever afraid of Ted. She never would have admitted to his dark side, but she obviously sensed it and had been alerted to it by teachers, neighborhood parents, and law enforcement all before he was 18. If I were her, I would have been secretly relieved when he went off to college and didn't come around much.

His mother diverted concern rather than being honest about her son. It is my opinion that even in spite of her moral efforts, she regretted the existence of and did not ever feel comfortable with Ted. He had been an excruciating inconvenience since she discovered the pregnancy, but she would never admit it in a million years. Rather, she tended to his practical needs meticulously. She regretted him and regretted herself for getting into this never-ending mess. That is why I think she never talked to her first born about his origins—her own shame of being the mother of this child that ultimately became her, and our, albatross.

Chapter Seventeen

What can we do about it?

Essential Narcissism Recognition and Management
Good Luck to us all.

Ted's narcissism was apparent early, even though his criminal activities were hidden. How narcissism comes about is generally one of two ways. Either the child is neglected, so is affected emotionally, or is overindulged behaviorally, which also neglects them emotionally. The child that is emotionally starved adopts a "me first" approach to self-esteem because they are hungry for affectional attention. Ted's first three months of life in the Home for unwed mothers were, although well intended, by their nature emotionally neglectful.

The sparse to non-existent emotional care at the Home was followed by free behavioral reign and praise in the Philadelphia home, which also neglected him emotionally. Like a puffer fish, a person who is that emotionally deprived expands and blows out arrogant spines as an offensive tactic, which is actually a defense when we think about it. If I believe I am perfect and deserve the best, I am protecting myself because you don't even get the opportunity to question it. This mindset is to protect narcissists from others who might detect their empty vulnerability. We have narcs—what some dub non-criminal narcissists—and narcopaths all around us. You have probably already thought of a bunch you know. It's the ones that evolve beyond being simply annoying to predatory that we want to be able to see and avoid because we cannot fix them.

So, being oriented to narcissistic behavior patterns is like sonar because the glaring giveaway that we might have a psycho/sociopath on our hands is their unchanging self absorption. Once we see the narcissism in them, we cannot unsee it. Again, if we spend enough time with them, their malignant self-interest will glow like a worm.

Since not all narcissists are psychopaths, but many if not *all* psychopaths are narcissists, sniffing out callous entitlement is the clearest way to protect ourselves from a potential psychopath. We want to limit interactions with narcissists as much as possible anyway, even when they are not full-on psychopaths or sociopaths, because they simply make those around them miserable. Even non-criminal narcs cause misery, either by being outright nasty like a bull in a china shop or going under the radar by being sweet and kind while peeing on your leg.

Since narcissists are everywhere, we can get a lot of practice identifying them. Learning to recognize this malevolent personality developing in our *children* is important. We see it early in the kid that is the bully, the spoiled brat, the needy victim, or the one that *must* be first at everything. The all-about-me ones tend to be readily evident. As insufferable as they may be, they actually appear to have friends, or perhaps "associates" is a more realistic term for their cohorts. They somehow manage to have their minions, but having support staff is different from having friends.

Some young narcissists choose to surround themselves with like-minded family members. It's an "us against the world," street gang type of loyalty. The associates, deputies, or family members of the alpha narcissist are sometimes referred to as *flying monkeys*, like those from The Wizard of Oz. They were on the witch's side come hell or high water. If young narcissists are following the footsteps of a family member, they stick by the leader's side. Likewise, when the young narcissists are in the seat of power, they expect their associates to have their backs. You may be thinking of this as identification with the aggressor, and you are right.

To clarify, narcissism itself is not a clinical diagnosis. We may refer to folks as narcissists, but the exact diagnostic term is Narcissistic Personality Disorder (NPD). A person must meet specific criteria in order to be given the clinical diagnosis of NPD. We refer to people as narcissists when they follow enough patterns of NPD that it's apparent to us that there is a problem. You will likely never get them to the psychiatrist for a real evaluation because they do not think they have a problem. How dare you suggest they do!

What we need to look out for is when they begin to follow a pattern of exploiting the lives of others in their own self-interest *or for their own enjoyment*, which is the next step toward the psychopath exit. Most of the time, narcissistic personalities are simply vexing, but we need to be aware when their actions have escalated to predatory proportions. Let's roll up our sleeves and talk about narcissistic behavior so we can recognize it in ourselves as well as others.

First, let's all take a Narcissistic Personality Disorder test. Think about Ted and even Louise as we ponder these questions.

- Do they boast or exaggerate their accomplishments?

- If not boasting about it, do they still consider themselves more talented or intelligent than others?

- Do they dismiss or one-up the achievements of others?

- Do they believe they are above rules or ordinary limits?

- Do they fail to recognize that they could hurt others?

- Do they lash out in anger when criticized or when a flaw in their plans has been pointed out?

- Do they have a need for excessive appreciation, praise or attention?

- Do they have a strong sense of entitlement, or a need to be granted special privileges?

- Is their sense of empathy lacking?

- Do they display jealousy, envy, distrust? Arrogance? Scorn?

- Do they have a pattern of manipulating others?

- Do they refuse to take responsibility for their bad behavior?

- Are they accountable?

- Do they feel better about themselves when hurting others or seeing others hurt?

If you see yourself in some of these examples, don't panic; we all have enough narcissism in our survival mode to keep ourselves from laying down in the middle of the road and being the speed bump. Self-interest has kept living organisms going for eons. Now, we also can't run around diagnosing everyone we don't like with narcissism. The more traits we have and the more we use them to promote ourselves over others, the more of a problem we are to society.

Ted had all of these traits early on, and we see them develop all along the way. Again, once we learn about narcissistic behavior, we cannot unsee it. Recognizing callous entitlement and learning to dodge manipulation should be taught in elementary school. Recognizing the fledgling criminal starts with understanding narcissistic behavior so we can at least avoid the ones that utilize the non-criminal methods. Taken to its ultimate extreme, Ted is what we get.

Those of us in the eye of the hurricane often don't see it, and do not want to see it, so ultimately prevention and early identification often comes down to the peripheral family members, neighbors, or teachers that are close enough to pick up on worsening aberrations that going unnoticed at home. For example:

- 12 year old Julia told her family about the knife incidents, but nothing was addressed or even discussed again. There was nothing much she could do as a youth herself, and then Louise scooped up little Teddy and moved away.

- Ted's parents overlooked the concerns described on his report cards. He disregarded other school authorities too. There was not much the teachers could do beyond enforcing their own classroom and school rules.

- Neighbors were aware of the injuries caused by Ted. Other youngsters that knew about his bullying and torturing of animals likely told their parents. that may or may not have told the Bundy's their concerns. I do not know if or how any of the neighbors confronted the Bundy family. How do you tell a parent that their boy is torturing animals and bullying other children? There are firm-minded people in every neighborhood, so I am sure some parents would have visited the Bundy's with a solid rap on the door. Since Ted's actions were still not addressed, remedied, and channeled, all that the neighborhood parents could do was help their own children understand that Ted's behaviors were wrong and encourage them to avoid him.

- The friends that went skiing with him on the weekends knew about his forgery skills. Ted would forge their ski tickets in spite of the rules. They didn't tell anyone about Ted's actions because they did not want to ruin their great ski weekends.

- People throughout his life knew he stole things he felt entitled to. Louise once said she thought the items showing up in his room were "gifts." In later years, Liz had a lightbulb flash when she saw a stolen stereo at Ted's apartment. When she remarked about it, he said that if she told anyone, he'd break her neck. She is the one who finally alerted law enforcement regarding her concerns about him.

As Ted got older, he knew peers were avoiding him and why. His entitlement and non-accountability moved from "harmless naughtiness" into crimes against animals and children. Remember, he believed he was a product of incest, so his sense of a contaminated self to conceal led to more social isolation. Feeling and being treated like a pariah reinforced having his own imaginary universe of his liking, where he was the "sun" dominating his cosmos powerfully, vengefully, even if it was secret—and given the content of his world, even better *for him* if it was secret.

His thieving progressed unabated from taking knives from the kitchen, to stealing mice from the pet store, to torturing neighborhood animals, to dragging neighborhood kids off into the woods to strip and terrify them (*where were their parents?*). He went on to steal stereo equipment, televisions, clothing, and ski equipment (very nice sporting equipment), then a child who lived along his paper route. Yes, I think he did take Ann Marie Burr. And once grown and strong, Ted regressed to stealing beautiful women, each of whose life essence he felt *entitled* to possessing and brutally destroying.

Ted later described that he would sometimes take home the heads of some of the bodies, shampoo their hair and apply some makeup. When he would go back to the deposit site and visit the bodies, he said, "I would look at their neck, breasts and arms; they were like marble." He took these goddesses that others wanted so he could toy with and groom them to his liking. No one could take these possessions from his god-like self. He had complete dominion over his universe.

Louise was quite narcissistic, as exemplified by her excelling at every endeavor and refusing to see any flaws evident in herself or her family members, especially Ted. This denial and compartmentalization was a coping mechanism she learned while living at the Philadelphia house in order to protect herself from revealing vulnerabilities and shortcomings. Ted absorbed Louise's influence by osmosis. Louise did not hurt others directly with her narcissism, but did hurt us all directly by the result of sharing these tendencies with her son.

Once Louise became free of her father's home, she could chart her own course. She was, however, already rather sealed over herself. She became her own sun, requiring control of her setting. That part of her was passed on by keeping herself arms length from Ted while expecting nothing less from him than the Boy Scout image.

Alas, Teddy was left to wander in emotional space repeatedly, as are others in this psychosocial condition, learning to rely on their own childlike (ie: self centered and "me first") devices.

The sense of personal essence likely was pretty much down to a flicker by Ted's early boyhood, and nobody saw it. Those that knew him were blinded to his arrogance by biases, wanting to give the benefit of the doubt, and blinded by, with the help of his mother, an impressive and deliberately crafted mirage that was always optimistically presented.

Another tool we can learn to identify narcissists is body language behavior analysis. I recommend watching The Behavior Panel on YouTube. These guys are the best of the best and inform us how to sense when we are being snowed by understanding because the *body* does not lie. They even analyzed Bundy once. Go check it out.

Here is my body language analysis of Louise:

Everything she did, everything she said, conveyed one thing about Ted.

He was the best son in the world.

The Tacoma News Tribune in October of 1975 featured Louise being asked about her reaction to Ted's arrest in Utah. Her reply was that she shakes her head day after day and says it just can't be. To explain her confusion about his arrest since *he was a normal, active boy,* she described her son as having played little league (*shoulder shrug*), football (*shoulder shrug*), and being a good student. When saying he was the best son in the world, she finished with an *apologetic laugh.*

For behavior analysts this cluster of unconscious tells suggests she was not convinced the reporter would believe her because either she wasn't sure herself or knew she was being misleading.

She very well could have been giving the reporters misinformation. Ted said he never played baseball because the uniforms were expensive and never played football because he didn't have the physique or his parents' seal of approval for playing sports.

Louise, in the interviews I have seen, has a habit of tongue jutting and lip compression. Tongue jutting and lip compression suggest "I don't like this" and "I am going to be firm about what I prefer." Having to reject unpleasantness, even unconsciously, was something she had to learn early at the Philadelphia house. Ted unsurprisingly did a lot of tongue jutting too, and likely for the same reason. It's a bit like sticking your tongue out at an idea you don't like, without fully doing so. She does a lot of eye blocking as well (closing eyes for longer than blinks in order to not have to "look" at something). It's only fair to say that, had I been in her position, I would have had my ostrich head *completely* buried in the sand while talking out the back end. Regardless of any grilling, however, she always managed to give a smooth delivery.

We all have our ways of expressing ourselves and unconscious signals that our body gives because the limbic system is not capable of lying. It is a truth serum that reveals deception via body language. When we have a gut reaction to someone, it is very possible that our mind picks up on their behavior or body language, even when we don't have the words to describe our feelings. Learning behavior and body language awareness will give you words for it.

During their last phone call before his execution, Ted told Louise he was sorry for all the trouble he caused her. He explained, "that part was there all along, but I was still Ted Bundy." We often see *that part* only through the psychopath's narcissism and lack of accountability that they are *unable* to hide. With psychopaths, we don't simply get the safe side or the danger-ous side; we get both. They are in no hurry to show us their dark side, but it does poke through even if we don't recognize those minutia at first. It may manifest into obvious signs such as delinquency, negative school reports, neighborhood complaints, and arrests that we cannot ignore. Managing the dark side with our children is *our* responsibility.

In her book *Resilient Adults: Overcoming a Cruel Past*, Gina O'Connell Higgins (1994) reminds us of certain ideas we already know and need to follow. She studied scores of individuals who had endured horrendous childhoods but grew up to be well-adjusted, self-supporting, socially interactive adults with strong relational bonds. In other words, abused children who turned out exceptionally well..

She asked them what, given their awful childhood circumstances, made the inspirational difference for them.

For each one, there was a person or activity that buoyed them all along the way. Whether it was a grandparent, neighbor, coach, or teacher, they had a person who took an interest in them, believed in them, and encouraged their natural interests, talents, and character. Be it in sports, art, music, academics, mechanics, building, horticulture, etc., their persons provided the youngster with supportive belonging and opportunities to excel.

Each child needs to be in someone's caring focus who will guide them in their goals, values, and achievements. When we have a safe, interested mentor, our ability to thrive is enhanced. The social setting is crucial for this flourishment as well. As we know, peer pressure is molding to a fault and so minors are easily swayed to conform to their peer group. Studies show that we become like the five people we spend the most of our time with. Caring about who our childrens' acquaintances are is key.

It is the child's job to grow up to not need his parents. It is the parent's job to ensure the child will reach adulthood not needing to depend upon them. There are fits and starts all along the way, but that is the biological route that ensures the health and survival of every species. Who is providing the *interpersonal influence* during the developmental stage is key to the child reaching independence.

Every child needs to be fostered toward healthy adulthood, so we need to be aware of our biases when we are alerted to the lonely child that is bullied or is a bully, doesn't fit in socially, steals things, or abuses property, animals, or people. We can be cognizant and seek help for the youngsters who are showing regressive signs. At the very least, we can keep our eyes peeled and discuss concerns with other adults or authorities.

The last thing we should do is turn a blind eye. These children born to neglect, cruelty, or abuse DID NOT ASK to be born. Whether we like it or not, we will pay for their outcome; either by providing supportive accountability and empathy guidance now, which are moderate financial and temporal expenses to us; or we can wait after the horse is out of the barn and pay $33,000-90,000 *per year per inmate* through taxes.

During Ted's incarceration on Florida state prison's death row, there were an additional 297 inmates, all supported through the low yearly estimate mentioned above of $33,000. That conservative calculation amounts to a grand total of $9.8 million dollars for Florida taxpayers *per year*. That's not counting the female population on their own death row. I don't know how much it costs to house female prisoners, but I certainly hope they get good shampoo.

When they were little boys and girls, these inmates, for the most part, did not stand a chance. Aileen Wuornos comes to mind. That little blonde haired girl was born without hope as well. She was an involuntary sex toy for every male, boys and men, who knew about her from the time she was little. No wonder she hated men. When Ted was little, his family was not attachment material. Kempers' mother was down right repellent, and his dad abandoned him. Ridgeway's mother was sexually abusive for starters. As for Charlie, his guidance came from various sidewalks, then juvie, and then prison.

The earlier, more consistent, and permanent the child's mentor opportunities, the less likely the child will face this outcome. Ted commented a few times that he appreciated when someone took an interest in him. We think of the detaching child's vulnerable narcissism that craves attention. Narcissism is exquisitely self protective, remember, even if it means you have to submerge someone else to keep *your* head above water. If no guidance is in place, the youngster does not stand a chance.

A child benefits from being in situations where it is safe to be vulnerable in order to develop psychological strength. They do best in settings that give them the freedom to be safely themselves warts and all, insufferable aspects and all. And they must be guided through vulnerability accordingly.

In our frenetic world, we are stretched so thin we have holes in the middle in order to keep our lives afloat. The more hectic our lives, the less attached we become, and attachments that are already there can be strained and loosened. Unless we pay attention, these children will fall through the cracks. Valuing each other above what we want is a challenge. A big challenge.

The missing sentiment and accountability are not up to the child to provide nor facilitate, nor is it the responsibility of their school. It starts and pretty much ends with parental and social support. Good enough parenting requires community interaction and support in addition to the parents concerned. We have to make time in our busy schedule for interpersonal influence. Ted did not have these opportunities to grow or a family and community on his sideline. We can see the impact it had.

Chapter Eighteen

My Amydala Made me do It

. . . This is a scary fun Chapter

Psychopaths have been shown to have under-active amygdalae. Inside our brain, we have two amygdalae located between our ears. One is located a ways in from the left ear, and the other is a ways in from the right ear. They operate within the right and left hemispheres of our brain and are part of the limbic system. Each acts as the smoke alarms for emotional reaction and the fight, flight, or freeze trigger. For example, folks with high anxiety on average have *larger* amygdalae, similar to when our heart has to work extra hard to get its work done and becomes enlarged.

Alternatively, psychopaths tend to weigh in with a *smaller*-than-average or sometimes *damaged* amygdala. More brain differences occur as well, but the red button regions are the amygdalae, which influence the entire conscious as well as unconscious portions of our brain. If the amygdalae are underperforming, so do the rest of the emotional contributors in gray and white matter.

I don't know if researchers kept Ted's brain. If not, I wish they had because I want to know how he measured up performance-wise in the amygdalae department.

No, the amygdalae cannot be fixed, but it can be considered as an important focal point in early childhood social development. Whereas extreme stress causes anxiety and an increase in amygdala volume, on the other side of this simplified coin, emotional neglect dumbs it down so that an individual's emotional responses are withered by comparison to other human beings.

Thus it takes more extreme experiences for the psychopath to get any jolts of thrill or even enjoyment so to speak. Remember branching and pruning. Ted's first three months did damage his emotional and empathetic abilities, as did the rest of his first five years. This is so, so simplified, but so, so important. Those first years determine the child's ability to relate to other living beings.

There is a new option for treating underactive amygdalae coming about that we might not mind actually spending our money on instead of schools and death row (like the 9 million dollar tax-payer bill for Ted's total legal actions, which in today's pocketbook would be $24,901,477.70).

This new exciting, promising, and slightly scary option for treating psychopathy is Deep Brain Stimulation (DBS). DBS has been around for a while now to treat all kinds of symptoms from Obsessive Compulsive Disorder (OCD) to very serious Major Depressive Disorder (MDD). The most reliably successful miracle to date is DBS modulation for Parkinson's Disease symptoms.

DBS is amazing. Electrodes are installed into the brain and attached to a battery pack. The pack is placed under the skin just below the collar bone, where it regulates the stimulation of specific brain areas to resolve symptoms. There is also a remote for manual self adjustments. Imagine if you will, as technology gets more sci-fi, we could possibly have a personal app on our phone that can be used to self adjust DBS conductions to wherever in our brains for whatever problems.

My mind is cloudy today. I need more focus, so I toggle the focus pathway and voila, I can sit down and figure out those taxes or clean out the garage.

Thankfully we are not there just yet, and as you can imagine, endless ethical gymnastics will follow these new innovations. But for treatment of psychopathic killers, further development of DBS treatment is worth looking into.

Brainstorming on neurological modulation for troublesome behavior originated in the early 1800's when a railroad foreman, Phineas Gage, had a yard-long iron bar driven through his skull during an explosion. After shooting through his head, the bar kept sailing through the air and finally landed in the dirt some 30 yards away. That exploding dirt made neurological history.

The launched rod destroyed much of his left frontal lobe, which is the part of your brain above your left eyebrow. This event has been long known as the American Crowbar Case. As it turns out, this was a very useful application of an iron bar to the skull because 25 year old Gage survived and became a modern medical marvel. To everyone's surprise, after he recovered from his injury, his personality was remarkably different. The man was rather obsessive compulsive before the impaling and hot damn, were things ever improved afterward!

Gage went on to become a stagecoach driver. A *much less* obsessive compulsive stagecoach driver. Up until that time, science wasn't sufficiently certain that the brain was all that integral in personality and behavior, but this got everyone's attention.

Various scientists in both Europe and the United States went right to work to uncover the reason behind Gage's altered personality. They have created various methods over the decades since Mr. Gage's fateful accident. Their first experiments involved removing the brain tissue that was believed to bring about certain behaviors in order to eliminate said behaviors, but they had mixed results. From these experiments stemmed the years of lobotomy treatments for psychiatric patients, patients such as Jack Nicholson's unforgettable sociopathic character mentioned earlier. Nurse Ratched, being the psychopath in that movie who was allowed to assist these treatments, is worth observing again. Her behaviors would *never* occur in a psychiatric unit these days, but she got away with it in that hospital and tortured everyone with a demeanor as smooth as glass. I think her little lip snarl was a tell, though.

When I worked in the Behavioral Medicine unit at our local hospital, a male patient that wanted some valium called me Nurse Ratched and slammed his hand on the table when I told him the doctor had refused. He might have been a candidate for e-behavior management if it had been available then. With the other patients tense from the table slap ringing in their ears, I would have headed right to the nurses e-station and toggled his currents. That is, I think I would have. I have mixed thoughts about this.

Currently however, it seems e-behavior is moving toward taking its place in the realm of anti-social management possibilities. Considering using neurological modulation via instrumentation to control personality rather than using it solely for physical symptoms and illnesses brings about frightening possibilities. The sobering possibility of Dr. John Q Jekyll creating an apparatus in his garage is just as scary as knowing our military can use this option for creating super soldiers. If combat soldiers were given amphetamines in the past (yes, they were), why not stimulate them with electrical current?

Also conspiratorially posited is the possibility of leadership deciding what is normal or abnormal behavior and wanting to adjust us accordingly. Do we make them religious? Do we lean their political thinking? Do we make them passive? Do we adjust it based on world events? The Moriarty's of earth would certainly brainstorm along those lines. As my grandparents used to say, *What is the world coming to?*

Now that I have us all completely freaked out, let's look at some more positive possibilities of DBS.

This new science *is* offering hope of getting these out of control individuals well under control. Had there been a behavioral probe and remote available to imbed in Ted's brain, it would have had to have been under someone *else's* management. Ted would not get to be his own doctor for this. Much like ankle monitors as an alternative for jail, this could be a tracking and *mediating* device. Ted did say he thought he could condition himself out of his behavior but was unable to do so. He might have been a willing guinea pig for this. Wow. But I believe the worm installed in his mind during early childhood would have found a way to fiddle with the mechanisms.

Still, both Ted and Charlie would have needed to be under layers of lock and key while electro adjustments were being calibrated.

To stay in this idea room for a bit longer, the talk in the tech world is that we will eventually use a *brain chip* rather than the current device for DBS treatment. Mr. Elon Musk (that guy doesn't quit!), along with a few of his co-developers, is making headway at his neurotechnology corporation, Neuralink. His team is currently engineering a brain-microchip interface designed to restore movement for the paralyzed and sight for the blind. My guess is they are just getting started. But if little Johnny gets his sight, it will probably be because of that science. Elon had better damn well see to it that insurance companies pay for it. Or maybe he will magnanimously pay for it. I guess we'll wait and see.

Once this technology is fully developed, scientists will likely alter the brain chip to treat other disabilities, including mental and social ones. At what point, however, and at what symptom concern level would one decide to use a behavior chip on a child like Ted? When Teddy was placing knives in his aunt's bed? When teachers noticed Teddy acting out in the classroom?

When other children saw him mistreating animals and building traps for little girls? When he was arrested for suspected burglary and car theft?

I don't think Charlie Manson could have been managed even by a behavior brain chip. When his little three year old feet began scavenging about the world around him, it would have helped perhaps. Still, he would have needed people that cared about him enough to stick by him and provide education, healthcare, skill opportunities, and encouragement.

When it comes to amygdalae monitoring, will we get to the point where we are scanning the limbic system to see if all is well? Will amygdalae scans be as common as using the developmental growth chart at the child's doctor appointments? I don't know the answer to that. The next generations will determine that course.

Electroconvulsive therapy (ECT), although effective for severe depression and other severe mental health conditions, is not effective for treating personality disorders such as antisocial personality disorder, psychopathy, sociopathy, or narcissistic personality disorder (NPD). Someone with a personality disorder and severe depression may recover from their depression following the treatment with ECT, but the personality disorder is not even touched. Rats.

Personality disordered folks cause the most social damage and misery. Many of them feel just fine until you make them mad, then it's your fault because you are the one that's *not* fine according to *their* assessment. There are other personality disorders that impact people as well, but the ones mentioned in this book are those that cause the most social disruption and expense. Mental health illnesses make *the individual* sick and can be treated. Personality disorders make *those around them* sick, and those around them wish the disturbed person were treatable.

Some people are in therapy for personality disorder, but the progress is glacial and sometimes requires a team approach. Talk therapy, meds, group therapy, and family therapy are recommended. It doesn't fix the patterns, rather helps reign the behavior in a little bit.

People who are unfortunately stuck with someone like this in their lives are usually the ones to seek treatment. The therapist's job is to help the client learn to recognize the negative behavior patterns of the disturbed person and how to give them as wide a berth as possible. Clients get lots of practice identifying the patterns because the disturbed person will repeat their unique symptom cluster over and over and over. That's why it's called a pattern. You can pretty much predict what they will do in most situations and not be as surprised by it.

So, what do you say we all take an *Adult* Psychopathy Test?

Remember many of us have used many of these strategies when finding ourselves between a rock and a hard place, but when thinking back are not particularly proud of it. The psychopath is gleefully smug about their skills and utilizes their favorite ones regularly on us.

- Have you ever been in trouble with the law? (I hope speeding tickets don't count!)

- Are you able to pursue one goal long term?

- Have you been in lots of shouting matches with people?

- Do you mind hurting others while pursuing your goals?

- Are many of your problems because other people don't understand you or are unfair to you?

- Do you feel bad if your words or actions cause someone else emotional pain?

- Do you let others worry about upholding values while your main concern is to get what you want?

- Do you think love is overrated?

- Do you think people who get ripped off usually deserve it?

- Are you often bored?

- Are you willing to lie in order to sell something or get what you want?

- Do you think that success is survival of the fittest and you are not concerned about the loser?

- Do you think cheating is justified even if unfair to others?

- Do you think that what's right is whatever you can get away with?

- Do you tend to not plan anything far in advance?

- When frustrated, do you become angry very quickly?

- Do you find yourself admiring a really good scam?

- Is making lots of money one of your top goals?

- Do you always consider the consequences of your actions?

- Do you tell people what they want to hear so they will do what you want them to do?

- Do you end up in the same type of trouble time after time? (Again, I hope traffic citations don't count)

- Do you enjoy manipulating other people's feelings?

- Do you care if your success comes at someone else's expense?

- Do you look out for yourself as your top priority?

- Do you feel justified doing whatever you can to succeed?

- Is your main goal in life getting as many things as you can?

- Do you quickly lose interest in tasks you start?

- Do you lack remorse about hurting other people?

- Do you like seeing other people hurt?

How did you do? What might occur is that you will identify six or nine of these items in your cousin Orville. If so, don't call the police. Unless he's holding a smoking gun, that is. Usually these people are simply miserable to encounter but that's the worst of it. When we are aware of the factor X's in someone, we should identify their specific behavior pattern and avoid being charmed, intimidated, or otherwise manipulated.

Dorothy Lewis MD, author of *Guilty by Reason of Insanity* (1999) has devoted her career to researching the brains of violent criminals. Criminals often have cerebral injuries that can account, for or at least contribute to, their atrocities. Teddy was hit over the head with something when he was six and had the scar to prove it. I don't know where located and what part of the brain may have been impacted, but I am convinced that he was already on the road to perdition well before that.

Before his execution, an Electroencephalogram (EEG) was done on Ted's brain. EEG's are performed by attaching electrodes all over the scalp that are themselves attached to a device that records the electrical activity currents of the brain. The tool can be used to decipher seizure activity type, propensity, triggers, and mood state. Ted's EEG was normal other than the suggestion of a mild depression. As a dangerous wild animal who had been caged, I'll *bet* he was depressed.

Researchers also performed an x-ray of Bundy's brain, and the only abnormality noted was a very small cyst. These are very common and typically harmless. We probably have some ourselves, and we are safe to be around (at least most of us are). Had they dared keep Ted alive, our current methods of PET scans, fMRI's and other noninvasive readings and imagery could have examined his brain better to see if there really was a worm in there.

Since the psychopath's amygdalae (the seat of emotion in the brain) is damaged or affected in some way, other limbic brain structures are impacted as well. The hypothalamus, which controls learning and memory, and the frontal lobe, which operates our judgment and behavior emergency brake, are affected. Bundy may have had some organic (physical) injury that exacerbated his aberrant behavior, but in my opinion, his early emotional attachment experiences *alone* are enough to account for it.

Was there a cure for his condition? *Is* there a cure?

No. Like any developmental disability, there's no cure for psychopathy and narcissism, and no pill for it either. Until that day, we must be attuned to recognizing the wiggling invertebrates that we have around us. Psychopaths are unlike other developmentally disabled individuals who have normal emotions and empathy. Others can be assisted to enjoy society, and we in turn get to enjoy them. In contrast, malignant psychopaths are completely disengaged, beyond enraged, feel vengefully *entitled* to their bad behavior, and savor the pain their actions cause.

Here is how disturbed personalities rationalize their awful behavior: think of when we see the bad guy in the movie finally get what he had coming. When we were kids at the cinema we would often cheer and clap when the villain finally got his due. Sometimes we still do as adults. The revenge psychopath, as we remember, feels like the target of his rage, his prey, *is the villain* that they are *compelled to do something about*. Being socially childish, they become delightfully vengeful when accomplishing final possession and destruction of the selected target.

Psychopaths accuse You, the Parent, the Company, or the Society as the cause of their bad behavior. NEVER to blame is the socially disordered person themselves. If they do admit wrongdoing, they will still blame others for having made them that way. Oftentimes, this is sadly true, but it does not constitute them blaming someone else for their own.

These criminals are similar to those who collapse economies and invade other countries, then ride off waving their self-congratulatory flag on their yacht. Tyrants practice another, more dreadful style of psychopathy because these disordered individuals damage entire populations. Richard Ramirez, the "Night Stalker," rationalized his bloody murders by saying he does on a smaller scale what countries do on a larger one. Sorry Richard, no free pass. Off to the slammer for you. Along developmental lines, Ramirez didn't spontaneously bubble up from the underworld as a spawn of Satan. He had a childhood history, too.

People who are on the same trajectory as Ramirez need to be kept *from* society. Period. We cannot unboil an egg.

However, we mustn't throw the baby out with the bathwater because we *can* make use of a boiled egg while it's beginning to boil. Again, *early* channeling of the child's aggressive, remorseless traits into skills that are useful sustain everyone's health and safety. For example, our Special Ops agents are *essential* for public, even national, safety. James Bond is a prime example of a socially beneficial psychopath. He's fictional, I know, but a great example. Watch a Bond movie again. He is a psychopath, but a socially advantageous one. He even got to guard the Queen.

The fictional 007 is that trustworthy, and just as essential as our callous, thrill seeking (not all) trauma surgeons, (not all) bomb defusers, (not all) front line workers, and all who relish doing the dangerously thrilling but distasteful jobs that would make the rest of us faint. They have the guts of steel to do the job, so we need them. Our beloved *Doc Martin* comes to mind, although we do get to see some emotion in him on rare occasions.

The genetic predisposition to limited empathy is referred to in a positive sense as "The Warrior Gene." The socially useful psychopaths can be thought of as warriors because of their prosocial fearless dominance. I think Louise was a warrior.

Let's look again at the fully developed feral criminal. Because of their positive presentation and ability to snow over the public, we want to think there is good in them that can be salvaged, encouraged, and helped. But even before early adulthood, that genie got out of the bottle. They learn to take advantage of our desire to see the best side of them and continue to role play for whomever their audience might be. This way, they might be able to *obtain* something from that audience.

Ted did so right up through his televised trials, in which he happily played the starring role. During his court sentencing proceedings for kidnapping and murdering a 12 year old schoolgirl and leaving her body to rot in a hog shed, Ted represented himself as his own attorney. You know the cliche about that—*whoever acts as his own attorney has a fool for a client.*

Bundy, playing lawyer with his childish self-esteem, staged a magic trick for the world. He called Carole, his current girlfriend, to the witness stand to give testimony and to assure the jury, the judge, and the world of Bundy's good character. She did assure all who were raptly listening of his fine qualities. Then, during a dramatic proposal, he used the televised courtroom to marry her in a brief perfunctory exchange before an unsuspecting judge. Abracadabra, Presto, Change-o—and they were married. He did this *during* his sentencing trial. The purpose of this was an attempt to appeal to all of us that *how can I be given the death penalty on my wedding day as a new groom with an adoring bride?*

Well, Judge Cowert did not allow his court to be wafted into Ted's attempt at a fairy tale. Considering the savagely cruel nature and behavior of the defendant standing before him, the judge agreed with the jury and charged Bundy the death penalty in spite of the ridiculously desperate wedding performance. Judge Cowert went on to refer to Ted as *"a total waste of humanity . . . extremely wicked, shockingly evil, and vile."* Still, Ted never gave up, continued to plead innocent, fathered a child while awaiting execution, kept in touch with whoever his supporters continued to be, and made positive public impressions whenever possible.

Bundy's swan song confessions immediately before his execution was another example of fake human compassion. *See, I'm doing the right thing, before God, for the sake of the families.* Of course, being Ted, he still held back most information in the hopes that they would offer him an extension. *You need to get the whole story for everyone, and I am the only one with all the information. So keep me alive.*

When talking with investigators who were desperate to learn where the children of these many families were, Ted hemmed and hawed. *Well, uh, I don't know, let's see, it's been a really long time. Maybe if we have more time later I will remember better, and I really need to see better maps. Can you get some better maps?* He threw out some descriptive confessions, but none resulting in more than a few remains being found.

To complete his ownership and dominion of his murderous universe, he requested his body be cremated and his ashes spread in the Cascade Mountain Range where the remains of many girls were found. Ted said that area was where he wanted to be dispersed following cremation because "I had some of the best times of my life there."

Now *that* is warped amygdalae.

Narcopath Preparedness and Handling

Preparedness and Handling Hacks

Y ou may notice that psychopathic elements are a step beyond narcissistic traits, and you now see how narcissism is a *surface presentation* given by the most dangerous people. Being aware of the condition and keeping these people at arms length is all we can do. Let's take a look at overt, covert, communal, and other manifestations of narcissism. This will help you spot a narcissist's assumed entitlement so you can protect yourself from their wiles.

Overt Narcissism

This one is the "bull in the china shop" kind of obvious. These bovines exude, "I am the best, I am the smartest, and I deserve the most. Follow me. I am better than everyone. How dare you question it! You are stupid to question it."

None of the people in these examples are physically harming people but *are* emotionally torturing the ones in their orbit.

In the movie *The Devil Wears Prada* (2006), Miranda Priestly played by Meryl Streep bulldozes along in designer clothes and pointy heels. Everyone kowtows to or scatters from her glamorously horrible presence. You can't miss someone like Miranda, so injury from an overt narcissist is easy to avoid. If one cannot avoid a Miranda, they should try their best to be callous against the narcissist's schemes while looking for employment elsewhere.

Ron Burgundy played by Will Farrell in *Anchorman: The Legend of Ron Burgundy* (2004) is a film featuring a grandiose character who displays infantile self-interest in a more artificially glitzy, gross way.

Gregory House on *House MD* is another unapologetic, in your face narcissist. (Fox)

I'm sure you are already having acquaintances come to mind . . .

Covert Narcissism

This is the under-the-radar fish that manipulates by feigning victimhood. They will charm with shyness, adoration, and even seduction to win your heroic assistance. Meanwhile, they are gathering all of your personal information in order to start working you, using you, and destroying you *behind the scenes*. Ted had this M.O.

They may seem sweet and solicitous, but they will assess what they can get from you, take whatever supplies they seek, and then discard you when you are "used up."

Scarlett O'Hara, played by Vivian Leigh in the film *Gone with the Wind* (1939), is another example of a person who *sees what you have to offer, takes what he or she can by seductively acting coy and needy, then discards you*. We all love the end of the story when Scarlett is pleading with Rhett Butler to help her sorry self. *Where shall I go? What shall I do?* Then dashing Clark Gable says, "Frankly, my dear, I don't give a damn." And we all clap.

Communal Narcissism

The public hero is best exemplified in an extreme way in *Mommy Dearest* (1981). The film tells the story from the perspective of the adopted daughter of the famous film star and pseudo philanthropist Joan Crawford. Crawford's part was played by Faye Dunaway. She presented as gloriously wonderful and selflessly giving to her admirers, but she was hell on wheels at home. These personalities give all of their kind energies out to the adoring public, and that's where it ends. A gut punch is when the admirers of the communal narcissist say to the children, "you are so fortunate to have such a wonderful mother." If they only knew.

Wrangling the Unavoidable Narcopath

Narcopaths present in myriads of ways. Another good movie to watch is *The Talented Mr. Ripley* (1999). Dickie Greenleaf played by Jude Law and Freddie Miles played by Philip Seymour present their self absorption and disregard clearly throughout their social interactions. Tom Ripley played by Matt Damon on the other hand covertly presents as passive, uncertain and needy. Although Dickie and Freddie leave social damage in their wake, Tom is a full on psychopath that only shows who he also is to his victims.

The television series *It's Always Sunny in Philadelphia* (2005-) has a group of psychopaths comedically pranking their way though life. The character Dennis Reynolds, played by Glenn Howerton is actually based on Ted Bundy. Danny DeVito plays a dad that has set the example for his offspring.

If we cannot avoid narcissists, they must be held at arm's length as much as possible. If it's a boss or co-worker, when seeking direction from or being directed by them, take notes or let them know you are recording them "to make sure you get it right." The manipulator will often distort exchanges you have with them and accuse you later of doing it wrong or saying something you did not. If they see you documenting for clarity purposes, it will reign them in considerably since they cannot deny what they said. They will not like you taking notes and may even accuse you of being silly or paranoid, but it's effective. You can also cc other parties during email directives. Even better, you can have a third party present during every meeting or exchange. Never having *private* exchange with a narcissist is best.

Accountability is your friend, not the manipulator. The manipulator will hate it when you do this, so be prepared for possible blowback. At the worst you might get fired or threatened depending how disordered the narcissist is. Choose your actions cautiously.

The Gray Rock Method

As mentioned frequently in narc management, learning to gray rock social predators is key. When going "gray rock," or what others describe as "pleasant walling," we only show pleasantness and nothing more. Narcissists are always sniffing for supply of something from others, whether it's your personal information or your admiration of them in order to better manipulate you. Gray rocking allows you to protect yourself in a way that subdues the narcissist's power over a conversation.

Here is an example of this method. You are at a gathering and so and so brags to you about the many properties they own. You might say, "Wow, how cool is that! You must be really rich and smart and more worthy than the rest of us." Personally. I have never tried that response, but that is definitely the impression they are trying to give.

If you do a gray rock reply attempt like, "That must keep you busy," they are likely to say, "Oh no I have people for that. I like to relax in the swimming pool." Narcissists are always sucking up for admiration or domination over another possible supply from you. Keep practicing.

What gives the vampires a satisfying zing is when they can make us mad or feel bad in some way. That is nectar to the narcissist and what they live for. Don't give it to them.

If stuck in conversation with this person, an even grayer rock method of *detail gathering* can be useful. "What is the climate like at your Costa Rica property? How well are the highways maintained in the area? What is your favorite time of the year to go? Are special vaccinations recommended?" . . . ad nauseam. They will get bored of you since you are focused on the property and not admiring them or feeling green with envy, and you will be dismissed. Good job.

Another fun response that works well is this: "When I visited Costa Rica, I loved it when the monkeys hung around looking for food." You then laugh and say, "I certainly had to watch my step though because they don't wear diapers!" The narcopath will usually bow out in disgust.

When interacting with the manipulator (aka. the invasive snoop, con, etc.), it is best to keep your responses brief and to the point. Don't explain or defend, which is the method used by royalty. It's counterproductive to try to clarify because, feeling fueled, they will continue with more vitriol. They can't help themselves because they love the challenge of evoking helpless emotion in you.

When holding your emotional boundaries, your dialogue exchange, although accurate, is quite boring for them. Some feel that it seems rude to keep things brief and to the point, but think of it as being professional. When the retail clerk or medical professional has important things to do, we do not expect them to apologize for bowing out with a brief interaction.

Any elaboration with a manipulator, controller, or con-artist (same things, different levels) risks giving them personal information that they will later weaponize against you, or they may use the information to wheedle into your privacy and control you there. Their tactics can be quite stunning.

You may have noticed this yourself during some of your own interactions with these personalities. People who invade your boundaries openly are not all that sophisticated so are pretty easy to spot.

The victim manipulators in your own life that haven't been successful at obtaining what they want from you may make accusations that you don't like them, that you have damaged them, or that you have been unfair to them in some way. Be prepared for that. They will even tearfully complain about you to other people. Narcissists do this in order to gain sympathy for themselves, thus controlling the *listener's* thoughts and emotions about *you*. They might even call *you* a narcissist or psychopath. No worries; just keep being yourself and doing what you do because they will keep being themselves and doing what they do and will *glow visibly* for the behaviorally astute. I find these people to be amazing specimens to study—from a distance.

Become attuned to narc clues and create as much of a distance from these individuals as early as possible. Sometimes we get into something before we realize we are in quicksand, and it can take some maneuvering to get out. Sometimes we cannot get out, and that is when we callous ourselves toward them as much as possible while looking for escape. I think that is what Louise did at the Philadelphia house.

If you have found yourself trapped in a situation like this, seeing a therapist that specializes in this personality disorder is crucial because our thinking has often been so manipulated that we cannot sort out what is going on and why we feel so confused and angry. But once you see it, you cannot unsee it.

How can you see it in the first place? Review the movies, YouTube channels, and books I recommend in the Resources section at the back of this book. All of the resources describe some level of narcissism. Watch movies portraying these personalities so you intuit them more easily.

Watch Youtube channels and read books about narcissism. There are so many professionals teaching about this subject currently because of the recognized damage narcissists do to the individuals around them.

Be a manipulation whisperer. Google "manipulation tactics" and you will discover a plethora of behaviors that bullies and con-artists use to control the people around them. Teach your children how to recognize when it is happening and call each other on it when it pops up spontaneously. Manipulation is a very Darwinian ideal that spans across cultures, and that is why the Golden Rule is spotlighted and emphasized as a combative measure in every major religion in the world.

The Golden Rule:

Do unto others as you would have them do unto you.

The Manipulation Rule:

Do unto others before they do unto you.

Chapter Nineteen

So What was the Deal with the VW's?

. . . Have bug will travel

Another claim to the Bundy infamy was being the serial killer in the Volkswagen.

The German Beetle was everywhere in the 60's and 70's. I had one myself. The popular little Bug was not the vehicle one would imagine as an ominous trolling set of wheels, but there were various reasons that brought about the evolution of Ted's transportation preference. The one Bundy drove was a bit riddled with rust and dents, the seats were torn, and looked a bit, well, ineffective. But it ran—he saw to that. He was quite good at working on Volkswagens.

Since he prowled college campuses and school grounds, which to him were candy stores full of women and girls, the buggy of death didn't look all that out of place since it's common for a poor college student to drive something rickety. Inexpensive transportation is a must while saving funds designated for tuition, books, food, and housing. With limited cash he became astute at stealing and living off stolen credit cards, shoplifting, and other people. For example, he was found with 21 stolen credit cards in his stolen VW during his Pensacola arrest, so he was obviously ever mindful of the value of a dollar.

Upon investigating his gas purchase receipts, police noted that he kept his tank on full as often as possible, fueling as little as 98 cents or less at a time. My thoughts on why he did this are that, given his proclivities, Ted never knew when he may have to make a run for it across a county, state, or jurisdiction when in a hurry to avoid detection. He had to do this, for example, after the Eastern Washington murder in Ellensburg. Ted high-tailed it across the Evergreen state and half way into the next state, Corvallis, Oregon to be exact, for his next hunt. He burned up the road some more after that murder because the Corvallis woman's skull was found on a mountain east of Seattle, 265 miles from Corvallis.

Regardless of where it was driving or parked, his buggy was a rag-tag contraption. Carol DaRonch, his kidnap escapee, said Ted introduced himself as an Officer Roseland who needed to take her to the police station to identify a person who had tried to break into her Camaro. When they got to his vehicle—his Volkswagen—she was surprised it wasn't a squad car. His intended captive thought it looked pretty beat up, but she assumed it was an undercover car. DaRonch asked him to show her his badge and he showed her one. It was either fake or stolen. Regardless, it was not his.

She had been taught to always respect and not question authority. She *did* hesitate, but lifelong training of submitting to authority overcame her, so she got in the bug. When he pulled over to a jolting stop and tried to handcuff her, the fight began.

Failing the handcuffs, he tried to crowbar her, but that girl fought, breaking nails and even getting some of his Type O blood on her coat. Fortunately, she was able to grab the door handle, open the door, and run for her Type A life. She was such a brave young woman. None of us know what we would do under an attack until it happens. She flew into action to save her life that night . . . and later identified Ted in a police line-up even though he changed his hair and parted it on the opposite side of his head. Her identification of him was the start of his finish.

Ever experimenting and adapting as predatory organisms do, Ted learned from the Carol DaRonch escape. He figured out how to remove that damn inside passenger door handle from the car.

With Volkswagens, at least back then, the inside door handle could be removed while still leaving the outside handle intact. He was probably quite pleased with himself for thinking of that. Since he had been a Boy Scout in his youth, Ted likely learned the motto "Be Prepared." Ed Kemper, being extremely long armed, would tell his passenger her car door was not shut, kindly reach across, open and shut it while slipping a chapstick into the door lever. This maneuver jammed her door handle without her knowing that she was trapped by this assumed gentle giant.

Another disturbing adjustment Bundy learned about was that the passenger seat was removable with these cars. The passenger seat even fit on the back seat if one needed the space for what he called "cargo." Adjacent to the driver, the cargo was easier to control than if tied up and covered by a blanket in the back seat.

Apparently he was also intrigued by the hand grip above the doors. I am not privy as to how he may have used it, but I am sure he certainly weighed its possibilities. His mental wheels were always turning, calculating, methodically trying things out. Abused kids do grow to be powerfully astute, hypervigilant observers. When watching footage of him, observe how his eyes were always darting elsewhere. He missed nothing. As Bundy's bad behavior accumulated, he would have been watching his back even more, and looking in every other direction for opportunities that might present themselves.

The sunroof feature of the bug even made it handy for transporting stolen goods, such as a 6 foot ficus tree he stole from a nursery. A final selling point for Ted was the surprise element. If you were going to guess what type of vehicle a serial killer would drive, what would you pick? Of course, our first thought is always the white serial killer van (which he did use in Florida). But if your guess had to be a car, what would you imagine? Probably not Herbie.

He taught himself to do the repairs and whatever upkeep was needed to keep the car running. He explained the variety of iron tools he carried throughout the car as needed for occasional repairs to anyone that found them suspect. Handcuffs, though? He had a story for that, too. Ted caught and tackled a purse snatcher in Seattle once, for which he made the news. He also received his second citation for bravery afterward, so of course Mr. Be Prepared had a ready explanation for the handcuffs. Also, there were riots and demonstrations in the 60's and 70's that could get rough, which was how he rationalized the crowbar. He also explained that his ski mask was for warmth, pantyhose with eye holes were for more warmth, and the rope and icepick were typical household items he wanted to have just in case. Many of these items were kept in what he referred to offhandedly as his "gym bag."

Another bonus Ted found from driving a Bug was that they got the best gas mileage. Having little money as a sketchily employed college student, the VW gave him the "best bang for his buck," as they say. Ted tore up the miles in that thing, throughout the University of Washington's U District, to Olympia, to Issaquah to Corvallis, to Ellensburg to Idaho, to Colorado, to Utah, to Philadelphia, the Jersey coast and who knows where else. It also carried him to his various disposal areas in the Cascade Mountains, where parts of his victim's bodies were eventually found.

Predators of Bundy's ilk put *hundreds of thousands of miles* on their cars *per year*. They burn gallons and gallons of gas and quart after quart of oil trolling for just the right victim opportunity. I suppose they wear their tires out too. I wonder if Bundy ever stole tires off of parked VW's.

They also search for new dumping sites and revisit former sites to see the progression of decay or check if police may have discovered their spot. Or they go there to reminisce. Due to all this travel, knowing how to maintain the vehicle saves money that could be better spent on trolling. If you are suspicious of a seedy someone's activities, check their mileage. The clever ones, however, are inclined to adjust their odometer.

We all grew up playing the Slug Bug game every time we spotted a VW beetle on the highway. Herbie the Love Bug has always been a hit with kids and grownups alike. The Bug represented the innocence of innocence, sort of like the assumed cheerful harmlessness of a clown (well, until John Wayne Gacy ruined that one for us).

Ted was big on making impressions. When he pulled up in a Volkswagen with his arm in a sling or walked an unsuspecting young lady to the little Bug, her first instinctual thought was likely not "I'm going to die now." When we spot a VW Beetle, often our first reaction is, *Oh, how cute and harmless.* That served him well, very well. So well that when preparing to go hunting in Florida, the car he chose to steal for transportation was, guess what, an orange one.

. . . and Roses?

Although roses have long been associated with love and romance, they also are symbolic of secrecy and blood. Ted had a certain affinity toward the flower, but the reason is unbeknownst. Still, I think it is important to discuss.

During his attempted kidnap of Carol DaRonch, he identified himself as Detective Roseland. To other individuals, he introduced himself as Mr. Roseland. He had worked as a campaign aid for Dan Evans in the Washington State Governor's race and surreptitiously trailed the opponent, Rosellini. He did that in order to get intel to report back to Evan's camp. He was caught and televised as boyishly laughing that he was surprised at the attention he was getting. Don't be fooled—he was reveling in that notoriety.

When escaping Garfield County Jail in Nevada, he traveled all the way to Ann Arbor Michigan to watch the University of Washington play the University of Michigan in the Rose Bowl. When in court as his own attorney, he talked and joked with journalists about the Rose Bowl. He could have joked about something else, but that popped out. His code name when calling Dr. Carlisle was "Rosebud." The finale was naming his daughter Rosa.

Certainly, introducing oneself as Detective Roseland rather than Detective Hatchet or Detective Lecter is better for reassuring the girl that it is safe to get in the car. It is no secret that women love roses, and the name Rose anything would have sounded more feminine and therefore nonthreatening.

With his flair for the notorious romantics, he would have liked variations of Rose as a name. Besides, the connotation is beautiful, soft, romantic, and loving. Aside from those pesky thorns, they are harmless. Or maybe he just really liked roses.

Early years in his grandfather's nursery may have influenced Ted's interest. There was a climbing rose bush on the outside of his grandparent's house. I'm sure the little boy certainly smelled them and his grandfather warned him about the thorns.

While at Temple University, Ted took some interesting classes that affirm his love for the Romantics. *Theatre in Western Culture* is the first one I find interesting pertaining to Bundy. Such classes typically included Greek Tragedies such as Oedipus Rex. Read the play and discover why he was named Oedipus, which means 'swollen foot.'

Here is a Thumbnail Summary of Sophocles' famous work:

Prince Oedipus learns that the king is not his real father. He then becomes apprised by the Oracle that he will kill his father and marry his mother. Spoiler alert: without knowing he is doing it, he does kill his father, who he thought was someone else, and does marry his mother, who he also thought was someone else.

As the audience follows the play with alarming concern, Oedipus and his mother have four children together. While all of us watching the play already know the sordid truth, Oedipus himself does not. The play evolves with Oedipus slowly coming to realize his true identity with horror. The audience (and Ted's classmates) witness and vicariously experience this dreadful paradox along with the unfortunate protagonist.

Lively disapproving conversation about the deviancy of the Oedipal life most certainly ensued in the classroom. With Ted sitting there. Likely silent. I would like to have been the proverbial fly on the wall for that class.

Considering the many similarities with Ted and his own confused parent-age, his recently confirmed illegitimacy, and the possibility of being a child of incest, I find him reading this to be significant. Other plays covered in these courses also may have influenced him. Perhaps the bard's beautiful, flowery words inspired him in his quest for self-realization as well.

"What's in a name? That which we call a rose by any other name would still smell as sweet."
Romeo and Juliet. **William Shakespeare**

What's in a name? Which name? Theodore Robert Cowell? Theodore Robert Nelson? Theodore Robert Bundy? *Who am I?*

[He did not know much about who he was, but he knew what he wanted to present, even down to the way he wrote.]

Ted's language and loopy scroll penmanship depicted literature to varying degrees rather than a friendly, informative, or business letter. I think he used the flowery style to impress upon others his facade of civility and softness. While awaiting execution, prison guards witnessed his growling filthy profanity that would have shocked, confused, and amazed any of these letter recipients.

Marcom Consulting Group did a handwriting analysis of Bundy. They noted that his writing demonstrated flagrant resentment and very low self-esteem brought about early in life. I don't know what methods they used to arrive at that conclusion, but I am not surprised.

The content of Ted's letter is of interest to me. He had been asked to write about what his attitudes and experiences with animals were when he was a child. He said of Louise that she talked and talked but never said anything. Ted similarly flatters and articulates, but never actually answers the question. Like mother, like son.

Shakespeare's style of writing was called Secretary Script. My great grandfather used the style when he was a scribe in Lansing Michigan nearly a century ago. We as school kids first saw it in history class when we studied assorted Founding Fathers documents. Ted used a similar style. I don't have any examples of Bundy's writing from when he was a youngster. It would be interesting to compare. My guess is, as we all do when learning penmanship, he developed the style deliberately for his own reasons.

Among his letters written from prison are some he penned to Liz in this same fluid handwriting. No matter how flowery they looked or sounded, they were not the roses he so admired. I think of what he wrote as paper rose bombs. Here is one of them. See what you think.

In this life we are fortunate to find one person to love and love completely. I am lucky because I love you in that way. Being in this jail has taught me this lesson. I think of no one else or miss no one else as I do you . . . In this hour when my whole life is threatened, the only thing I regret losing is you and Molly. So I give you one more thing. It is the one part of me that cannot be taken away. I give you my love as deep and as powerful as any human being can have for another.. I give it to you as the woman who has captured my very soul. Every last grain. There's no one to whom I could give my love for the rest of my life. My love for you is life itself. Without you there would be no life.

Ted
From The Phantom Prince (2020)

I wonder if Liz ever felt like he was her own Shakespeare writing love letters to her. That was very possibly another one of Ted's manipulative intentions to keep her as his supply source. Yes he would do that.

Chapter Twenty

Con Man Ploys

Nothing to see here . . .

As you may recall, further exploration into his foundational origins is what took Bundy to Philadelphia in 1969 to visit his grandparents and other relatives. He also impulsively enrolled in law school without having obtained a Bachelor of Arts degree, which is what he later obtained at the University of Washington. Remember that impulsivity, disregarding rules and demonstrating a lack of forethought, is a trait of psychopathy, except for when psychopaths are calculating. Magical thinking regarding himself is also something Ted never matured past. He utilized magical thinking rather than developing a capacity for insight.

When Ted was formulating his lofty Temple University plan, he wrote a five page letter to his grandfather. The letter, Bundy being now in his early 20's, was a loquacious introductory resume to impress and garner approval from this man who was his first role model and, for all Ted knew, possibly his biological father.

In the letter, Ted addressed Samuel and Eleanor Cowell appropriately as his grandparents. I wonder if this was his way of telling them he now knew his relationship to them. Ted wanted answers, and this lovely, impressive letter was working at endearing himself to the Pennsylvania relatives who had answers to every secret.

Bonding with his kin was not his intent since he wasn't capable of such, but in his mind he wanted answers and the admiration of his first father figure. Ever the troller, Ted knew connecting with that side of the family was also a good opportunity to access whatever might be useful to him materially. His Pennsylvania relatives were a means to procure the scaffolding he needed to stabilize his always precarious foundation.

While telling his grandparents that he intended to go to Temple's law school, he strove to impress them by recording his many experiences in politics. He described at length his trip to Florida during one campaign, a convention for Nelson Rockefeller when he was running for the United States Presidency. Among his impressive sentences regarding his many successes and affiliation with various government officials, he referred to the city of Miami as resembling a spleen at bursting point. A what? Apparently, a favorite pastime that he was actually candid about was that he would often go into the medical libraries at universities and peruse pictures of autopsies, bodies at crime scenes, and organs.

Whether he heard someone else describe the city of Miami as such or if he came up with it himself, who knows, but it is rather garish among the ornate articulations throughout the rest of the correspondence. I wonder if Ted had an imprint of someone suffering a ruptured spleen during one of the beatings witnessed at the hand of the father. I'm really going out on a limb here, but I wonder if this was Ted's way of letting his grandfather know he remembered the injury to demonstrate his prowess by holding secret information over them. *I know this and could make trouble with it, but I won't if you will give me what I want.* Yes, a narcissistic psychopath will do that sort of veiled intimidation when not wanting to be blatant about it. Who knows if that was the case, but that is a possible example of what a disordered individual will do to accomplish an intention. He will use a rock.

As John E. Douglas, retired FBI Profiler, teaches us, "Everyone has a Rock." The example he gives is from when he was having a conversation with a suspect regarding a child whose skull had been fractured by a rock. Mr. Douglas does not interrogate; he is more conversational with perps and gets the most information that way. Because of its effectiveness, his style changed the way police interview suspects forever. Some still use extreme methods of interrogation like shouting, table pounding, even waterboarding, but none on Mr. Douglas's watch. I would not have minded investigators using the water method with Ted. He certainly didn't hesitate using it on other people.

Anyway, the back to the rock guy Douglass investigated. He had murdered a little girl with a big rock but insisted on his innocence. Well, Mr. Douglas made sure that *the rock* itself was in sight when the sicko was brought into the interrogation room. The guy crumbled when he saw it. Case closed.

A psychopath is astute to an individual's vulnerabilities and secrets, and he will use those secrets against the victim for his own purposes. In his uncanny way, Ted may have been using whatever he could to manipulate his grandparents to get what he wanted. Yes, he would even stoop to manipulate his own grandparents.

Who knows whether Bundy was using this spleen imagery in his letter for dastardly purposes, but regardless, we do know that Ted did have a craving for horror and perhaps let it leak from that compartment in his mind.

Being naturally wordy, Ted speaks to them throughout the long letter with resolve of his intention to move to Philadelphia. He told them he had bought a one-way ticket and already paid for pre-registration at Temple. The three classes he ultimately took during his semester at the college were not law classes. He possibly hadn't learned yet that he did not meet requirements for entering Temple's School of Law. Even if he knew, it would be like Ted to let his family think he was taking law classes.

Also typical of the parasitic psychopath, you may notice that his letter left space for family members to volunteer to pay for some expenses and offer housing. We mustn't assume that when a college student is hoping to stay with family that we have a psychopath on our hands. Remember, this is Ted we are talking about. He was "close" to his family mainly for the benefits. The framework of his life plan was still making his way by feeding off of others. Bundy was always erratically on the make and always would be since future plans were for the most part nonexistent.

Ted was ravenous to BE somebody. Somebody others would admire. But he, as psychopaths do, could not stick to something to completion unless it served his personal interests. Even then, he used others until they were all used up. When a paper was due in a class, he would wait until the last minute and have Liz type while he dictated. I imagine him feeling a bit self-important having someone typing for him, like his mother had when he was in high school.

He created and improved upon (at least in *his* estimation) his personal identity as he went. Ted, due to the black hole that marred his social intelligence, was not able to interpret how others perceived him, so he made it up for himself by guessing what *they* wanted him to be or do. Because of his lack of sense of self and purpose, he made swings in many directions with no lasting results. Socially disordered persons are unable, or at least don't try, to sustain goals or accomplishments. The only accomplishment he completed was his Bachelor Degree in Psychology with Distinction at the University of Washington.

Ted studied psychology for a reason, but not to help others. He wanted to learn the best ways to manipulate others. He didn't complete much of anything else in his life except the dreadful vocational Bullseye at which he proudly became a world-wide expert. His strategies made him the global poster boy by which all other serial murderers would be profiled against for the years that followed.

Ted stayed with his aunt and uncle while attending Temple University, as his grandparents didn't have room for him in their now smaller housing arrangement. I would guess that he was helpful and entertaining during his time with any of the Philadelphia relatives. I do not know whether family members helped pay for any of his expenses. He was adept at shoplifting and stealing credit cards, so was probably able to cover most of his personal provisions and keep himself somewhat afloat in that way.

He was only at Temple for one semester before he quit and returned to Seattle. I do not know the reason why or what his reception had been by the grandparents during his stay in Philly. The only reference to interaction with his grandparents of which I am aware is Ted mentioning during his visit that he planned to go up to Burlington, Vermont. He recalled they both looked sideways and said nothing. His foundation here, as everywhere in his family closets, was air. I wonder if his grandfather worried that Louise could have left indication that he was the father in some of the Lund Home for Unwed Mothers' paperwork.

Ted likely left because he was following the pattern he always had. The psychopath pattern is to see what is available, try it out to see what can be gained, and then move on when it has been used up or cut off by the suppliers. Ted had gained all he could from the city of Brotherly Love, so it was time to go home.

Tools of the Trade

The term "Con Man" evolved from the old fashioned term of "Confidence Man." The behaviors of these manipulators are customized to build and ensure our confidence *in them and what they are selling us*. They are really good at reading people and planning their most convincing ploys. Once they have a sense of what will be required to love bomb us, their pattern kicks in.

Con men entertain us by convincing us that we need them or what they have to offer in our lives. They are salesmen selling *themselves* to us so that we will give them what *they* want. Or they present downcast puppy eyes begging for help. That method can work just as well; with some victims it works even better than the sales pitch. Whichever approach they use, once we see the pattern, we will always see it.

When the FBI called Ted's aunt when investigating the Jersey shore murders, she denied that it could have possibly been him. Our human nature instinctively denies the possibility that anyone associated with us could be capable of committing such awful acts. We especially don't want to believe it if that person had been kind to us, was fun, or at least nice to have around. The aunt, although aware of his preschool antics at the Philadelphia house may have thought, *But look, he has turned out just fine.*

It seems the only family member that acknowledged and expressed concern about Ted's aberrant behavior was his Aunt Julia. As we know, her concerns about Ted when they were children were never acknowledged by the rest of the family. Years later, she revealed her earliest concerns about Ted with the world. When Bundy's crimes came to light, if I had been Aunt Julia, I would have thought, *Well dammit people, just like Ted said, it was there all along. Why couldn't you believe it?* Again, when it came to building a foundation for Ted, the family offered empty air other than Aunt Julia's unbending rebar.

This experience exemplifies how individuals can differ greatly in response to abuse, even in the same family. Where one individual tends to be the 'truth teller,' which I think Julia was, others differ. Often, the truth teller is the one that calls a spade a spade and rips the wool off our eyes, so to speak. Sometimes we are not too happy about having the wool ripped off. Although family members, co-workers, or any other close associates would rather not notice or talk about their issues, the truth teller simply can't help themselves.

As you might guess, I am the truth teller in my family.

The truth teller is often kept at a distance by the avoidant others because the truth can be *very* uncomfortable and at times even risky. The truth may require some action, and if the possible outcome of the action is not something we want, we naturally find a way to avoid the discomfort.

Conveniently, or at least convenient for the others in the group, the truth teller becomes the scapegoat because if the secret keepers can invalidate them in some way, it will mean what they have to say has no or at least less merit. *She's a pretty mixed up gal.* The *scapegoat* becomes the *problem* for the group rather than the problem being the problem. The individuals that would like for the elephant in the room to simply evaporate are the ones who let sleeping dogs lie. If we don't want to get involved, strategies for successful noninvolvement can be to *not notice* what's going on, *minimize* the importance of what's going on or flatly *deny* that it's going on. Any of those actions allow us to keep our false sense of peace.

As a child, Molly chose the non-involvement strategy of minimizing the importance of her situation to protect her beloved father figure.

Little Molly did not want to lose the wonderful times she had with Ted, so the little girl waited decades to tell her mom about his inappropriate games. She was afraid he would have to leave if Liz knew the truth, and that would break her mother's heart. Many children in family situations like Molly come to the same conclusion. The Con Man knows this and plays upon that vulnerability.

At the same time, Liz did not want to lose her dream of being with this man who presented himself so irresistibly to her. He knew exactly what she wanted and used fake promises to give them hope that things were going to be wonderful for the three of them as soon as . . .

Every once in a while Liz would step up as the truth teller and call Ted on his shit, but he was SO good at crazy making to alter her perception of him and win back her trust.

Crazy making is when we deny another person's reality, causing them to question themselves so as to give up their idea. In spite of all of Ted's emotionally hurtful behaviors, he would insist how much he *loved* Liz and Molly. Being quite the influential talker, he was able to make the people around him question their own thoughts and observations. They are successful at duping us because we *want* them to be who we want them to be. Imagine Molly hearing Ted tell Liz an innocent version that they had played hide and seek and that he read Molly his favorite bedtime story. He might have given Molly a wink and then distracted them from the truth by taking them to the zoo for a wonderful afternoon, making light of or even trying to delete what really happened. Crazy making, at its core, is dismissing, minimizing, or denying the hurtful things and redirecting someone's focus on promising times to come.

'Gaslighting' is another form of crazy making. The term comes from a 1940's Movie called *Gaslight*. The plot is about a man who is trying to convince his wife and others that she is crazy so he can have her committed and gain access to her inheritance.

Ted gaslit Liz, Molly, and almost everyone else in his path constantly. Another example Molly gave was when Ted deliberately threw something at her face. She knew it was intentional, but he insisted it was an accident. If the subject is not dropped, the perpetrator will distort what happened and accuse the child or whomever it might be that they are overreacting, trying to get them in trouble, making them look bad in some way, or lying. The injured person becomes the bad guy. It's called "Blaming the Victim."

This will result in the victim questioning their own thoughts about what happened and coming to rely on the controller's description of reality, believing their own to be faulty.

When the manipulator is called out for distorting the truth, they often will blame the victim with, "Don't get so upset! I was only joking," or, "Well, if you had only . . .," or possibly question them with, "You're so perfect?" The manipulator may even try to threaten the victim with something like, "Well if that's how you feel, I guess our vacation plans are off."

We don't intend to make it easy for perpetrators to con us in these ways, but we often unknowingly do. Kemper and Ridgeway were approached by their victims. With Kemper, he saw girls hitchhiking and all he had to do was come to a stop so they could get in his car. He had a university parking sticker on the back windshield, so they probably assumed he was an instructor. It was the same way with Ridgeway. Street workers would come up to his vehicle to offer services, get in, and go. Sometimes he would return them unharmed so they might tell others he was safe. When one of them disappeared, they assumed it wasn't Gary because he always paid them and brought them back.

Ted, on the other hand, approached his victims in a variety of ways. It's called "Criminal Versatility." The final confession he gave Bill Hagmaier describes him overhearing a beautiful woman in a phone booth telling the listener that she was worried about her father, who was having heart trouble. The ever-prepared former Boy Scout took out a badge and told her he was there to take her to the hospital, as her father had suffered a heart attack. Being in a state of shock, she agreed to go with him. As she stooped to get in his car, *wham*.

Gacy lured victims with an offer of a job. Dahmer got them to his apartment by offering to photograph them. Charlie just sat on the sidewalk singing and smiling. They came to him, too. Psychopaths, having started out life at the miserable mercy of other psychopaths, grow up narcissisti-cally *deciding* to dominate the world around them. Feeling like such losers, they want to equalize the scale. Even more, they have every intention to win, if not destroy, so they set lures that entice.

That's how it's done in the world of a Confidence Man.

Chapter Twenty One

Up Close and Personal

. . . Trust the leaks and the tells

Now that I have sharpened your *Faulty Amygdalae Antennae* (I made that up), we will talk about the telling behaviors that seep out of psychopaths. Regardless of how charming or disarming the psychopath may be, if we spend enough time with them, many nooks and crannies of their true selves will show.

Carole Boone, Bundy's death row wife, said that as time went on, Ted became more and more exhausting, obsessive, and demanding. Remember the lazy, selfish phases after love bombing. Carole was seeing it. She was finally experiencing the side of Ted that the prison guards knew all along. I suppose those guards have seen it all.

We saw a living color video display of his childish narcissism in the courtroom after he had refused to turn up for court proceedings during the Kimberly Leach trial. In his cell, he broke a lightbulb, crammed toilet paper in the cell door lock, and refused to leave for trial appearance. Three guards could not get into his cell because of the TP obstruction trick. Imagine what Louise had to deal with.

Judge Cowert handled that trial tantrum soundly, as if setting a spoiled child right. That is what the Judge had in front of him, after all. Remember, narcopaths are at the emotional maturity level of toddlers, and when push comes to shove, you will see it loud and clear. We also see it with his outbursts challenging the Judge and prosecutor. "You want a circus? I'll give you a circus. I'll rain on your parade, Jack. It will be a thunderstorm. This will not be the little drama you've arranged." I wonder if he talked like that to his elementary school teachers. Apparently he could be difficult.

As Ted was being escorted to his cell once, a passerby said that instead of the gentle American Boy expression Bundy typically presented, he had no pretense. The witness said it was a cold, murderous face. Occasionally, this face would burst out in public, but only rarely. Then he would have to regather himself to present the American Boy countenance again, gaslighting us as though the other face had never leaked.

Speaking of leaking, I'd like to share various water related stories regarding rather frightening appearances of Ted's dangerous personality. The first one to explore is a *presumed* hero story. Remember his early hero fantasies.

When he was mixed in with a crowd of people at Seattle's Green Lake on a beautiful summer day, a little three year old girl went missing. Of course, all were frantically searching for the child and authorities were notified. In the midst of the crowded panic, lo and behold came Ted, walking out of the water with the drenched and dripping little girl in his arms. He was the hero of the day and given his fifteen minutes of fame. He may have been on the news for this, but don't quote me on that.

Nothing in this example is an obvious "I am a psychopath" tell, but human behavior specialists would love to look into it further. Perhaps his love of attention and self-absorption were easy tells. If there is video coverage of an interview with him afterward, I would like to see it. Without being solicited, he may have said he was a law student, or college student, or worked for the governor . . . not mentioning the little girl he saved but bashfully reveling in his *own* attention.

Regardless, he fulfilled his own hero fantasy. How the child nearly drowned we will never know, but I think he had come up behind her and pushed her off the dock, started dunking her from behind, or swam unseen underwater and pulled her under. Ted told Bill Hagmaier a story about the biggest fish in the deepest water waiting for the best prey, referring to himself of course. And here we have the heroic you-know-who, bringing his prey out of the water and returning her to her distraught and eternally grateful parents. I'm sure he racked up a really big pile of good guy points for that one. In fact, he won another Citation for Bravery Award for it. Why do I suppose he staged it? First of all, because he was Ted, and also, there's more stories following the same thread.

Once, he and a woman were on a date at a secluded spot along a river when he suggested she climb up on a branch that was hanging out over the river. She refused, and he was not happy about that. Ted started getting ticked and kept insisting she do so. Was he bored and hoped she'd fall in? Remember boredom comes quickly to these guys.

Ted's date, rather than climbing out over the river, waded into the water thinking that being out in the river would satisfy him. He followed behind, trying to untie her bathing suit top. They played a bit in the water and then got out of the river and had sex.

She said she expected sex, but he was so aggressive she thought it might be what rape is like, and then it occurred to her how far out in the middle of nowhere they were. Afterward she had cuts and scratches on her back from the twigs and jagged stones in the soil beneath her. She never went out with him again. Did you notice how many tells he gave us in this incident?

Another time when on a rafting trip with Liz, he came up behind her and pushed her off the raft into the water. The water was shockingly cold and she had difficulty reaching the rope to pull herself back on to the raft. She said during her struggle he watched her blankly, flatly, and did not help. She had to manage on her own. What tells did you notice here?

Continuing with the water-related red flag ensemble, he cheated on Liz and took a date on a rafting trip with another couple. They were floating down the river on a blowup raft that *Liz* had bought him for his graduation. Admittedly, it was a gift so technically he could do what he wanted with it, but still. One of the others on the outing was a professional journalist, which meant that any bizarre or frightening behavior would have been *noted by the writer.*

When his date got out of the raft and waded in the water, he dunked her head under. For a long time. He finally let her up gasping and then did another dunk, and another. She thought, *is he trying to drown me?* But then she reasoned it away with, *oh he's such a nice guy, he does not realize what he is doing.*

Next, she got onto an inner tube floating along the side of the raft and he untied it, knowing she couldn't swim. One of the others re-secured the tube, and she got back into the raft. Ted got in the inner tube and drifted into the faster water, pulling the raft with him. He nearly upended the raft.

When they landed on shore, it was up to Ted to go back to get the car. It took him over an hour and a half before he came back to pick them up. When he finally arrived, he was angry and wouldn't say a word about what he had been doing during all that time. When they all went to eat after, he sat silently during the whole dinner and on the way home. His presence was so shockingly different to the Ted they thought they knew. Afterward, they wanted nothing to do with him. I'm sure when the criminal Ted was seen by the world, they looked on that day and his behavior. How many tells did you count here?

"First grade, I was somewhat of a champion frog catcher. I was a frog man. Prided myself on my ability to spot that pair of bulging eyes, which would bob just above the surface of a murky pond."

~Ted

There is a poolside pose from *The Phantom Prince*. Molly and Liz are sitting at the edge of the pool, Ted is standing above them, both of their heads are capped by his big hands. Liz is leaning away from him, Molly is looking down. Ted has a distorted look on his face. I wonder what Molly and her mother were sensing if anything. It may have seemed funny at the time. Liz eclipsed any concerns about him with optimistic love, until she didn't. Molly kept secrets about him, until she didn't.

"You're like a fisherman who fishes for years and catches a small fish.

Sometimes a medium fish. You get lucky and get a big fish. But you know that there's a real big fish under there that always gets away. You and your group are going to get a lot of serial killers and they're going to help you. But with the real good ones, the only way you're going to know what goes on under the water is to go under the water. The fisherman drowns going underwater. But I can take you there without drowning. *If* I trust you. And *if* I decide."

~Ted to Bill Hagmaier, FBI

In college psychology class, Ted had learned that women were more likely to trust and want to help a man if he were injured, so of course he promptly incorporated that approach into his kidnap and murder repertoire.

At Lake Sammamish State Park on a beautiful, very crowded summer day, Bundy approached several women in the crowd. He had his arm in a sling and asked them to help him load a small sailboat onto his car. Some women who were initially willing to help got suspicious when they saw there was no sailboat by his car. He told them the boat was actually at someone else's house, and when realizing the extension to his request, most of the women refused to help.

Two young ladies still agreed to help, however, and were never seen alive again. As one of the women was leaving with him, an onlooker commented that it looked as though she wasn't pleased about doing so. If that is true, I wonder if her gut was objecting.

Another psychological trick he used was targeting women in a crowded area, where they were more inclined to feel safe with so many onlookers. To his benefit, the onlookers would not think anything at all of two people chatting, getting into a car, and driving off. Nothing. No one would take a second look or give it a second thought.

"Since this girl in front of him represented not a person, but again the image, or something desirable, the last thing we would expect him to want to do would be to personalize this person. . . . Chattering and flattering and entertaining, as if seen through a motion picture screen."

~Ted

Even if there had been any suspicious activity or scuffling between them, onlookers tend to dismiss it as couple turbulence that is none of their business. *Oh, it's just a couple having a fight. Uh-Oh, they're having a domestic. Hope it turns out okay. Somebody (else) needs to call 911. I don't want to ruin my beach day by getting involved.* This phenomenon is called the Bystander Effect. It is always a good idea to alert authorities to something unusual rather than hope someone else will.

If no one comes to the rescue, when they get out on the highway and the crowbar comes out, it's too late. He practiced his method with each hunt and learned with each blunder and success.

"The organism does what has made the organism successful."

~Greg Hartley

Ted was feigning being on crutches when he approached one of his first publicly known Seattle victims. He asked her for help getting his books to his car. Her mistake was being kind and willing to help him. He was hoping for that. Her body, or parts of her body, was found eventually.

A few weeks prior to that, in the same vicinity he had used an arm in a sling-balancing-books ploy to get a woman to help him. She helped Ted to his bug, and when he asked her to bend over and adjust something on the dash, she got a gut alarm and left. She was able to get away and tell the story, but she didn't report it because he never actually attacked her. She second guessed herself until the aforementioned woman went missing weeks later, and then more disappeared afterward.

Had she gone to the police once she realized what was happening, she could have filed a report including a description of him, the car, and what they talked about. Ted said later that he *missed one* (like fish or game) when she got spooked and left. He berated himself because he had told her he was a law student working in Olympia for the government, which he was at that time. I wonder if he spilled personal information about himself because he liked to talk about himself, had a grandiose sense of entitlement, and he was certain the women would never live to tell about it.

As far as anyone knew during his reign of terror, Ted attacked women he did not know, but that was not always the case. Ted didn't stumble across

Susan Rancort the day he abducted her. He had been visiting a friend in Ellensburg and participated in an early morning running group in which Susan was a member. He *stalked* her in that way. He knew her activities, and his being a familiar friendly face would not have alarmed her when he did approach.

Linda Ann Healy was in three of Ted's psychology classes and they shopped at the same Safeway. One set of check-out receipts show him checking out behind her in the same line. His fellow student could have very possibly recognized his face from class and said hello to him in the grocery line.

To the casual observer, these women did not seem connected to him in any way. However, he often knew all about them and stalked them for days, if not weeks, so that he knew their routines. Yes, he was that creepy. Psychopaths often have a sinister list of well-researched individuals, and when the planets line up, it's game on. This might have seemed like a change in M.O. for Ted, but part of the reason why he was undetectable was because he would deliberately vary his mode of operation and signature (Killing Habits). Polishing his methodology and altering it at times to throw us all off, he was able to remain well concealed. I'm sure he was quite pleased with himself for that.

What do we do with this information?

First of all, we need to know our own biases and how we are blinded by them. If Ted had been sketchy looking or less groomed in appearance, if people knew that he was chronically unemployed, or that he had an expunged criminal record, we would have more easily recognized him as the distorted human that he was and women would not have been as likely to trust him. They would have been more wary. But he presented the opposite of all that and, as the cherry on top, he presented the coveted position of *law student*. He carried the law student persona all the way through death row by "helping" other inmates with their cases.

Even when you knew he was a killer, you could not tell he was a killer. A pleasant head tilt suggesting friendliness, sort of when a kitten or puppy looks at you like that. When he appeared in court wearing that ridiculous bow tie, I disgustedly thought, *Oh, please. We are supposed to be impressed with that?* It was like wearing a chef hat when fixing a sandwich.

Had it not been for our biases, Bundy might have been investigated sooner. Had he not mastered the art of portraying a dazzler when he chose to, we would have given him a more critical second look. His foundation, as it turned out, was more crumbled than it looked. It is interesting that, on close inspection, Mr. Up and Coming did not stay with any employment for long.

He dropped out of Law School after a few semesters without finishing his final exams. He dabbled for one or two semesters at different schools without accomplishing requirements or turning up much for class. He did stay with his Bachelor's of Psychology diligently and graduated with distinction from the University of Washington. But how he was using that education with distinction is now infamous.

His employment background was scattered and brief, with many various and sundry jobs for the short term. Ted was fruitless when it came to professional productivity, but there was a method to his madness. When he worked for the shoe store, he stole shoes. When he worked for the medical supply company, he stole crutches, surgical gloves, and plaster of Paris. And a speculum. A speculum for the uninitiated is the very private instrument used for examining the feminine vaginal canal and cervix. It is made of metal, or sometimes plastic these days, and looks like a huge duck's beak. Like dental instruments, it is something we do not want to see, much less think about or submit ourselves to.

The first Seattle crime *for which he was known* was sneaking into a woman's apartment and viciously brutalizing her. When a profiler is investigating a crime, the number of times the victim is shot, stabbed, etcetera is meaningful for profiling the attacker. When a person is stabbed 10, 20, 40, 50 or more times, it is considered 'overkill'. In this case, Ted first used a metal bar from her bed frame to *fracture* her skull. She suffered 50% hearing loss, 40% vision loss, and she had to learn to walk again. Then with the stolen speculum he attacked her womanhood.. Ted pulverized her reproductive organs into uselessness, and he even split her bladder and GI tract. Then he left her to die.

Overkill.

Thankfully she lived. When she woke up out of her coma several days later, her sweet dad was there. She asked what happened and he said, "Honey, you got a little bump on the head." A dad should never have to figure out what to say to his beloved daughter in a situation like that.

Later he was hired for the Seattle Crime Commission *by a psychiatrist,* who was later as astounded about his behavior as the rest of us. Ted's job there was to gather information regarding clue detection and the conduction of rape crimes investigation. He was always learning on the job. *Ted never left clues.* He knew how to do that thanks to the information for which he was paid to glean from crime scenes. He really liked learning and shopping on the job for *his own benefit.* I think he was smug about it. Learning and stealing from the job was fundamental for Ted. When he had a job that is.

While working with Ann Rule, an author of crime books and articles, at a Crisis Call Center, he portrayed the foundational marvelous guy involved with his parents and siblings. At the same time, Anne thought he was taking urgent calls and saving people's lives. Meanwhile, undetected Ted was also making obscene phone calls to coworkers.

Coworkers at Harborview Medical Center Psychiatric Unit described Ted as showing up only when he wanted to, and being rude and dismissive to patients who he referred to as "Schizos." He was also accused of stealing patient's charts. For stalking purposes? They fired him. Why he took the job in the first place was possibly for more access to vulnerable women to put on his mental list for future possibilities.

The yacht club where Ted was a busboy fired him after they discovered he would take desserts and put them in his locker. He worked at Safeway for a bit, then went home one day and never went back. When one of his housemates found out he was applying for a position with a political campaign, she called the campaign headquarters and *warned them* that he was an odd one, a sneak, and a bit crooked. They hired him anyway. That's politics. While working with them, he attended and recorded the opponent's speeches so his party would know what issue arguments to counter with. He was on the news for that too, smiling, laughing, looking all sheepish and innocuous.

Ted was always on the job of seeing what others had to offer. A house-mate who often loaned him her car said he would be gone until three or four o'clock in the morning with no explanation. After his own housing rental arrangement fizzled, he went knocking door to door asking if the homeowners knew of any rentals available. An elderly couple took in Mr. Humble, Poor, Starving Law Student, and he enjoyed their gracious charity for some months.

Ted was not at all impressive if anyone looked close, and few were close enough to look close. He showed up when he showed up, but he was always well groomed, articulate, and shining his orbital charm. He would leach from those around him, but go above and beyond while people were watching. Our assumptions and biases dummy us up. Too often we dismiss the red flags, much like Louise(!) saying that he meant no harm; he was just humble, shy, helpless, poor little Ted.

Until he wore out his mask, he was undetectable most of the time. *Hello, I'm Detective Wonderful trying to help you. Hello, I'm Mr. Injured, can you help me?* I would have fallen for those ruses, too. Being helpful at heart, I would have wanted to assist, especially if the guy was cute and seemed harmless.

When he was on the lam in Florida after some years in prison, Ted finally looked like who he was. One evening, a group of women from Florida State University were enjoying their time together in a nightclub near their sorority. Up against the wall was a sallow, staring man. He asked one of them to dance. She whispered to one of her companions, "Look at this guy I'm going to dance with. He looks like an ex-con." Yes he was, and he had already been watching them, learning where they lived and what their routines were.

Several hours later, he attacked the sleeping women at the nearby Chi Omega sorority. Then several blocks away, he snuck in and bludgeoned another female student. His last murder that we know for sure about did not require any charm either. He left the stolen white van running in the middle of the street with cars accumulating behind it and ran into a school yard, grabbing a 6th grade girl and pushing her into the vehicle. An onlooker assumed Bundy was an angry parent.

"Where do you think you're going?"

~Ted

No special skills were required for any of that, just bloody greed. Photos of him on Florida Death Row show him as the ragged soul he really was. There was no mistaking him for Mr. Nice Guy now.

Various individuals that were in close contact in the prison interview rooms said that Ted would undergo a personality shift like we heard regarding the raft trip. There were times when he didn't even *try* to conceal himself. An acquaintance of mine worked in the Dean's Office at the University of Washington during the time Ted was home on bail from Colorado. She said he wanted to be able to use the library. He was forbidden, and his eyes went black. Our pupils dilate huge when we are perceiving a threat in order to take everything in. The adrenaline can cause the pupil to almost overtake the iris. Our eyes can be rather kaleidoscopic, changing depth of color depending on our mood. Ted's eyes were either blue or black. Bundy, at times, would also emit a smell when his mood would shift, as noted by interviewers.

Had he only presented to all the girls *that* way. Some near Misses said there was something really creepy about his eyes. They are windows to the soul if we get close enough.

My own instinct spoke up in an olfactory sense once when I was in an appointment with a handsome adult kid, much like Bundy in the way that his self description was *poor me, but look how great I am and my plans are, except for this . . . and I was almost going to accomplish this except for that . . .* As my patient talked about himself, I became uneasy and was surprised by an ammonia-like smell coming from me. I had heard dogs can smell fear, after all, they can smell cancer and diabetes can't they? I wondered, *am I oozing fear?* I excused myself, left the room, and called my husband. When he arrived, they greeted each other because the patient happened to have worked at my husband's place of employment for a while. They had a "Hi, how ya doin? It's been a while. Whatcha up to these days?" kind of conversation as my husband escorted him out the door.

Remember, there are all different levels and goals of psychopaths. My guess is that my patient would have tried to get financing from me for his "really great ideas" that he would in turn abandon because *nothing was going right, people were letting me down.* At the time I couldn't help but have a heart for him, but my body told me differently.

Had Ted's prey been the elderly, or prostitutes, or homeless women, we still would have found it startling that it was him. This seemingly solid appearance was observed on the outside, but inside, he was an unattached human who saw the world with murderous entitlement. Look at any of his pictures taken before Chi Omega. Can you see who we now know he was? No. Remember, it's the behaviors we observe when they think no one is watching that tell us. The face these people present publicly is a mask. If they are trying to convince you into something that takes you out of your comfort zone, beware.

Bundy said he sat himself down one night and decided that the image he wanted to *sell* to the public was aloof, arrogant, and intelligent. It seems to me that instead of arrogance he would have wanted confidence, but arrogance was all he could come up with given his limited understanding of what makes up a healthy personality.

Chapter Twenty Two

Baby Boys Gone Bad

. . . what do you want to be when you grow up?

Gary Ridgeway

Gary Ridgeway, a small, ordinary looking man responsible for the murders of nearly 20 years worth of women, was a bit unexpected when he walked into the courtroom for arraignment in his orange jail suit. The fact that his prey were prostitutes and runaways did not slow the Seattle law enforcement investigations. They doggedly tracked the Green River Killer for almost two decades. He had been arrested for soliciting a prostitute early in his murder career. They hauled him in and found no criminal record apart from this incident, so he was released.

Fortunately at the time of that arrest, they took saliva samples before releasing him and put the evidence on ice as they say. Science finally caught up with the spit, and his DNA exposed him. When accused of his crimes after the DNA tests, Wary Gary tossed his head and said that it didn't prove anything because he left semen in lots of prostitutes. Looking closer, detectives noticed paint debris on one of the bodies and had it analyzed. Bingo! It matched paint splatters on his work coveralls and that slam dunked him into conviction.

We were all surprised that this bland, long-term employed, religious, married, nobody of a man and *father* was the one who evaded detection for *all those years*. He was not impressively obvious as a successful serial killer due to his ordinariness, small stature, and IQ in the low 80's.

Biases get the best of us every time. Gary's childhood was warped by his mother hand washing his genitals "because" he was a bedwetter until age 13. To my way of thinking, that is enough to explain his disgust of women. He started to act out his frustrated rage as a youngster by committing arson and torturing animals; for example, killing a cat by trapping it in a freezer. He then moved on to the prototypes of his rage—women who, in his mind, represented his lecherous mother. He was painfully aware of his limited intelligence and like Ted felt that his only way of *excelling* above others was by committing crimes that no other killer could match.

Charles Manson

Unattached and absolutely crazy Charles Manson was visibly emotionally detached and dangerous. No one ever questioned that. His prostitute mother, when arrested, left him to whatever family could help. Due to the adversarial behavior he had already assimilated in the Red Light District and the fact that his relatives weren't exactly child psychologists, they were unable to effectively parent him. His hyper-religious aunt was no help, and his uncle dressed him like a girl and beat him. He was in and out of juvenile facilities all of his youth and then in and out of prison during adulthood.

No bonding or attachment with that little boy occurred in any way, shape, or form. Charles was a small boy who grew to be a diminutive man. At first, he was absolutely desperate to be in control for his own safety and survival purposes. Remember, the organism does what makes the organism successful, and he developed his rapid nonsensical rants because people would just give up when they were unable to argue or persuade him with logic.

Like Ted, Manson eventually became his own Sun, drawing hippie men and girls (mostly girls) to him and impressing them with his disconnected monologue salad. To them, his rants possibly seemed like wisdom beyond their grasp. He certainly would have made them believe that.

The reasoning abilities of Manson's followers were seriously impaired further since he kept them stoned on pot, LSD, and who knows what else in order to brainwash them. He was safe in his own kingdom of a personally manufactured family where he was worshiped by devotedly brainwashed subjects. Little Charlie was finally in complete control, and his followers were willing to do whatever he suggested, all the while thinking it was *their* idea. Remember identification with the aggressor and Stockholm syndrome. That is what Charlie accomplished with those young adults.

Ed Kemper

Next, let's get reacquainted with Edmund Kemper. For all of his childhood and early adolescence, Ed's mother Clarnell berated and harped at him for being a boy, looking like his father, and being so big. He was 6'4" by the age of 14, as if he could have helped that. After a decade of Clarnell's vicious haranguing, Ed's father left when he was nine. The boy didn't get to go with his father so was forced to live with his vicious mother and his two sisters.

His destructive acts got off to an early start when, as children, Ed dismembered his sister's dolls and played "gas chamber" with them. As siblings do, they likely sparred, and the girls would have been conditioned by their mother's behavior to think less of Edmund and to tell on him for his bizarre behavior. Certainly he resented that, and his behavior increasingly illustrated that resentment.

Regardless of any genetic slant toward psychopathy, I believe Clarnell's actions pushed him the rest of the way. His mother moved his room to the dark basement, where he slept in a sleeping bag on a cot. There was a bare lightbulb hanging from the ceiling. The basement was frequented by rats, and at times his mother would lock him down there because she was certain he would do something awful to his sisters. She read him right; he may have been entertaining such ideas by that time.

Ed's dad did absolutely nothing to protect his son. His father worked as an electrician at a nuclear facility and said the risk of exposing himself to nuclear disaster was easier for him to bear each day than living with his former wife, Clarnell. *Yet he left his son there with her.* Thanks, Dad.

Remember, it is repeated rejection that berates the disturbed person's identity and brings about human detachment and revenge-seeking rationalizations, especially if they are cursed with a genetic vulnerability to begin with. His father, having abandoned his family, married a somewhat glamorous woman. I wonder if Ed's dad thought Clarnell was glamorous at first. Behaviorally speaking, Clarnell may have love bombed the father at first and then turned on him once he was in her net. The second woman seemed to have ruled the father's roost as well, but that is another study.

At 14 years of age, Edmund, abandoned and abused, ran away from Carnell. His [already] 6' 4," 200 lb self appeared on his father's doorstep, hoping he would give his son refuge from Carnell's tortuous behavior. After 14 years with atomic hazard Clarnell, young Ed was already pretty well seared off emotionally. To make things worse, he arrived at his father's house to find his father had a new family. While staying with them, he kept staring at his stepmother, creeping her out. Remember the narcopath stare. They cannot stop looking at and obsessing about what they cannot have. His stepmother, being unnerved by Ed, prevailed upon his father to get rid of the giant youngster. His father took Ed to "visit" his grandparents on Christmas day and left him there.

Before long, Ed murdered both of his grandparents. He said later that he shot his grandmother to see if he would feel something. Ed then shot his grandfather because he didn't want to upset him when he saw the dead grandmother. Ed called his mother to tell her what he had done, and she told him to turn himself in. He did. Robotic, no? He was incorrectly diagnosed with paranoid schizophrenia and sentenced to a hospital for insane juveniles. Lovely. He remained there from the age of 15 until he was 21.

During young Ed's psychiatric hospitalization, he assisted psychiatrists by passing out and grading psychological tests for other inmates. Although a teenager, because he was so intelligent with an estimated IQ of 147, the psychiatrists were open to his input. He was very polite and helpful, and by the time he was 21 years old, they released him from custody convinced he would not be a danger to himself or others. They even expunged the double murder of his grandparents from his record. During a visit from his parole officer who documented that Ed was doing well and was not a danger to others, Kemper had a girl's head in his backpack. I think we need to rethink expunged records.

After his release, he began killing college coeds. He said his mother, who worked at the local university in Santa Barbara, always told him no intelligent woman would ever want him. By the time he was released from the psychiatric hospital, making any social connections with peers, especially women, felt hopeless to Kemper. He felt the only way to possess a woman would be if she were dead and, unlike his mother, silent. Before he killed his grandparents, a school mate suggested Ed kiss his teacher. His answer was along the lines of "I'd have to kill her first."

Ed had no hope that he could ever receive voluntary affection from a woman. Upon release from the mental facility, he moved back in with his mother *against* the firm recommendations of his psychiatrists. Where else was this [gigantic] *socially dwarfed* kid of 21 going to go? Even though he was extremely bright and articulate, Ed had no perceivable way of charting his own social and relational course.

Ed ended his co-ed murder spree by finally killing his mother, the original object of his rage. His last straw reaction was triggered when Clarnell had come home from a night out and was in her bed reading a romance novel. She had said many times that because of him, she would never be able to have a relationship with a man, and she said the same thing to him that night. Then she said, "Now I suppose you want to stay up and talk all night."

We all have insufferable aspects of our personalities. Ed was a concepts conversationalist and could explore ideas for as long as his discussion companion participated. Many of us would be intrigued by his knowledge and ability to compare and contrast ideas.

Clarnell, however, wasn't interested in her son and may not have been bright enough to keep up with his ideas anyway. Evidently she would tolerate and participate with him at times, but other times not. Once again, this time she cut him off. She just did not have any interest in him and therefore none in his interests. Oftentimes his intellectual reveries were more than she felt she could bear and when that was the case, it sounds like she was not merciful about it.

Ed had decided a week earlier that he would have to kill his mother in order to stop his murder spree, or at least he told himself that. He did kill her that night and subsequently turned himself in.

I sometimes wonder if, once released from custody at age 21 and sent back out into the real world, Ed realized he had nowhere to go. Aware that it was just a matter of time before he got caught, he decided he fit best in a psychiatric hospital setting where he felt useful. He referred to turning himself in as deciding to *"come in out of the cold."*

He has remained in custody since that day, a life sentence without parole, and is once again a model prisoner. Kemper even narrates audiobooks like *Flowers in the Attic, Petals on the Wind*, and *Star Wars*.

Jeffrey Dahmer

Jeffrey Dahmer's beginnings are intriguing to me. His mother, according to Jeff's father, was mentally ill, not wanting to comfort Jeffrey when he was a baby fearing she would contract a disease. She was treated with tranquilizers for this anxiety. I believe, however, that she was mainly experiencing postpartum depression, which can be a medical emergency. Tranquilizers might have soothed her anxiety some but would not have fully ameliorated depression symptoms. Sleeping pills would not have treated depression either, so as far as depression goes, she would have had to wait for the ability to come out of it on her own. If she ever did make it out, it must have cycled around again because we do know she attempted suicide at least once when Jeff was a boy.

Being home alone with a baby much of the time with the father loosely involved due to his work and study would have been difficult for Jeff's mother. It would have prevented bonding between the mother and her baby. I would *so* like to have a conversation at the dining room table with her as to what experiences with baby Jeffrey were like for her and how her symptoms were influenced by him.

These young men had a bewildering lack of identity and sense of insignificance. I wonder if Jeffrey was on the autism spectrum. If so, he would have needed even more consideration as a kid. He was sidelined at school, and his lack of being emotionally successful with others would have likely been picked up on today with our new understanding of the spectrum. It makes me think of Jeffrey Dahmer when at school, flipping out and faking a seizure or other bizarre behavior that came to be referred to as 'doing a Dahmer.' That didn't win young Jeffrey any friends.

His father Lionel does not strike me as overly warm, which an autistic child would not require anyway, so I don't see that itself as a factor of concern. Jeff's mother was seemingly overburdened and mentally fragile, so she likely wouldn't have noticed anything unusual in her son's behavior. In that period of time, autism was not frequently recognized, diagnosed, and tended carefully as it is today. Whatever degree Jeff was on the autism spectrum, he may have been guided in a socially useful way had he been born in the 2020's. His intrigue with dead animals, entrails, and chemicals could have been channeled in a variety of directions. But no one knew that then.

With the understanding we have today, Jeffrey's natural propensities could have been channeled for developing healthy, useful interests. For example, he could have become a cook, a butcher, or a taxidermist.

In our current culture, his homosexuality would not have had to be secretive. If Jeff as a youngster was displaying homosexual tendencies, that would have also presented a problem socially in the '60s and '70s, especially depending on how his family perceived homosexuality. Jeff's sexual identity was surely thwarted culturally, but it could have been within his family as well. This subject is not anything that has been addressed by Jeff's parents in memoirs or interviews that I know of. Lionel gave Jeff books about Creation Theory when Jeff was in prison that Jeff seemed to take to heart. Creation Theory subject matter is meaningful to evangelical church leanings, which suggests to me that Lionel may have been concerned about Jeff's homosexuality.

Whether or not the spectrum child was unable to tolerate being thwarted because of his sexual preferences, we know plenty about the other situations that led to his outcome. Jeffrey would have been absolutely rattled by the parental arguing, overdose attempts, separation, and uncertain living situations that the family *has* discussed publicly.

John Wayne Gacy

John Wayne Gacy had an apparently solid foundation. He was a plump, outgoing, Citizenship Award holding community pillar who by all public awareness was attached to the humanity around him. Publicly, he was boastfully proud of himself, promoting his privately owned construction and designing company.

Gacy participated in many community events and cheerfully visited children's hospitals costumed as Pogo the Clown. Gacy, given his position in the community, even had his picture taken with First Lady Rosalind Carter at a fundraiser. I suppose she cringed later when watching the news like all of us who were oblivious to his activities.

His detached upbringing began with his domineering, degrading father that felt young John was a sissy since he wasn't athletic and "manly." His father beat and tormented him, accusing him of being homosexual. That was in fact correct, but John held that secret through all his developmental years of rejection and abuse. Years later, John's sister, told the public how their father treated John.

Gacy started out adulthood as a married assumed heterosexual male. After being arrested for sodomy, however, the secret was exposed and his wife divorced him. He was sentenced to 10 years in prison but was released after 18 months for being a model prisoner. I repeat, being a model prisoner is no guarantee that the person is safe.

He married again but covertly continued his homosexual activities. In order to keep his secret under radar, Gacy murdered the young men he lured to his house, raped and then buried one after another after another in his basement and other places on his property.

His new "companions" were permanently possessed by him beneath his feet, and no one was the wiser. His wife divorced him due to the horrible smell in the house that he refused to remedy. Eventually Gacy was caught, absolutely shocking everyone that knew him because he had established and maintained such a great foundation.

Foundations served some of these guys well. Except in Manson's case of course. There was no disguise mistaking Charlie, and no foundation there either. The others we are looking at learned early to build an "acceptable, if not admirable," platform from which to survive and prey upon the weak.

If you ever want to go to a costume party as a serial killer, dress Friday casual in clean jeans or dockers, a cotton shirt or a flannel, tidy tennis shoes or oxfords, and be quietly polite. You probably won't win the Best Costume contest because people will not see the monster–which is the point I am trying to make. Nevertheless, if your name tag reads Serial Killer, you just might win.

When the developmental histories of these men were researched, the common factors besides the Big 5 (bedwetting, torturing small living things, arson, stealing, and destroying property) were the interrupted bonding and pervasive rejections we have discussed at length. Both factors create ultimate emotional detachment which in turn *brings about the big 5.*

Notice the many commonalities between these killers and Ted. As children, they were all helpless in the care of the adults that shaped or, unfortunately, misshaped them into deadly individuals. People often asked, regarding these misfortunate souls, "But didn't they at least love their spouse? Didn't they love their family?" Yes and no. It was not a love they experienced. It was more akin to loving the wellbeing of what they saw as an extension of themselves. They loved them like a prize possession, like a set of golf clubs or a boat or a motorcycle, of which they are proud, protective, and preserve *for themselves to utilize.*

They learn early not to trust others emotionally, not to trust enough to love vulnerably. Rather than remember their own terrifying vulnerability, the serial killer manipulates, possesses, and destroys those they resent in order for them to feel absolutely in charge of others. This outcome is complex, disturbing, and unavoidably permanent.

Again, the killer obsesses over what they cannot have. For Bundy, his obsession was the possession of a smart beautiful woman and personal significance. For Kemper, it was the same. For Gacy, it was the desire for significance as well as possession of a homosexual companion. For Manson, his distorted obsession was fame and to create a devoted family. Each man plied his craft of deception to obtain his originally unobtained desires. At least that was the goal. When accomplishing a project, in their mind it was an "I Dominated, I Win."

Since their prey were objectified symbols of the origins of their rage, they compulsively killed said objects in order to have the complete and permanent control they were originally denied. Bundy said the killer in him took out the inner turmoil he felt on the "objects" he obtained.

In the public's impressions, when it came to bright, smart, popular, upcoming leader Ted Bundy, the perception of him as a hunter took quite a while to clarify. Once law enforcement got a true impression of him, they were on it, but it was still unbelievable to many right up until his confessions. His supporters were stunned because they thought they knew Ted. Well, they knew a *version* of Ted. No serial killer is going to act like a murderer when they are with you, well, unless it's your turn. If it is your turn, they will be convinced that *you* deserve it and so they deal with you accordingly, and will *relish* doing so. For some serial killers, it is like killing exotic game.

Ted was quoted by Michaud and Aynesworth as saying, "Society wants to believe it can identify evil people, or bad or harmful people, but it's not practical. The thing is, that *some people are just psychologically less ready for failure than others.*"

Chapter Twenty Three

But for the Grace

. . . *Some Near Misses*

This collection is of women I personally know who escaped or managed to avoid predators. Carol DaRonch made headlines with her escape; these women did not.

Marcia

In her own words:

I felt I must get to the hospital before visiting hours ended to spend as much time as I could with my boyfriend, Greg. He was in the Harborview Burn Unit with damage to 30% of his skin from an acetone fire at work. I was riding the bus back from visiting my sister overnight near Tacoma. The bus ran along highway 99 south of Seattle at that time, in 1977. I wanted to be sure to get there on time because poor Greg, I thought, was estranged from his family and really needed my support. Sure, he seemed to have mental health issues, but nothing I could not deal with. I was often depressed myself. As that spring and summer went on, however, I realized his problems were way worse than mine. I discovered that he was . . . [smoking] lots of hash. When he got out of the hospital he hit up every pharmacy he could with his opioid prescriptions. But that is a whole other story.

At any rate, I was in a hurry to get to the hospital, so when the bus broke down and it was announced that it would take a couple of hours to get a new bus there or get it fixed, I decided to stick my thumb out on the highway. So, there I was, a teenage girl, long flowing hair, braless, in a skirt and sandals, waiting for whoever would take me closest to the hospital. I did not need to wait long. A guy in his early 20's in a well-maintained classic car pulled over, leaned over, and opened the door for me. I told him where I needed to be and he said, "Climb in," so I did.

You might be wondering, possibly harshly, why a young gal like me would be willing to take this risk. And why would I for a guy like Greg? Like many girls, I had been taught to "be nice" no matter what.

When I was about 3 years old I had a "boyfriend." My oldest sisters were 11 and 13 years older than me. They would have their friends over to the house for games and dance parties. One of the guys took a special liking to me. I would sit on his shoulders as the teens sat on the floor gathered around a game board. He doted on me, and would tickle my feet and kiss the soles. I would giggle and wriggle delightedly. I have no idea how long this went on, but everyone called me his little girlfriend. Suddenly, one day I refused to see him. I hid in my room. My older sister came to get me, saying he wanted to see me. I screamed and cried and held on to the bedpost when she tried to drag me out to see him. She told me I was stupid not to come. As often happens, my brain blocked the traumatic memory, but years later I remembered the event that caused this complete change in my attitude toward him. He had snuck me out to the garage and into a storage closet where he raped me anally, my head repeatedly banging into the wall.

It goes without saying, but I'm going to say it anyway. Marcia's preschool age experience was so unfair and painfully overlooked by the group surrounding her, well meaning though they were.

In monkey terms, they needed to pluck that lousy teen out of there, but they did not know he was so dangerous.

This is a good time to talk about grooming. With the term, you may get the mental image of chimps that comb through each other's fur to clean and remove parasites. Grooming between humans is when someone goes out of their way to be extra nice to you. It might come in the form of a coworker grooming you to be prepared for a job promotion or a coach preparing an athlete for competition. We love grooming because it's flattering and reassuring to have someone paying personal unrequested attention to us. Flattery does two things. Feeling flattered, we automatically want to bask a bit in their presence, and as they continue to hopefully add more nice comments, we feel a bit indebted to them. Or the attention increases our trust and sense of safety with them, which is what happened with 3 year old Marcia.

For the church going reader, I recommend you grab your concordance and look up every reference to the flatterer or flattery. Like charm, flattery is not your friend. Ted said he didn't like solicitous people, perhaps because that was one of his tricks and he knew what was possibly behind it.

Marcia refusing to go near her assailant was not understood by her sister. In a kinder world, Marcia would have felt safe telling what had happened even if she had been threatened. Kids can deal with and recover from just about anything as long as they are believed and feel justified. Supporting and affirming the child about what has happened does wonders. They should know that was not fair, they did NOT deserve that, and that we will see to it that the perpetrator is held accountable for what he did. We must follow through and support the youngster even if their accusation has not been proven. Too often, it cannot be proven, but that does not mean the child lied.

Marcia continues:

Some people may wonder why no one else realized this happened. For one thing, I suspect he threatened something to keep me quiet. For another thing, I lived in a big house with a big, busy family with six kids, and one was younger than me. Whatever was going on with me was never a priority. I just had to deal with it. But, believe me, I got the message that #1, I had to comply with the request of the male, #2, I was stupid if I didn't, and #3, my feelings were not important to others. These messages were reinforced by my father's behaviors over the years, too. He molested women, young and old, and treated my mother poorly. He tended to treat women as objects. As a result of the pain I was in, I learned to eat like crazy for comfort, which helped me hide from possible unwanted fondling from men. I became an obese child (unfortunate, especially because then I became the target of all sorts of harassment for years).

I remember once, when I had slimmed down at age 14 or 15, my parents had a party at our house with a bunch of my father's long-time work friends from GE. As I came down the stairs in a cute plaid miniskirt, a man leaned over to my father and asked if that was me. My father nodded and the guy said, loudly enough for me to hear, "Well, she certainly has become quite the prick tease." My father nodded and chuckled in agreement. That is the sort of anti-self-esteem training I had growing up.

> *It's common for someone that has been brutalized to lose self confidence. The remarks from trusted people around Marcia reinforced her impression of having deserved what had happened to her. They made her feel as though she did not have the acuity to easily discern mal-intent or use her self-protective instincts.*
>
> *This example of family collusion coupled with fear of punishment can settle deeply into an individual that has been traumatized by a loved one. We can have a desire to please so as to not be left behind or punished. Thinking back on Marcia's introduction to relationships, it makes sense, no?*

Marcia continues:

So, back to 1977. I climbed into the guy's car but felt uncomfortable the minute I got in. I broke into a nervous sweat. Something felt very wrong. The guy didn't look very bright, but I thought I should not judge him by that. I wanted to get out but wanted to be polite. Maybe it was the way he looked at me, I am not sure, but I immediately wished I had noted the license plate number and was feeling sick to my stomach. We drove about 20 to 25 minutes with little talk. When we got to Capitol Hill, I asked him to drop me off at a friend's house to pick something up. He said it was no problem. When we got closer it occurred to me briefly to have him drop me at a well-traveled intersection with a stoplight, but I changed my mind so I could save time.

I hopped out fast when we got to my friend's place, walked quickly to the door, and knocked. Silence. I tried the door handle and it was not locked, so I went in and locked the door. I called for my friend, but no one was home. I figured the guy had driven away, but I peeked out the window and saw that he was there, staring at the door. I worried that other doors might be unlocked too. Then I noticed he was getting out of the car. I briefly thought of getting a knife, and even went to the kitchen to check for one. I heard him knock on the door and decided against the knife (he could probably use it against me if it came to that . . .). To be "polite," I went to the door and opened it a bit. He asked to use the bathroom. I hesitated, and then he pushed his way in through the door. He immediately grabbed me, knocking me up against the wall and down the hallway . . . He threw me to the floor, knocking the air out of my lungs. Then he hit me and started to rape me.

Oddly, I decided I was not going to act scared. My thinking was that if I could make a blank face and start asking him questions, he might rethink what he was doing and I might be safe. I started asking him things like, "Don't you have a girlfriend?" [Yes.] "How would she feel about this?" [Ummmm.] "Do you live with your girlfriend?" [Yes.] "Where do you live?" [On my mother's property.] I was interviewing him, basically. He would get mad and continue his assault, but then try to answer me, then get mad again . . . Eventually he went flaccid.

Right about then my friend's 9-year-old son came home, looked down the hallway and saw what was happening. I cried out to the boy to get help, he ran one way (to get help?) ... [The man] leaped up, zipped up, and ran off. I am pretty sure I spent at least the next hour crying, shivering, babbling, and pacing the house, up and down the stairs. Eventually, my friend's husband got home with his buddy and they took care of me, wrapping me in a blanket and calling the police. The police weren't much help. With no license plate number, rough description of the car, and bland description of the guy, they said there was little they could do. It did not help me at all that when my girlfriend arrived, she was not sympathetic. She seemed to think I was just trying to get attention. I ended up walking to the hospital because I knew there was a little more visiting time left.

That was just about the worst thing I could have done. I tried to act normal, but I guess Greg could tell something was off, so he kept asking me about it. I finally told him what had happened. He told me that I was an idiot for getting into that guy's car. Wow! Talk about getting hit when you're down. I was crushed again.

PTSD due to sexual assault is real. The combined effect of my early life experience and this rape has been difficult to heal from. I have found many pathways and strategies over the years that have led to healing, thankfully.

But something kept plaguing me. When I first heard some details about the Green River Killer and the killings (mid-1980's?), I thought that my perpetrator could have been him. Of course I thought that was absurd, that just the coincidence of the location and timeframe was not enough to justify these thoughts. But they lingered. And no one had figured out who the GRK was ...

I shared this story and my persistent fears with one of my sisters at some point. She is deeply empathetic and a wonderful confidante. Many years later, in 2001, I got a call from this sister while I was driving through

Lynnwood. She suggested I pull over. I pulled into a strip mall parking lot. She said that they had just caught the GRK, and I should get ready for her to send me photos from the news stories. The recent pics meant little to me. That was just some middle aged man. However, when there was finally a picture of him as a young man I had a terrible jolt. Gary Ridgeway had definitely been my assailant. After the visceral shock, an immense wave of relief passed through me. Next, I felt intense gratitude for Dave Reichert, the King County Sheriff, who never gave up hunting for the Green River Killer. He is my hero.

Rachael

On Valentine's Day of 1997, Rachael and her friend, both 17 years old, went to a grocery store in Redmond, Washington to get something to eat. When the two were walking through the parking lot, out of the store came Gary Ridgeway. He was carrying roses and heading for his car.

At first glance, Rachael equated him to a random dad-type getting roses for his wife. It didn't seem to her as though he was looking for anyone.

And then he spoke.

He asked them what two beautiful girls were doing alone on Valentine's Day. Something felt off. Something about him made her hair stand up.

He had a twinkle in his eye and said something along the lines of: "If I wasn't headed home, I would take you guys out." Rachael made a comment about having to go back to school, and the twinkle instantly went away.

This incident stayed in her mind for many years.

I wonder what Ridgeway did with those roses. I am guessing he gave them to his wife and she loved him for it. Women and roses.

Cathy

Cathy's former husband went to law school with Bundy in Utah. He helped raise money for Ted's defense. A whole group of law students did not think that nice, quiet, smart, good looking Ted could be guilty of all the crimes he was accused of committing. Men typically don't pick up on this stuff quite so well because a male psychopath normally won't turn on the charm for a man or stalk him.

Cathy's friend met Ted at a church party (great trolling grounds) and he offered her a ride home. She declined by giving him some excuse. Later that night, Cathy's friend looked out her bedroom window and saw his Volkswagen Bug parked just across the street. She closed her curtains and it's not certain that she told anybody. She had no idea that he was a serial killer, but she certainly got a creepy feeling around him. When she looked out her window a little later, his car was gone.

Janet

Walking on her way to work at SeaTac one morning, Janet was approached on HWY 99 by Gary Ridgeway, who tried to give her "a ride to work." SeaTac was supposedly right on his way. She didn't know how else to describe the look in his eyes other than "glittering," and not in a good way. When she refused a couple of times, he sped off in the opposite direction. So much for "right on his way." That was the closest Janet ever came to violent crime.

She didn't think it was Ridgeway necessarily at the time but recently when she and her sister were watching a documentary about him. There was a single suspect drawing of him with longish hair. Most depictions of him when being sought for capture were short hair composites. When Janet saw this drawing with longer hair, the picture gave her the chills. THAT was the guy. Till then, she didn't really think it was him.

She did report it to the police at the time at the prompting of a coworker. Three years later, even after having moved to another city, she got a call from the Green River Task Force saying they had followed up on her tip.

Carol

As youngsters, when it came to stranger danger, we were always taught the importance of safety first when we were out and about. Back then, we freely ran all over the countryside when at our country house and all over town when at our city house. None of us ever had a near miss except me, one time, when I was 11 years old.

One day, I was walking along a country road from my house to meet a friend who lived about a mile away. The road was lined by woods on both sides. Being five miles from the nearest town, there was never much traffic along the way. While walking up a slow hill, a car came up from behind and drove by me. For some reason I took in the back of the car and still remember it today. The model was a 1960 Belair. It was white. The driver pulled into a driveway up the hill from where I was walking and came back down, driving slowly past me. He had dark hair and was wearing a white T-shirt. The hairs on the back of my neck were standing up, but my mind was clear. I had time to plan what to say if he actually stopped. Ted's method with his last girl was to leave the vehicle running in the middle of the street, jump out, and grab the child. This guy was more cautious. He passed me again, went on up the hill and again turned around in the same driveway. He headed slowly down toward me again. I knew this time he was going to stop.

My heart was pounding so hard I remember I could feel it in my eyes. His window was down, and he leaned out and asked me if I'd like to get in. I said, trying to sound angry rather than terrified, "Listen buddy, my dad's a cop and I live right up there in that house (I had no idea who lived in that house) and if I were you I'd get out of here." He replied, "Well I just thought you might want to go have a coke or something." Thanks be to God, he left. I didn't wait to see if he was really gone. I ran as hard as I could up to the house where "my Dad, the Cop" lived. In case he was still watching me, I was going to open the front door and walk right in as though I lived there. Like Carol DaRonch after she escaped from Ted. She just opened the car door of an elderly couple's vehicle and jumped in with them.

When I got to the house, the door was locked. I banged on the door and thought, well if I really lived here, I wouldn't bang on the front door. I'd run around back. So I did. That door was locked, too. Nobody was home. I was supposed to meet my friend on the road, and we were planning to walk together back to my house. I didn't want to miss her and was afraid he, the driver, had approached her. I didn't know whether to keep walking to meet her or run the half-mile back home. I decided to keep walking toward her. When I got back out to the road, I could see her coming and ran to her. We walked back to my house watching every car that happened by, looking to see if it was by chance him again. I don't remember if we had a plan for what to do if he returned and stopped again.

The driver never came back, and when we got to my house, I frantically told Gramma what had happened. I asked her if we should call the police. Gramma said no because he didn't really do anything. That being settled, something else was on my mind. We were Catholic at the time, so I was really worried about the three lies I had told the guy.

1. I had indicated I had a dad. I didn't have a dad.

2. Because I didn't have a dad, he certainly wasn't a cop.

3. I didn't live in that house.

Gramma opined that under the circumstances, telling the lies was necessary and probably saved me from something awful. She added that I should probably tell the priest at my next confession just the same.

So I did. I was almost as nervous giving my confession as I was when experiencing the situation itself, eyes pounding and all, but bless him, he said the same things Gramma had. He did admonish me, however, that it would not have been okay to lie had it been a safe situation.

For penance he gave me two Our Father's and three Hail Mary's. Usually he gave me two Our Father's, five Hail Mary's, and one Act of Contrition, so I lucked out. I was never, before or after that day, so relieved to do penance.

Laura

Laura was unable to sleep one night and so decided to go out for a run with her big, gruff, barking dog near her home in Murray, Utah, the city where Carol DaRonch escaped Ted's grip.

While out running through the park, a car pulled up and she slowed her pace. Her dog went running ahead. The driver was a nice looking, dark haired man who was very well dressed. He asked for directions, opening the passenger door for her to look in at the map he was holding close to himself.

She leaned in to see, and when she did, he grabbed her shirt to pull her the rest of the way in. The fight was on. Laura was able to struggle free, leaving her shirt behind, but he came out of the car after her. He tackled her to the pavement and her hands were bloody from fighting with him. The dog finally showed up, barking like crazy.

Her assailant, our very own Ted Bundy, quickly got into his car and fled. I wonder what Ted thought about the blood she got on his nice clothes.

Laura did not report the incident either because he was not successful.

When in doubt, report.

Debbie

"When I was a teenager in New Jersey, I was hitchhiking and a guy in a station wagon picked me up. He kept giving me very weird vibes with his questions and talk. I looked in the back of the car and it was crammed with fishing poles and gear. I was street smart but very naive sexually. He asked me if I wanted to make some money and I didn't know what he meant. He then shoved my face in his lap as he was driving and continued his 'routine.' I ended up jumping out of the car while going 35-40 mph and another person saw me jump, turned around, and pulled over to bring me to the hospital.

"There was another time when I was hiking at Torrey Pines Park in San Diego with a girlfriend. She was quite dramatic and kept telling me there was a man following us and every time she turned around he would duck off the trail and he was naked and masturbating. He followed us to the cliff where it was high tide and we couldn't get down to the beach. It was then that I saw him and she was telling the truth! I started yelling to some imaginary people, saying, 'here we are,' and 'we're heading your way,' and other nonsense. We made our way back to the parking lot and the police were all over the place. Turns out the man had raped a young girl earlier that day. They had us identify him in a lineup. We were lucky that day!"

Carol

When I was in second grade, I was attacked by school mates when we were outside for recess. There was a random refrigerator-sized cardboard box on the playground. Two fourth grade boys teased me to get in it. I refused. First one of them got in it and came out, then the other got in it and came out. Next, they said it was my turn. *See, it's no big deal.* I got in it and they came in after me. They lifted my dress and tried to pull my underpants down. I gripped the sides of my underwear, but they tried and tried to pull them off.

Someone must have seen the cardboard box bouncing around and heard me yelling because a teacher appeared and sent us to the principal's office. I don't know what punishment they received, but for me, the principal told me to never get myself into a spot like that again. For the rest of my time in school, I did not talk to either of those boys. I was relieved when they graduated two years ahead of me. The older of the two boys was the instigator, and the younger boy went along with him. Looking back, I think the younger one might have been salvageable, but the older one was mean.

Often a psychopath will find a weaker partner to do crimes with. It gives them a sense of power and shared responsibility. Not that they would ever *admit* responsibility. They would be more inclined to shift blame entirely to the follower. Manson comes to mind here.

The weaker one would not have necessarily committed a crime if not spurred on by the stronger one and ends up where he would never have on his own.

These are only women I happen to know. There are so many more who have had such experiences and miraculously lived to tell about it. A book of Near Misses could be put to good use for educating young adults.

Near Misters

These stories will be near misses of a different kind.

Near Misters are the men I know who could have gone Ted's route but did not. Although en route for "detachment boot camp" since they were preschoolers, they each had loving people and expectations of accountability, which I believe is their saving grace.

Micah

Micah is a huge, muscled, African American gentleman who grew up in the "hood" of a large city. He was the youngest of five children raised by a single mother. Welfare and food stamps were her only means of support after the father abandoned all of them, never to be seen again. Like Louise, Miss Mary was a petite woman who didn't lay around all day watching Soap Operas. She worked at the community center making sandwiches, serving milk, and overseeing the behavior of the kids who would come there to hang out and play pool.

What seems to have differed from Ted's world is that she loved her children warmly and whooped their butts whenever necessary. Any misbehavior on Miss Mary's watch was dealt with soundly. The only butts she whipped were her own, so when at the Center, the unruly kids would be set out of the building, including Micah. He remembers peering in the window from outside watching as the other boys played pool and ate sandwiches. When Miss Mary allowed him back in the center, he behaved.

Micah says he never questioned whether his mom loved him and is still ticked that his dad ran off. They have no idea where the father is or if he is alive. He describes his family sans the father as very close. His mom comes to visit Micah and his wife regularly and freely vocalizes admonitions to their two kids. It sounds like she can't help herself, it's how she is built and is probably what saved Micah's bacon.

In his growing up years, his entire neighborhood was "really tight." They still are in communication with and care about each other. Miraculous given that he lived in a "hood" complete with Bloods and Crips who even had their own dance.

Myself having a white majority upbringing in a homogeneous country-side, I am rather naive regarding gang life other than West Side Story. Considering that, I'm sure my eyes were pretty round while we talked about life in his neighborhood. The stomping grounds were so rough that a police precinct was installed into one of the neighborhood apartments on the upper hillside of the housing cluster. The police woman that ran the station was called "Missy," and she didn't suffer young fools gladly either. Two maternal figures were the law and order in Micah's world.

Life in this neighborhood was poor and the refrigerators were often empty. Kids barely had money for food, much less clothing and school supplies, so stealing and selling items and dealing marijuana was the go to for many of the kids rather than the measly pay for paper routes and lawn mowing.

What was different about the street gangs where Micah grew up was that they were thousands of miles from LA, or NYC, or Philly, so they were less impacted by the big city criminals. The way of thinking in Micah's world was that since the kids were all from the same environment, when it boiled down to it, they would back each other like brothers. As he talked about it, I thought of football teams that trash talk and pummel each other on the field, but when it comes down to it, they call time out for each other. Micah said that's pretty much it. As mad as that sounds—except on the ball field, that is—there is a reason for the madness.

They are divided into different gangs for protection. Remember identification with the aggressor and safety in numbers. Each gang protects their "turf," their neighborhood microcosm.

Fortunately, accountability was a dominant feature in Micah's family. He could not get away with anything. His mother found a couple of guns in his room once "and she whooped my ass up the hill to the police station and turned me in." This neighborhood was different. The kids for the most part grew up different too. Although many served stints in Juvie or prison, in turn, many of them like Micah grew out of it.

Now, many men from his neighborhood are self-supporting adult citizens with families of their own. Micah even married a yoga instructor. It would be interesting to do a study similar to Gina O'Higgins work looking at the ones who turned out great and what made the difference for them. My hunch is love and accountability, neither of which Ted seemed to get nearly enough.

There was plenty of darkness in Micah's neighborhood as well. One boy, Jamey, lived in his house alone growing up after both parents had left him there. He had an adult brother who would come visit him two or three days a month, but otherwise the boy was alone. Micah said he did not come out of the house much. The kid submerged himself into running drugs and weapons and of course ended up in prison. After release, some guy hit on his girlfriend and Jamey exploded. While he was beating up the guy a friend of the person he was assaulting shot him five times in the face. Right there on the sidewalk.

As you can imagine, the girls in the neighborhood didn't fare so well, either. One girl, Lindy, was sexually molested by a male friend of one of her family members. This went on for years. Although she told her mother repeatedly, her mother didn't believe her and so did nothing to protect her daughter. While growing up, Lindy developed a behavioral habit of fastening her long shirtsleeves down over her hands, hiding them if and when she came out of the house. Micah has no idea why the girl did that. I think Lindy would have been better off with the alleged Wolf Girls of Midnapore and their family.

When she was older, Lindy killed her mother, chopped her into tiny pieces and put her bits into plastic grocery bags. Nearby children helped her put the bags into various garbage bins. I wonder if knotting her sleeves over her hands as a child was her way to keep her hands from doing something awful.

Angel

During Bundy's reign of terror that had expanded to the Southwest, Ted found himself in jail in Utah for possession of burglary tools and attempted kidnapping. He was released after many who believed in his innocence raised money to pay his bail. He then flew from Utah to Seattle where there had been no disappearances of women and girls since he had left for Utah. Although many were willing to vouch for him, even with their money, everyone else in Seattle was on edge knowing Ted was among them again.

The news media had broadcast Ted's skinny white photos, and the entire PNW was on the lookout. Police knew Ted was back in town, so they kept their eyes peeled. There were even surveillance cars following Ted when he was out and about, and occasionally he would give them the slip. Since Bundy knew he was being followed, he taunted them. He even went so far as to wave at them or strike up glib conversation. Arrogant bastard.

One night in a local music venue, one of my dance buddies, Angel, was out for an evening of dancing with his friends. Angel, being a muscled block of brown Puerto Rican courtesy, always found ladies who were happy to dance with him. Out of the blue, two police officers approached and directed the bewildered dancer through the crowd and outside for questioning.

During the inquiries and verifying of his identification, Angel was in a bit of a sweat, not knowing where this encounter was going or why. Once the officers were satisfied they could let him go, Angel asked why they had been questioning him. They told him a woman in the club had called in and reported that he was Ted Bundy.

Angel's mistaken identity is another example of how we see what we don't see and don't see what we see. At the same time, Ted was such a master of disguise we would not put it past the chameleon to be able to play himself off as Puerto Rican. Given Bundy's shapeshifting proclivities, Law Enforcement could not be overly dismissive of any reports.

Joseph

One of my friends adopted an orphaned eight month old Ethiopian baby. The newborn boy had been found when he was only days old, along with another baby, a girl, in the woods behind the police station in a village on the Horn of Africa. It was common for abandoned babies to be left among the trees behind the station, similar to our local fire department, hospitals, and police stations that offer safe haven for abandoned children. Any of these sites have a "no questions asked" policy for overwhelmed mothers who surrender the infant into their care.

He was placed in an orphanage along with eighty other babies and even more children of all ages. They named him Adem and the girl baby Eve.

They were not simply numbered which is a good start, and they were named which is a step up from the warehousing of little numerical beings. However, as with orphanages worldwide, the care-giver to infant ratio was immensely imbalanced, which means the *needs* of the children and babies were vast and largely unmet. It comes as no surprise that compassionate adults from all over the world want to rescue an infant or two from such daunting circumstances and so many couples apply to adopt. These parents are hopeful and eager to bond with and provide a good life for the infants and children in such need.

Pictures sent to my friend from the orphanage were of a very small baby boy. She became smitten online and chose to rescue him. The infant was brought to her nearby city where she received him at the airport. As with all emotionally bereft infants, he had already been in the process of giving up on ever receiving affection. Being a tough little guy, he survived well past the four month mark we read about earlier.

Upon assuming care, she was puzzled that he did not cry. He did not ever cry, in fact. He learned this behavior from getting no response when crying. He also seemed immune to pain, probably for the same reason. She says on the first night home together when she put him in his crib, he pulled his blanket up over his head and went to sleep. That was a learned behavior from always going to sleep on his own. She adored him and hoped to love and care for him out of his marooned start in life.

In spite of fifteen years of TLC, he has been in and out of juvie multiple times for aggressive behavior. She and her husband that she married when Joseph was eight years old continue to provide not only affection but also consequences, hoping to instill responsibility in the boy.

Joseph and his stepfather get along great. However, that does not keep Joseph from testing the water. When Joseph messes up, off to juvie he goes. This young man seems immune to discipline, and he is so handsome and charming that he can manipulate others successfully. Channeling his anger into sports and activities at which he can excel is not easy, but his parents keep at it. After such a searing start, any of us would pray that our love would be enough to help the boy thrive.

They have been completely forthcoming with Joseph regarding his beginnings and have told their son his entire story, so there is no confusion of betrayal among them. When collecting saliva in order to trace his DNA origins, the first words out of his mouth were: "Will this help me find my mom?" It's biology; we want to know where we came from.

A glitch in the system is that Joseph's adoptive parents divorced when he was five, so his first dad lives outside the home. Although the divorce was devastating for Joseph's older sister who was 15 at the time, his mom says it never seemed very hard on him. Once his parents divorced, his father began badmouthing his mother. Remember identification with the aggressor: when one parent teaches disrespect of the other parent, it affects the children profoundly.

His counselor describes the youngster as 60% Joseph and 40% his first dad. Another dynamic to understand is *Parental Alienation Syndrome*. It is a form of child abuse where one parent degrades the other parent. A risk factor of an absent father is *less* risk than a father who denigrates the mother or for that matter a mother who either disappears or denigrates the father. When parents vilify the other, or are downright fighting, the children are better off if the parents divorce so that there can be peace at least half the time. That's statistics.

When one of the parents is berated by the other, the child is pretty much psychically split in two and must divide loyalties. Ted had to do that at the Philadelphia house, and we know how well that turned out.

The saving grace of in-home parenting is when the adults set a responsible example for the child and delight in him. At the same time, they must also hold him accountable for any unacceptable behavior.

Bonding is crucial. When we have a child in which affectionate interchange did not occur early on or it was insufficient, causing the affiliation cord to be frayed, the child has very little to lose. Unless a child is well bonded to a caregiver early, accountability can be ineffective. So for the receiving parent of a delayed bonding child, there is much work to be done. Joseph's parents are doing their best to undo and repair whatever imprint was downloaded his first eight months before he was brought into a loving home. Not all orphans are given that opportunity. Too many of them don't stand a chance.

Eddie

Our *young,* unmarried mother became pregnant with Eddie with the whole town watching in 1947.

Unlike Louise, she braved the laundry lines right there in her small home neighborhoods. The father of her baby crossed the street when he saw them coming, but they went to the store anyway. Soon after, my mother married a good man who wholeheartedly adopted Eddie. I am told that my father adored all of us. I don't remember, but Eddie remembered. When Eddie was four and I was almost two, we were in a car accident and both of our parents were killed. Eddie had fallen asleep in the car and when he woke up, he and I were busted and bandaged up in a hospital room together, suddenly without parents. He never fell asleep in a car again. After a week or so in the hospital, relatives we had never met that lived in a different state took us home with them.

We were with our aunt and uncle and their three children for less than a month and then passed into our paternal grandparents' care. To this day, no one is sure why that transfer happened, but it did. We were somewhat burdensome, being busted up and grieving, but we were taken in by our grandparents. This extended family was our home base throughout our developmental years. Different from the free affection from our parents, Eddie was a bit hesitant about living with them. He was our unwed mother's son and try as one might, in those days there was an unavoidable cautionary element in place with bastard children. Grandmother said before we arrived, "I'll take the girl but not the boy." A judge ruled that we be kept together, so we were. Kids feel it. Eddie felt it. I felt the strain that we brought into their lives, but Eddie felt something just barely palpable in addition to that. Like something was wrong—with him.

When he learned of his illegitimacy, much later than Ted, he was almost relieved at finally knowing. When I learned of it after he had, it made sense to me as well because we sensed that unexplained crack of separation. When I was told, Eddie looked at me with bitterness on his sweet face and said, "I always knew I wasn't part of this family." As the years went by, he was always welcome to family functions but rarely showed up. Thankfully, he did stay in my world. What kept Eddie from going down a dark path was the solid love he had first from our mother and then from "our" father for his first four crucially formative years. Their affection kept his empathy and desire to connect with others intact. His little growing brain absorbed enough love and safety early on to sustain him through the many disconnects to come.

Eddie was loyal to his step-grandmother and she to him, but her dissonance was sadly there although she tried her best to hide it. During a trip to visit and meet our many aunts, uncles and cousins States away, each time we drove off from a relative's house she would ask both of us, "How would you like to live with that family?" Grandfather made her stop doing that.

Some decades later, Grandmother's priest advised her to write a letter of apology to Eddie. Penance was not something she could ignore and she wrote the letter. Eddie told me he had gotten it with that bittersweet look of his. He said he had not answered it. The day before she died, he telephoned her to say goodbye. I was with her when she got the call, she could only weakly talk so the conversation was brief. Neither of them wept.

Chapter Twenty Four

Catch Me If You Can

. . . I gotta get out of this place

Before his expulsion from the womb, Ted was already genetically vulnerable, so his release into socialization was a huge flop. He experienced failure after failure with humans, culminating in him needing to be locked up for society's safety. When it comes to the slammer, most prisoners who did the crime do the time and make no bones about it. I think for Ted, many things influenced his unrelenting compulsion for escape. For starters, his malignant narcissism certainly made him feel like he deserved better treatment than being locked up with men he considered as his "inferiors."

From the very beginning, he was handled by inadequate caregivers, 'tis true, but becoming downright arrogant and indignant about his surroundings didn't help either. He felt stuck everywhere he found himself and was itching to get out.

Elizabeth Lund Home for Unwed Mothers

Imagine being a helpless newborn abandoned for adoption, named a number, spending hour after hour, day after day, week after week imprisoned in a bassinet with excellent but *non responsive* care. If the infant could talk or even know how to organize thoughts, the communication might be,

"I'm not a pancake. Is anyone out there that cares enough to get me out of here?" That period of time did serious damage to his trust and attachment potential, which would only worsen over time. Louise did, somewhat as an afterthought, come to collect him after he had spent three months in his first introduction to rejection. As we already covered ad nauseam, these environments impact the relationally grasping infant as surely as frostbite freezes their toes. He did not need to understand what was happening for it to affect him.

What a start.

The Philadelphia house

This address consisted of an unwed mother, a mentally ill grandmother, a frightening grandfather, and two teenagers who were volleying care of and influence for the baby. Rather than the regimented aloof care at the Home, this setting for the infant was the opposite but equally as traumatic. Ever changing supervision in the turbulent household meant Ted was always met with unpredictable moods.

We all differ in our parenting perspectives, and in those first four years, Ted likely got mixed messages frequently from his various attendants. The caregivers themselves, as well as *giving* mixed messages to the little one, were certainly *getting* mixed messages from each other. Unavoidably, the individuals in the household were at an increased risk for differing opinions, thus producing arbitrary interactions with and expectations of the little guy.

For a little one sponging up his environment over which he had no control, it would have been terrifying to see, hear, or even anticipate witnessing or receiving punishment without knowing the reason why. Little children do not understand arbitrariness and trying to figure it out can be tormenting.

What's okay, what isn't? How do I know what's right or wrong? What does a relationally adapting brain do with that? In those extremely formative early years there was no way for this little boy to escape the involuntary absorption of this setting either.

If we can't escape, we do what we must to survive our environment.

If you can't beat 'em, join 'em.

We know for certain by three and a half years old, Ted had joined them. In the Philadelphia placement, he had learned at the very least how to acquiesce, charm, and form alliances in order to ensure food and safety. His antics were overlooked, or at least not addressed, and so the little boy interpreted them as okay.

SisterEleanorMotherLouise's House

About age four, he was extradited once again by Louise and they moved from Philadelphia to Tacoma. A new city, a new part of the country, *always* more unfamiliar people; he was still trapped by all of those uncomfortable realities of new people and various expectations to try to assimilate and navigate around them. In spite of Louise's outward public devotion to her son, she strikes me as an arms-length constraining parent. Just for the sake of it, read about obsessive compulsive personality (OCP). I think many of the traits describe Louise. I really wish I could have evaluated her, but I would have gotten nowhere. Her life was bolted shut. I think of a Female Warden keeping everything possible in precise order, under lock and key.

Individuals with OCP are preoccupied with rules, orderliness, and control. They tend to be strict, supremely task oriented, emotionally withholding, and morally stringent. Anyone who has someone with this personality in their world can feel simultaneously constrained and put off by them. At the very least, the person will notice that any reciprocity has to be on *the obsessive compulsive person's* terms, so we don't get much, if any, warmth from them.

According to relatives, Ted knew he had to be good in order to be accepted by his family. That is miles away from unconditional love.

Bundy described running away at the age of four because his mother expected him to take a nap and he did not want to nap. He said he was gone for about two hours, got hungry, and went home. When he told his mother what he had done, she said she hadn't noticed him being gone. More often than not, when a child tells their parents that they are going to run away, the parents actually give them permission, knowing they will not be gone long. Perhaps Louise was thinking along those lines.

Any lukewarm or cool parental framework the child is reliant upon does not leave much along the lines of emotional reinforcement. The dynamic is enigmatic: always earning, never obtaining. What does a youngster do with that? When detachment takes place in the child and longings for personal worth, identity, safety, and freedom are unmet, he has to come up with *his own* means of satisfying those cravings. Any coolness from his mother would only increase his self-reliance and need for creating his own relevance.

Escaping *non*-identity to find *significant* identity would be the genesis of Bundy's lifelong operating system. Even before his nighttime peeping, Ted said he would escape the house in the wee hours of the morning, go into the woods, shed his clothes, and run naked through the forest. To my way of thinking, he was unconsciously tossing propriety, tossing human identity, and running free of it.

Ted was a night troller all of his life. Night trolling is solitary, secretive, unseen. We can imagine him creeping behind houses, between houses, checking doorways and windows while clothed entirely in his darkest colors, then riding by the same homes the next morning, tossing the newspaper and waving at the unsuspecting tenants. They may have thought *Ted's such a nice boy* with no idea he knew which of the doors and windows they left unlocked. It would not surprise me if he had discovered some days earlier during his Tallahassee night trolling that the Chi Omega back door was left unlocked for sorority house late comers, and that there was a pile of fire logs sitting there.

Ted's first remarkable attempt at freedom from captivity was auto theft when he was 15. One source said Ted wanted to head back to Philadelphia to confirm who the heck he was since no one in Tacoma was telling him. He was arrested before skipping town, and who knows how Louise and Johnny reacted, but I would guess that they didn't have a talk with their son. That would have been *a really good time* to sit down with young Ted, face facts, and get him some help. I think at this point Ted was way beyond help, but they could have stopped covering for him and saved untold, unimaginable grief for themselves and everyone else.

First Louise, and then Louise and Johnny, did not talk about what had been crucial to *Ted's inner world* from the get go. Rather, they seem to have been addressing what was crucial to them as parents, hoping that would be enough. Did you make your bed, did you finish your paper route, be courteous, time for dinner, is homework done, watch your brothers and sisters while we are gone for the afternoon. At the same time, Ted's narcissistic entitlement, like young Adolf, may have caused him to resent such directives, as he believed he was above such tasks. Who knows, but clearly adolescent Ted was able bodied enough and politely angry enough to try to make a run for it.

Part of Bundy's quality escape skills was to use *extremely clever means* to bust out of any place that was binding him. When one strategy didn't work, he would try another. And he would suck it up when he got caught because he could use that time without privileges to think up a new game plan. His adolescent experience of getting arrested was an opportunity for him to try out ways to keep free of the slammer. During the remainder of his adolescent years, he used persuasive vocabulary and eyebrow raising to talk himself out of being held responsible for forgery, burglary, and car theft.

So don't tell us you were a good, all-American Boy Scout, Ted. Since Ted's records were expunged when he turned 18, the crimes didn't come up on his background check when the Seattle murders were happening. That background check snafu kept him free and clear for a few more years into early adulthood. The concealed record was yet another escape from justice.

When old enough, Ted moved out, got his own place, started going to college, and was making his own rules, which we know he'd already been doing stealthily for some time. But now, as long as he presented as polite and friendly in public, he would be free to do otherwise elsewhere. During the early part of his killing career, Ted smugly enjoyed the anonymity and freedom to operate in the PNW unhindered and, personally at least, molestation free. He steadily became more skilled and bolder. He was pleased as punch to be so good at it.

However, being overly cavalier, after the Lake Sammamish murders, Ted had blown his cover. Everyone was looking for a curly brown haired Ted who owned a Volkswagen and faked an injury. He was too close to risking capture after that arrogant blunder, so he got out of Dodge. Ted packed up and left the state of Washington, hauling his belongings in a pickup truck to Salt Lake City. After settling into a place in SLC, he returned to Tacoma to quickly retrieve his Beetle, then motored confidently with each mile away from the West Coast.

When in Eastern Washington, Idaho, Utah, and Colorado, his disposal methods had to change. The terrain in these areas was not blanketed with lush undergrowth along random side roads like his forested home territory. Wide open spaces left fewer outdoor hiding places, so he began leaving his discards in rivers and then closer along the roadside in an unavoidably more open view since it took too much time to find a spot secluded enough to his liking.

Also different in these new areas was that he never established a dump site, so the remains of his victims were never together. The only profile similarity these crimes had to the PNW crimes was the attack itself.

Utah State Prison

Ted was finally locked up in Utah State Prison after the conviction for Aggravated Kidnapping of Carol DaRonch. A kidnapping is deemed to be of an aggravated nature when the purpose of the kidnapping is to force, do harm, or demand ransom. He was given a sentence of 1 to 15 years. With that sentence, horror of horrors, he *could* have been released within 18 months for good behavior. Recall that being a model prisoner is not a gold star. Having *been* a prisoner and for what *crime* is not to be overlooked on someone's resume.

To Ted's amazement, he found himself actually locked up, in a cell, in a prison. This was new. But Ted was undaunted and as always schemed confidently throughout his inmate days toward escape.

Tirelessly being a life-long learner, he was ever shopping, ever stealing, ever researching, ever honing his talents. He never stopped thinking.

Ted was allowed to do a work rotation in the Utah prison print shop. Ever creatively deviant, while in the shop–get this–he forged a social security card, sketched an Illinois driver's license, and printed road maps and airline schedules. Although off to a hopeful start, Ted was caught and punished with "the hole," a solitary cell where the prisoner is kept for 23 hours per day. No worries, more time to connive.

Pitkin County Courthouse

We all know about Ted's leap out of the top story window at Pitkin County Courthouse. He had been transferred from Utah to Colorado and jailed on suspicion for the murder of a nurse in Aspen. He created this escape from the courthouse because he knew that if he represented himself in court, he would legally require access to the law library. Even if it was not granted by law, it wouldn't have been a problem for Bundy because he was too good at wheedling people around his long, skinny fingers.

The guards didn't believe he would jump, because who in their right mind would do so, but of course this is Bundy we are talking about. For weeks, Ted had practiced jumping from the top bunk to the floor in his cell in order to strengthen his legs for the impact when he would jump from the courthouse window. What did the jail staff make of all his jumping and thumping?

Repeatedly, on each of his escorted walks around the courthouse grounds, he would pause for several minutes while the escorts watched him focus on the slopes of Smuggler Mountain that loomed beyond the Roaring Fork River.

Here's a Ted Tip: The more out-of-cell time one has, the better the opportunity to see what escape routes there might be, monitor if or how well the inmate is guarded during the time out of lockup, or snitch needed items to sneak back to the cell to squirrel away.

Ted knew there was an open window in the top floor library. We even have footage of him crouching to obtain a book from a bottom library shelf right next to the window. Meanwhile, he was able to learn the local terrain by studying the *maps he was given access to as the defense counsel.*

June 7 was the day he decided to make the jump. He courteously left a sweater behind in the courtroom for the bloodhounds (he was thoughtful that way) and psyched himself up for the jump. He had put on a second layer of clothing under his presentable-for-court outfit. During a court recess, the guards thought nothing of him going to the law library to brush up on this or that, but when he was alone, he jumped out that window.

In spite of all those preparatory jumps, he did roll his ankle, but he didn't stop and ran straight to the Roaring Fork River. He hid in some brush by the river, reversed his clothing, and rearranged his hair (he was always rearranging his appearance–a bit of a diva that way).

He watched from his hiding spot as the melee of law enforcement and tracking dogs gathering outside the courthouse prepared for the chase. Once they dispersed with the dogs trying to find his trail, he said he leisurely backtracked his own steps right up the center of town and past the courthouse, heading in a *different* direction from Smuggler Mountain toward Aspen Mountain.

At least that is one of a few stories he gave. Psychopaths will lie when there is no reason to, so the fact that he had various stories about this does not surprise me. He still mastered an escape and disguise regardless of the route he took out of town and up into the Elk Mountains range.

Amazing how when in a frantic chase (not that I've been in any), we only see what we *expect* to see. Ted didn't look like he had 45 minutes ago in the courtroom, with different clothes, different hair; now, he may have looked somewhat touristy. Nobody "saw" the man who fancied himself as Mr. Concealment, the Master of Disguise.

In his escape outfit, he climbed up the mountainside and the higher he got, the colder it got. Then a rainstorm rolled in, and as a Colorado storm will do, it poured cold rain down for hours and hours. Ted looked for shelter. After long hours in a sleet storm wearing street clothing rather than cozy weather duds, one becomes wet, cold to the bone, and nearly in shock. Teeth rattling and body shaking, the fugitive was desperately seeking a cabin. Poor him.

Imagining this brings to my mind the lovely, innocent Nurse Caryn Campbell, who was the reason why Ted was jailed in Colorado. During the night after being dumped on a roadside snowbank while still alive, Caryn succumbed to exposure and the several injuries caused by Ted. Her autopsy report indicated she, like so many others, had multiple injuries, was partially fed upon by animals, was frozen solid, and was buried by the road plow and falling snow. He had disposed of her only nine miles from where he was "suffering" in the sleet storm.

Desperate for shelter, Ted found a cabin that had been locked and boarded up for the winter. It took awhile to break into, but he finally got some plywood loose, broke a window, and climbed in. After staying in the cabin some days, he politely left a note for the owner of the cabin that he had broken the window to get in out of the storm, eaten some canned food, and apologized. On the plywood that he replaced over the broken window, he also left a note of apology. Unmentioned in the letter was that the thief also stole the cabin owner's .22 pump rifle.

Ted, having left the cabin, hiked and wandered some more, but the weather again got the best of him, and he returned to the edge of the cabin property. From the treeline, he spotted the cabin's owner and law enforcement outside the home. He hoofed it elsewhere with his rolled ankle and blistered feet. Overcome with the elements, he limped back to Aspen. He spotted a light blue Cadillac with keys in the ignition and off he drove. Roadblocks had already been set up because of guess who, so he was unable to leave town in his stolen Caddy. Being disoriented and unsure of where to turn, the officers pulled him over because they thought he was a drunk driver. Realizing who he really was, they arrested Ted on the spot.

Garfield County Jail

Due to his high escape risk, law enforcement transferred Houdini to the more secure Garfield County Jail. Ever watchful, ever astute, the quick study learned his surroundings and drew a diagram of the exits and ventilation systems. He observed the ongoing jail routines and learned Garfield security staff habits and weaknesses. In retrospect, the guards said he always had jovial questions for the passers by. *When is your shift over? What are you doing for New Years? It's just me, friendly, polite Mr. Con Artist.*

Knowing the layout of the building design is what made escape possible. There was a 1x1 foot (which doesn't seem possible, but every report I have read is consistent as to its size) light fixture in the ceiling of Bundy's cell.

No one would consider that little potential hole an escape route– except for Bundy. Lying on the top bunk, over a period of time he kicked the fixture plate repeatedly until it loosened. An inmate in the next cell reported the noises and while Ted was in court, the ceiling was inspected. A welder was called to repair the damage. The welder did not return the call, and the concern was forgotten.

I would be horrified if that were neglected on my watch. At the same time, who would think anyone could squeeze through that hole? Ted said he wore all of his clothes during the times he was going to court so that his dramatic weight loss would not be noticed. He had already dropped 20 pounds during his days on the lam, but at Garfield County, he restricted his food and dropped an additional 10 pounds.

Ted stacked law books on the top bunk to make a handy perch to hoist himself up at night so he could explore and familiarize himself with the possible route. Fellow inmates reported they could hear him crawling around up there. They reported it to a guard, but perhaps the guard thought *let him crawl around, he's not going to get anywhere except claustrophobic, or better yet, stuck.* To the officer it may have been amusing at best, but it got worse.

Ever the intruder, he found or created (reports differ) a drop down from the ceiling opening into the jailer's apartment closet. Mr. Covert Narcissist knew the jailer's schedule from pleasantly gathering personal information.

Back in his cell, when he was ready to escape, he stuffed a blanket full of books in his cot so it would look like he was sleeping. Since he often didn't touch his breakfast, the guards wouldn't try all that hard to wake him and so it would be hours before he would be discovered missing. Ted crawled along his usual route to where the vent opened into the apartment, got into the jailer's clothes, and cool as a cucumber strolled out the front door of the building. Just as he had planned, he would be long gone and on a plane before anyone would notice he had escaped.

What he did not know, since there were no windows in his cell, was that a blizzard was swirling outside. After traipsing around in the snow looking for a car with keys in it, he found a rickety MG. An MG is about as good in the snow as a sled, and before long he slid into a snowbank.

A highway patrolman came along and helped the poor, unfortunate, starving law student out of the snowbank. Ironic. Sickeningly ironic. Of course, the patrolman had no idea who this was because no one had yet discovered Bundy's absence from his cell, and they did not discover it for many hours. After Ted was some miles back on the highway, the MG finally broke down, so he hitched a ride with a trucker to Denver where he boarded a train to Chicago.

From Chicago he flew to Ann Arbor, where he stopped in a bar and cheered as his alma mater, the University of Washington won the Rose Bowl football game against University of Michigan. He was, of course, among Michigan fans and nearly got himself beat up. From there he stole a car and headed south toward Atlanta.

The car broke down in Georgia's capital city, so he hopped on a bus and headed confidently into the death penalty state of Florida. He learned which states utilize the death penalty, so Mr. Chess Player surmised law enforcement would be least likely to look for him in a Capital Punishment region.

After arriving in the Sunshine State, he said he loved being warm after the cold, cold Ann Arbor and Denver climate for which he didn't have proper clothing. Poor Ted, he had been exposed to the elements again in Michigan. But now in Florida on New Year's Day, he was laying on the beach, soaking in the sun and getting a tan. He said he felt really great starting the New Year that way.

He had a new ID and a new name (he had learned early on to adapt new names), so the old life was gone. But it was troubling for him that he wasn't *the* Ted Bundy. He was a nobody there and could not handle the insignificance.

"It was New Years Eve . . . I was waiting for the bus . . . there were all these people going to a Hawks game. And I was watching these people—these people who had real lives, backgrounds, histories, girlfriends, husbands and families. Who were smiling and laughing and talking with each other. Who seemed to have so much of what I wanted! All of a sudden I felt smaller and smaller and smaller. More insecure. And more alone! Watching groups of couples talking with one another, strolling toward the gate. Bit by bit, I felt something drain out of me. And by the time I got off the bus in Tallahassee . . ."

~Ted

Within a few weeks, he took his insignificant self out and had himself a slaughter. Then another one, then a week later, his last one.

I so wish his parents hadn't been covering for his behavior early on.

Upon his arrest in Pensacola, Bundy was taken to Leon County Jail. The Sheriff was Ken Katsaris, a dapper dresser, and news footage shows him in a fancy black suit and alligator (maybe snakeskin) boots. I think Ted hated that the Sheriff looked so slick and he was stuck in a frumpy jail suit while the world was watching. Ken made damn sure that Bundy was not going to escape from *HIS* jail. He had installed solid steel walls and several padlocked doors, each with a separate key assigned to a separate person, and Ted didn't escape. Ever the opportunist, however, when Bundy was led out for the reading of this several page indictment, he turned and looked in every direction, taking in all possibilities. Katsaris had armed guards on all sides.

"Okay, you've got the indictment, that's all you're gonna get . . .
I'll plead not guilty right now."

~Ted as Leon County Sheriff Ken Katsaris reads
him his indictment for the murder of the Chi Omega Sorority girls
(July 27, 1978)

Florida State Prison

Once convicted and on death row thanks to the Florida legislation, Ted didn't settle for his new predicament. He was at Florida State Prison for some time before he managed to obtain a hack saw blade. He then set out surreptitiously, sawing bit by bit through some of the bars of his cell. As he finished each bar, he dabbed it with paste to conceal the cuts. Meanwhile he was again dropping weight.

Ted had a wife and daughter by this time. His wife, Carole, being completely convinced of his innocence, was likely fraught with worry and confusion regarding his behavior. I wonder if Carole noticed his weight loss. He certainly would have had a good excuse by blaming the jail food. Being yet another kind soul, she might have sympathized and tried to comfort him by satisfying his sexual needs. Remember, to the psychopath it's considered a mistake *not* to take advantage of someone.

As is done randomly in prisons, the guards did a cell toss. They flipped mattresses, looked in every conceivable hide away, and even banged on the bars. Guess what? Ted's plan was foiled when his bars went flying. This didn't help his chances of appeal either.

Ever the researcher, Bundy's favorite books included *Papillon* by Henri Charriere, the story of an impossible prison escape from Devil's Island. The student of escape read it four times. Another favorite of his was *King Rat*, the story of Prisoners of War in a Japanese prison camp. What he probably liked about that book was that the "King" had become a major power in the POW camp through his charisma and intelligence. Having come from a working class family, he was undistinguished in civilian life, so being King in the camp was a proud power position for King Rat.

Ted said that when he was in prison was the first time he felt that he had a social identity of status. He conned the other cons, usually by offering cigarettes or other small luxuries. In one of the jails where he was held, there were not enough bunks in the cell for all the individuals, so he voluntarily slept on the floor. I wonder if Papillon or King did that to win over their peers in order to take timely advantage. Ted was always building likability points with anyone who could possibly serve him in some way when he decided to call in favors.

In spite of his best efforts, Ted found himself up for the death penalty. One of the final witnesses at the sentencing trial gave a blow by blow account of what an electrocution is like. Ted's face twitched and he clenched his jaw when hearing about what awaited him. The witness went on to number the number of death row inmates that have, through good behavior, true good behavior and honest parole, gone on to be genuine contributors to society.

Surprisingly there have been some. I had no idea that was possible. But apparently it is.

Ted's fellow news and political cohorts in Washington State believed in his criminal acumen as well. A letter from Richard Larsen, who was then the Associate Editor for the *Seattle Times*, described the possibility of preserving Ted's life for the sake of utilizing his unique expertise at Quantico. He envisioned Bundy helping law enforcement and society to better understand, identify, and handle personalities prone to criminal behavior. He was considered by psychiatrists and law enforcement as a walking treasure trove of knowledge. Those Feds desired that Ted be spared and placed at Quantico as an interstate information resource.

This smacks of Ed Abagnale, the versatilely talented career criminal played by Leonardo DiCaprio in the movie *Catch Me if You Can*. Tom Hanks played the FBI agent who finally got his hooks into Ed and decided that Abagnale would be placed at Quantico as a consultant under house arrest. Apparently there was some hope that Ted would have a similar future. But that was not to be.

On his last and final day, Ted waited for the phone call granting another execution stay. But it never happened, so burly guards walked his still hopeful self down to the death chamber. He called out more victims' names along the short thirty foot walk from the death watch cell. He kept calling victims' names, desperate for a chance for more time, hoping those women could help him. Again. Come to the rescue for him again. How dare he.

They strapped him in the chair and clamped the scalp piece on. Still, he hoped the call would come. It didn't. So he made his *final* escape. Televised around the planet, with crowds cheering him on, he went rather spectacularly, right through the exit jaws of Old Sparky.

Bundy's last words have a twinge of irony: "Give my love to my family and friends."

What Love?

What Family?

What Friends?

Bundy managed to keep his optimism right up until the executioner flipped the switch.

Chapter Twenty Five

Was Bundy Insane?

. . . Crazy like a Fox

After Ted's execution, Louise continued facing life with her same steely determination, aiming to keep her personal and family dignity intact. Johnny remained at her side unfalteringly as she continued to serve her home, church, and community. I wonder if, like her son, she considered it as an acting role? If she did, hats off to her because she was incredible. Perhaps because of her own emotional gulf she could devote herself to being a mother and housewife without going south. I don't know.

Louise was more determined to defend her child than any woman I've ever heard of. Strong minded like her father, she *never* crumbled. In fact, after Ted's first conviction, she said, "I'd like to throttle the prosecutor." It makes me think of her father and the chickens–even her son and his victims. She never gave up even after Ted confessed. Louise was televised saying with self-defensive and distancing language:

"This hit us right between the eyes. We don't know how this could have happened. He wasn't raised that way. Something happened after he left this house to unleash this madness."

Not so, Louise. It had been building all while he was in your devoted care. You didn't see it. Optimism does not change reality.

Like his mother, Ted was optimistic all the way to the chair. I do not know anyone who can sustain that level of persistent confidence. Yes, it was to a pathological extent, but I don't think either Louise or Ted were clinically delusional. Their rose colored vision was not due to a thought disorder, but a self-protective decision.

I hope upon receiving the information in this book no one says again that Ted or any of the others were born evil. They were not. We have a hand in making them this way, and we are still creating these empty souls starved for affectionate, interpersonal connection. Ted starved for it and, in his own disturbed way, he tried to fill that void .

Ted himself denied that he was insane, even though one psychiatrist, Dr. Dorothy Lewis, diagnosed him with Bipolar Disorder and speculated that he also had Multiple Personality Disorder (aka Dissociative Identity Disorder). Ted insisted he was not crazy—even though convincing a jury that he was mentally ill might have saved his life. Bundy was not a good lawyer after all. My thoughts are that, because of the deep family stigma regarding his grandmother's mental illness, and grandfather's near psychotic behavior of brutalization, he didn't want to be thought of as having a "mental weakness." For whatever reasons, apparently Ted would rather die than be thought of as mentally ill.

Ted's childish judgment in the courtroom manifested itself when playing at cross examination to his own detriment. The psychopath, being a narcissist, could not obscure his preschool emotional development level. He made me think of a persistent little boy when questioning the detective on the stand who had been first on the scene at the Chi Omega slayings. Bundy wanted the detective to describe in inappropriate detail the horrific crime scene, then he wanted the witness to repeat it a second time.

Look! See this amazing picture I painted all by myself? See?

In order for a suspect to be found insane and deemed not responsible for a crime, it must be proven that the individual was not able to determine that their actions were wrong at the time of the murder. Make no mistake—Ted was well aware of his actions. He not only researched and stalked selected individuals before hunting his chosen prey with tools he kept inside his vehicle; he lured his targets, raped and butchered them, went to great lengths to hide the remains, and even left fake clues to throw off investigators.

He wore wigs, grew a beard, shaved a beard, got a haircut, let his hair grow, dyed it, greased it back, wore fake glasses, had a false mustache, plucked his eyebrows, used medical devices, slings, surgical gloves, crutches, three piece suits, tennis wear, and various names *to deceive.*

His boarding house roommates that shared the bathroom commented that he had a makeup kit he would take into the bathroom with him, and occasionally he wore a fake mole between the left side of his lip and his nose. Sometimes he wore wire frame glasses and other times tortoise shell glasses. One fellow student saw him leaving the boarding house on his bike with a board and a saw sticking out of his backpack. Who knows what plans he had for that.

When using his stolen crutches and walking a girl to his car, one Near Miss said he wasn't putting weight on the crutches or even limping, so she told him he was full of shit and left. Later, she saw him still waiting for "help" in the spot she first saw him.

When planning, he waited for a clear night to strike. If it was a full moon, all the better. His various lures worked so well, he said, *they didn't have to come with me, I didn't go after them caveman style, they came to me.*

That is not insane. That is calculating over a period of time, researching his captors' personal info, hunting his prey, covering up the evidence again and again. He compared it to sportsmen that hunt big game and mount their kills proudly on the wall. Those sports are not considered crazy, and he didn't think his pastime was crazy, either. He was proud of it. Rationalization of his crimes accompanied his urges as they came to fruition. Ted was honoring what he had always thought was the purpose of women: to be possessed, controlled, subservient merchandise for violence.

"I deserve, certainly, the most extreme punishment society has . . . I think society deserves to be protected from me and others like me."

~Ted

So no, Theodore Robert Bundy was not insane, even temporarily insane, but was permanently, incurably dangerous.

Throughout his life of always longing to be someone significant and famous, he rubbed shoulders with Governors, Presidential Candidates, Commissioners, Lieutenant Governor Candidates, a very famous crime writer, and more.

When his killing became public and he found himself getting media attention, he vowed to himself that if he could not be famous in politics, he would take a shortcut to fame by being the best at his other hobby. He bragged that he had a PhD in Serial Murder.

If he even knew about it, he was probably proud that a folk song was written about him by a Colorado musician:

Let's salute the mighty Bundy
Here on Friday, gone on Monday
All his roads lead out of town
It's hard to keep a good man down.

Upon deciding to take the shortcut to fame (you know what they say about taking shortcuts), he became Seattle Ted, Utah Ted, Ted the Troller. When he introduced himself to Florida law enforcement as Ted Bundy, they did not know who that was. Being a bit chagrined that they did not know of his fame, he said at long last,

"I'm THE Ted Bundy."

After 40 years of waiting, Ted was *finally* somebody. That shortcut to fame did, after all, bring him the power and control he needed to make his mark on the world. He now had an identity—a solid identity that has stood the test of time. At long last a *famous* identity that society would take seriously and *never* forget. Now the world would forever recognize his face, and he would be a household name for what he had accomplished in history.

You Can't Go Home Again
-Thomas Wolfe

There are times when we feel compelled to look back while looking forward—back to what cannot be changed and forward to what we hope to learn along the way. In our lives, we will suffer some bumps and scrapes when we travel new, untrodden paths. For that reason, we should give ourselves some grace. In our desire to survive well, we try to learn from the unfair circumstances of others with our own interpretations of why things went wrong. Sometimes we are right on and other times we can only give an educated guess. This book is meant to help us survive well by utilizing what we know about Louise and Ted and applying it to how we conduct ourselves in life.

When we are forced to live with and stumble through unfair or unwanted destiny, we should do so with the sincere desire to survive well. Some become resentful and full of murderous rage, but others put their head straight into the wind and endure. Still others stay in smooth currents—doing well and being done by well. Fortunate young starters often have aspirations that propel them into their promising futures and sail along beautifully unmolested. Until they don't.

None of the young starters Ted took get to go home again. Each individual within these pages deserves another start and a different finish. But we don't get any do-overs, unless reincarnation actually does occur, and even then we would likely wish for still another do-over.

My daughter Shawnee and I decided to google locations in the Seattle-Tacoma area where some of the discussed incidents occurred with Bundy and those in his grip between the years of 1950 and the summer of 1974. He was in these parts from the age of 4 until he made a run for Utah at age 28, one month after tipping his hand at lake Sammamish.

We started our exploration in a little SUV with our Starbucks and water bottles. It sounds trendy, comfortable, and somewhat inappropriate given the unpredictable self-charted day we encountered upon, but that is life, no?

Our first stop was Crescent Lake, a sweet little lake inhabited today by watercraft, nice homes and gated driveways here and there. During Ted's growing up years, Louise and Johnny owned a little piece of property here where they put up tents and built a platform for an off the dirt cooking area. They must have covered it with a tent as well because they referred to it as "the cookhouse."

They also built a little dock and had a row boat. In later years, Ted both reminisced and resented (as he was prone to do) the family get away spot on the small lake. He talked about the rowboat derisively and gave the fishing experience a sense of dismissal. I am confident the rest of the family loved it. Kids love dirt, water, boats, and food cooked over the fire, so the family site their parents provided for them would not have disappointed Ted's siblings. Conveniently for the family, it was only 20 minutes from their city home just across the Tacoma Narrows Bridge.

We circled the lake, being misled by a GPS that was even more disoriented than we were. Being curiously uncertain of what else to do, we followed satellite guidance and embarked on trails that, as we discovered, led away from, rather than to, the shoreline. As you may surmise, with thick undergrowth between the very nice homes we were unable to find a possible campsite with a little dock. At one home surrounded by a concrete barrier, we could see a good share of the lake. I hopped out to take a picture and a young man approached me to ask what I was doing. I suppose it looked to him like I was casing the joint and so bowed out as gracefully as possible. One can't blame him—nobody wants someone all up in their business.

Had the lake properties in the Bundy's camping days been as nice as they were when we pulled up in 2023, I think Ted would have approved.

I don't think he approved of his house 20 minutes away. It was, is, a very small four bedroom, one bath, 1,452 square-foot house that accommodated his parents, young Teddy, and his younger siblings.

Although the house was freshly painted and nicely maintained by Johnny back in the day, today it looks strikingly similar in upkeep to Louise and Teddy's starting place, the Philadelphia house. The stairs and rails wobble as you climb up, at least now they do, and there are scattered rags and cellophane wrappers of some kind scattered on the wooden porch. I thought the old door being displaced by the new one was solemnly suggestive of how we often reject the original for something we deem more desirable. Perhaps the previous owners hoped the newer door would give the place more sidewalk appeal. Maybe it just needed a new door. A lock box was on the door knob with no indication of the realtor. Limp curtains covered the windows, weakly attempting to keep the inside to themselves. Two columns like the ones at the Philadelphia house braced the upper front portion of the roof. A rumpled backer board skirted the base of the front to keep out weather and anything else that might disturb the foundation.

When looking at the two flights of steps leading up from the street to the front door, I thought of Louise bustling from the car up the stairs with bags of groceries in her arms or holding a child or two. Or maybe Johnny made the grocery and child trips. When Ted got older, perhaps he brought in some groceries or herded siblings up and down the steps.

The sides and back of the house were supported by pocked concrete. Every basement window was covered from the inside with paper. A narrow stairway with narrow steps led down to the basement that was blocked by the original door. Basement windows were hung half heartedly with some kind of cheap material. It felt to me as though this house had completely given up hope with a last gasp of the new door. On a realty website, I was able to find notes on when it most recently sold and for how much. Are you sitting down? Bundy's childhood home sold for nearly half a million dollars. It is currently off the market.

Never shy about research, I knocked on several neighboring doors. One didn't answer the door although there was a car out front, one had a permanent sign saying DO NOT KNOCK, BABY SLEEPING. Across the street however, was a nicely cared for little home so 1950's-ish it looked like there might be cinnamon rolls baking inside. We knocked and waited minutes for someone to open the door. We were halfway back to the sidewalk when out poked the face of a sweet elderly African American woman.

Asking if she knew anything about the house across the street, she said that when she moved in there was only a man living there and didn't know anything about the family prior. She didn't look like the nosey type.

Overall, the neighborhood may have become absolutely sick of people like me knocking on their doors. I don't blame them.

Looking back at the Tacoma house as we left, I thought again how similar it was to the Philadelphia house; it too seemed dejected, forlorn, and absolutely worn out among its neighbors. Louise would not approve today, and she and Johnny certainly had it ship shape when they started out there.

When Teddy was seven, they sold this house. I do not know the price but it was enough to buy another home. A rather charming one, I'd say.

East of the house is a sizable plot of woods that Ted and his neighbor described. Ted haunted those woods and the surrounding neighborhood. Ted built the tiger traps in those very woods. Today, however, the woods and streams are cut through by a rushing freeway.

As I examined the forest, my thoughts turned to Louise. Ted said his mother didn't do things with other women like have coffee or join clubs. When we have coffee or spend time with other women, that means we have to talk. I'm sure Louise didn't want to be forced to talk about how her son was terrorizing the neighborhood. The houses were very close together and the streets were narrow. I imagined Ted at night creeping among the surrounding homes in the dark, and children screaming from the woods across the street.

Parents *HAD* to have come knocking on her door. The detectives certainly did. I wonder if she gave the same answers to them as she did the Tacoma News Tribune during her interview following Ted's first arrest in Utah: "We still don't believe it. It just can't be. I keep shaking my head day after day, saying how can this be? Our son is the best son in the world. A very normal, active boy."

Our next stop was Lake Sammamish State Park. When Ted first saw the huge body of water, he probably thought. "Now THAT'S a lake." Expansive beach, no brush anywhere, sparkling ripples sliced through by water skiers, music, and bikini's galore—a young man's paradise. As it turned out, he had other things on his mind.

We spent the day at the lake with our jackets on because the sky was cloudy, with rain drops and wind here and there. On the day Janice and Denise enjoyed the water and sand amidst a crowd of over 40,000 people, it was 90 degrees. Summers at Lake Sammamish were absolute Heaven for the young people of King county. But it turned out to be absolute Hell for the two young women on that day. They each kindly accompanied the cute, injured fellow across the expanse of lawn to the jam-packed parking lot. As he drove the helpful girls out of the parking lot, someone was likely quick to grab the newly empty spot.

From the lake he took them about five miles to what is now a huge Swedish Medical Center Campus. It took us a while to get there because the GPS was yet again even more disoriented than we were, but we luckily found it. I don't know if it was the designer's intention or requirements of the highway department, but there is a groomed stretch of green lawn between the medical center's buildings and the lanes of the Highland Drive highway. This is where Denise and Janice's bodies were found. It has a memorial feel, so I think it was intentional to preserve the spot.

In 1974, the grass-only parcel was covered with trees instead of a medical complex. Below the site where the girls were dumped, through the trees that were there at that time, was a condemned and vacant house. Perhaps he brought them there first before disposing of their remains. I'll leave it for you to sort out. I will not recount the facts of that day—there are several books listed in the bibliography that will do that for you.

We looked for markers or a respectful acknowledgment of the young women as we walked the small area. We philosophized many reasons why the space is simply kept quietly green and undisturbed.

While the "Memorial Lawn" of Janice and Denise was rather close to the lake, the Taylor Mountain dumpsite was up a mountain pass.

The Bonneville power line towers up the face of the foothills and through adjacent Tiger Mountain and Taylor Mountain. There are lots of places to hike in the nearby area and as it turns out, Ted and his cousin spent lots of time hiking the landscape together. His cousin said Ted knew the area very well. Of course he did.

When we got to the turnoff onto the power line road, we parked and looked up the hill. The road curves up the hillside incline and we got out of the car and walked to the top of the summit We turned around and looked back down to the road entry. It was at that spot where Bundy said he parked because he could see any headlights turn onto the road below. Moonlit nights were his preference to stop at the dump site so he didn't need his own car lights on. If someone did come up the hill, he could pretend he was taking a leak.

The remains of the four girls were found scattered into the brush and trees there that are now impenetrable.

Although it was rain jacket and hat weather for us, poor us, each of the women found there and at Issaquah were abducted in moderate to warm spring and summer months. Their remains, however, were left there to be dominated by the ever repeating seasons. What Ted described as nature's disposal methods which were weather—warm, cold, freezing and rain, and 'beasties'. I have images of a coyote with a leg bone, a bobcat with a hand, a cougar dripping entrails, a sniffing black bear. The girls, their obliterated dreams and futures, were scattered and lost.

These women are famous now in a way they would never in a million years have chosen for themselves.

Those were my thoughts as we walked back down to the car, and they even hang heavy upon me now.

From Washington, to Oregon, to Idaho, to Utah, to Colorado, to Florida and who knows how many . . . those countless lovely women and girls, because of him, couldn't go home again.

Bibliography

Athens, Lonnie H. *The Creation of Violent Criminals* (1992) *London: New York: Routledge 1989*

Barth, Christian *The Garden State Parkway Murders* (2020) *WildBlue Press*

John Bowlby *The Making and Breaking of Affectional Bonds,* (1979) (Taviston Publications, Great Britain)

Carlisle, Al PhD *The Case of Ted Bundy I'm Not Guilty,* (2016) Genius Book Publishing, Encino CA

Carlisle, Al PhD *Violent Mind, The* (1976) *Psychological Assessment of Ted Bundy*, Genius Book Publishing Encino CA

Candland, Douglas K. Feral Children and Clever Animals (1993). Oxford Press

Dekle, George R. Sr. *The Last Murder* (2011) Prayer Santa Barbara, California, Denver,Colorado, Oxford, England

John E Douglas, Anne W. Burgess, Allen G. Burgess, *Crime Classification Manual, A Standard System for Investigating and Classifying Violent Crime, Third Edition* (2013) *Wiley and Sons New Jersey*

Fromm, Erik PhD *The Anatomy of Human Destructiveness*, 1973
Picador, NY

Hare, R. D. (1993) *Without Conscience: The Disturbing World of the Psychopaths Among Us*. New York, Pocket Books

Hi, I'm Ted, A Killer in the Archives Patreon

Impact of Maternal Stress, Depression and Anxiety on Fetal Neurobahavioral Development

Kendall, Elizabeth *The Phantom Prince, My Life With Ted Bundy*, with Molly Kendall (2020) Abrams Press NY

Keppel, Robert D. PhD., with William J. Birnes *Signature Killers* (1997) Pocket Books

Kernberg, T. A. (1994) *Psychoanalytic Theory of Personality Disorders* in Clarkin and Lenzenwanger (Ed's.) *Major Theories of Personality Disorders* New York, Guilford Press

Kinsella,Clin Obstet Gynecol. Author manuscript; available in PMC 2013 Jul 14. 2009

Larsen, Richard, *Bundy The Deliberate Stranger* (1980) Pocket Books NY

Lewis, Dorothy Othow MD *Guilty by Reason of Insanity* (1998) Ballantine Publishing Group NY

Lynam, Childhood Psychopathy Scale (CPS; 1997). URL

Michaud and Aynesworth, (1999) [1983] p. 263 *The Only Living Witness A True Account of Homicidal Insanity*, Signet Books 1984 Chicago

Bibliography

Michaud and Aynesworth, *Ted Bundy: Conversations with a Killer.* (2019) Paperback ed., New York City: Signet Books. Transcripts of the authors Death Row interviews with Bundy

Myra McPherson *The Roots of Evil*, Vanity Fair 1989

Nelson, Polly *Defending The Devil* (2018) Echo Point Books and Media, LLC Brattleboro, Vermont p198

O'Connell, *Gina Resilient Adults Overcoming a Cruel Past,* (1994) Jossey-Base Publishers San Francisco

Ronson, *The Psychopath Test* (2011) Picador

Rule, Ann *The Stranger Beside Me,* (1989) Pocket Books, Paperback updated 2009 ed New York City: Pocket Books. p.14

Sullivan, Kevin *The Enigma of Ted Bundy* (2021) Blackstone Publishing

Sullivan, Kevin *The Bundy Secrets* (2021) Blackstone Publishing

Viorst, *Judith Necessary Losses,* (1986) Fawcett Gold Medal Ballantine Books NY

The Behavior Panel (You Tube)

Ted Bundy America's Boogey Man (2021) Hulu

The Ted Bundy Tapes (2019) Netflix

About the Author

The author achieved the Associate of Science Nursing degree from Peninsula College School of Nursing where she also has served as an adjunct professor. The Bachelor of Arts Degree in Human Services Counseling she received from Western Washington University and was chosen Outstanding Student for that year. A Masters Degree in Nursing Science was awarded from the University of Washington in Seattle.

She worked at Peninsula Behavioral Health as initial psychiatric intake evaluator, Olympic Memorial Hospital as Charge Nurse in the locked Behavioral Medicine Unit and at Psychiatric Associates clinic. The last 30 years have been spent in selective private practice.

This book came about after years of researching and thinking about the burgeoning subject matter and finally, like throwing up or having a baby, it just couldn't be held back any longer.

Hopefully the reader finds the necessity of studying the developmental years of apex killers and individuals with destructive narcissistic patterns enlightening and useful.

When not traveling, Carol resides among friends and family near Seattle.

www.ingramcontent.com/pod-product-compliance
Ingram Content Group UK Ltd.
Pitfield, Milton Keynes, MK11 3LW, UK
UKHW050703230125
4254UKWH00020B/82

9 798989 139804